Language Experience Activities

Second Edition

Roach Van Allen & Claryce Allen

Language Experience Activities

Language Experience Activities

Second Edition

Roach Van Allen
University of Arizona

Claryce Allen

HOUGHTON MIFFLIN COMPANY BOSTON
Dallas Geneva, Illinois Hopewell, New Jersey
Palo Alto London

Cover photograph © Elizabeth Hamlin, 1976. Stock, Boston

Printed in the U.S.A.

Library of Congress Catalog Card Number: 81-83688

ISBN: 0-395-31802-5

Contents

Preface

Audience and Purpose

Language Experience Activities is intended to serve both as a resource text in undergraduate and graduate classes and as a personal reference for teachers in service. Each of the more than 250 activities is related to a basic language concept for developing literacy. These concepts form an intellectual base for a language arts program that balances thinking, listening, speaking, and reading and writing.

Design of the Activities

1. The activities and questions promote divergent thinking and divergent responses. There are few "correct answer" activities. Rather, students draw upon their own experiences and their own language to respond within a pattern or a design that is provided. They practice being creative in their language responses at the same time as they encounter basic language concepts in many situations.
2. The activities emphasize three major language learning processes for the student: (1) communicating in a variety of ways—talking, discussing, acting, painting, sculpting, singing, chanting, and writing; (2) studying communication processes—how language works through the use of names for things, words of movement, words of description, words of structure, the study of words, the study of sentences and sentence patterns, and the repeating patterns of language in poems and stories; and (3) studying how other people communicate through language, literature, and the arts.
3. The activities develop, as do many activity books, recognition

abilities for reading. In addition, however, other language abilities are extended, such as those that promote language acquisition, language prediction, and language production. Throughout, students learn to become authors of books and of other materials that are useful in the instructional program.

4. The activities develop and strengthen a linguistic base for reading. Phonological structure is strengthened through listening, repeating, chorusing, dramatizing, and reading orally individual compositions built on language patterns new to the author. Morphological structure is extended through word analysis and word synthesis. Syntactical structure is extended and highlighted through the use of patterned sentences and patterned poems that stimulate students to speak, read, and write in ways that expand their home-rooted language.
5. The activities represent a wide range of difficulty and permit a variety of responses. The same activities thus become useful at many levels of placement in schools.
6. The activities and selections are original and encourage originality. The authors developed the activities as instructional material that encourges students to launch out on their own. Students learn to use their own ideas and experiences within linguistic patterns that are new to them.

Features of the Second Edition

Organization

The second edition has a completely new organization. Rather than the three large sections of the first edition, the book has been divided into several chapters. Each chapter focuses on one type of learning center and activities appropriate to it. Within each chapter the activities are now arranged according to group activity or individual activity. Additionally, the number of group activities has been expanded; there are now 58 selections to draw students into groups.

Format

The new grouping of activities by type of learning center has eliminated the need for the complex cross-referencing code of the first edition. The new format allows teachers to locate easily activities relevant to particular language concepts and skills.

Expanded Treatment

Learning Center Concept

As mentioned, each chapter now begins with a section that explains the nature and purposes of a specific type of learning center. The activities suitable for use in the center, the language skills they will develop, and the basic materials needed are all identified in these opening sections.

Dictation

Within all the activities, the process of dictation has been further developed as a means to involve students in the production of reading materials drawing on their own interests and vocabularies. This assures that students sense the relationship of what they read and write with what they think and say.

Student Authorship

Students' writing has been expanded into a basic language experience. Literary language patterns are introduced in oral activities and then extended into writing and reading so that students will grow to understand and appreciate literature. Developing this new awareness, detailed suggestions for a Publishing Center are presented in Chapter Five. Students here learn how to edit, illustrate, and bind their own literary productions for use in the school curriculum.

Test Taking

Test taking, too, has been developed into a language experience. More than twenty basic language concepts involved in major reading tests are identified in Chapter Eleven. These concepts are related to students' personal language production through activities presented in a test-taking format.

Activities and Basal Readers

Explanations are presented for integrating language activities and the learning center concept with basal readers. Concepts introduced in those texts can be extended and enriched through the activities presented here. Readers will also be shown how to coordinate the use of learning centers with reading instruction.

Self-Growth and Language Growth

All the activities have been designed to develop and maintain the self-concept of each student who participates actively. Students encounter and learn from questions that shape their lives.

Who am I?
What can I do?
What can I observe and hear in my world?
How can I find out about what others have thought about and shared?
What is in my imaginary world—the world beyond experience for me or for anyone else?

These questions are integrated into the activities in ways that help children grow in their abilities to communicate with others as literate members of society.

Acknowledgments

We would like to extend our sincere thanks to: Dr. Sara Davis, The University of Alabama, University, Alabama; Dr. Charlotte Hess, Bloomsburg State College, Bloomsburg, Pennsylvania; and Dr. Ursula Simonson, Eastern Washington University, Cheney, Washington. All provided helpful suggestions as *Language Experience Activities* made its way to a second edition.

R.V.A.
C.A.

Chapter 1

How to Use This Book

Use as a Resource Book

Language Experience Activities is a resource book to be used with a variety of school programs and classroom organizations. The group and independent activities can be used as they are presented or as models to follow in designing one's own activities. They represent two major strategies in introducing, repeating, and making useful some of the major language concepts required for literacy. First, they introduce language concepts through group activities in which students can participate successfully without having to be good at reading and writing. Second, concepts are elaborated and practiced through independent activities. All these relate stated language concepts to topics that are covered in most instructional programs dealing with reading/language development.

The concepts used throughout this book are organized into nine major categories, which are listed in Table 1. Under each major concept is a listing of subconcepts with references to specific activities that develop them. Table 1.1 can be used as a guide for selecting purpose-related language experiences for students no matter what teaching style or classroom organization is in operation.

Table 1.1 Table of Language Concepts in Group* and Independent Activities

1. Code: concepts dealing with the alphabet as a *code* for recording speech sounds.

The English alphabet has twenty-six letters.
- Cinquains from A to Z 83
- Alphabet Puzzle 189
- ABC Montage 214

Each letter of the alphabet has a name.
- Alphabet Shopping 154
- Eat Your Own Words 176
- ABC Montage 214

Each letter of the alphabet has a recognizable shape.
- Eat Your Own Words 176
- ABC Montage 214

Capital and small letters are used in writing.
- Words that Begin like My Name 176
- Who Am I? 177
- Alphabet Puzzle 189
- ABC Montage 214

The words we say are written with the letters of the alphabet.
- "Limericks" 74
- Eat Your Own Words 176
- What Do You Hear? 271

The letters of the alphabet are used over and over to write words.
- "The Amorous Octopus" 160
- "At the Circus" 165
- Antonym Train 184
- What Is the Word in That State? 192
- Just One! 194

Some letters are called consonants and some are called vowels.
- Puzzle Announcements 193

* Group activities are built on selections whose titles are in quotation marks.

Reproduction of simple letter forms and letter sequences in words is basic to reading and writing.

2. Communication: concepts highlighting language as a *process* of human interaction.

People communicate in many ways through many media.

Meanings change by voice inflection, rate of speaking, and other oral characteristics that do not show in print.

People use common courtesies when communicating with other people.

People communicate by speaking and writing in sentences.

(*continued*)

Table 1.1 *continued*

Two-faced Words 173
Join Us 177
Sports Words 179
I Don't Like Blanks 183
The Opposite Pocket 185
Discovering New Friends 192
I Heard Music 273

People communicate some information in sequence.
Push the Button 87
Growing Up Stories 150
Recipe Exchange 235
Filmstrip Stories 277

A sequence of pictures can tell a story without words.
Growing Up Stories 150
Filmstrip Stories 277

We can use language for fun and nonsense.
"Limericks" 74
Take a Pill 91
Slurvians 195
"The Zingitty Zangetty Zoo" 204
Newspaper Costumes 218
Ridiculous Recipes 233
A Clown Act 258
Animal Party 260
Timed Activities 301

The same picture suggests different words and ideas to different people.
Comic Stories 86
Growing Up Stories 150
Comparisons Using As . . . As 164
Imaginary Walk 273
What a Contrast! 274
Filmstrip Stories 277

Abstract forms may suggest ideas that can be expressed in words.
Illustrating Manuscripts for Publication 102
A Triangle Hunt 186

Want Ad Art 210
Clowns 215
Cook Some Clay 219
What's Hiding There? 221
Scissorettes 222
My Own Slides 276
A Mood Picture 279

Language can be expressed in rhythmic patterns.
"Tanka" 69
Modern Mother Goose 84
Name Chant 172
"We Are Making Soup at School" 226
"With a Friend" 245
Ish Dance 255
Mother Goose in My Town 272
Folk Songs 275
Syllabication 295

Some symbols other than our alphabet communicate meaning.
Feet Riddles 84
Big Numbers 85
Illustrating Manuscripts for Publication 102
Can You Name It? 150
Number Posters 154
A Triangle Hunt 186
Number Hunt 189
Family Food Budget 237
"When Can I Eat?" 268
Filmstrip Stories 277

We perceive our own meanings from our experiences.
Comic Stories 86
The Missing Person 88
"Green Desert" 141
Can You Name It? 150
I Don't Like Blanks 183
Discovering New Friends 192
"Beauty Is Blue Sky" 205
Transparent Illustrations 207
Want Ad Art 210

(*continued*)

Table 1.1 *continued*

Masks for Me 211
"Ish Time" 253
"Bill Henley and the Magic Bus" 269
What's the Title? 278

People express feelings and emotions through creative activities.
"Terquain" 56
"Tanka" 69
"Sijo" 71
Stories from Classified Ads 91
"Click! Click! Click!" 137
Transparent Illustrations 207
Popcorn Clowns 215
A Feast for Birds 241
Over and Over 246
Mirror Acting 257
Paper Sack Plays 257
A Clown Act 258
My Own Slides 276
A Mood Picture 279

Greeting cards and letters are special ways of saying things.
Take a Pill 91
"But I Smell Good Morning" 132
Special Occasion Mobiles 212
Greeting Cards 216
Nature Greetings 217

Replicating information requires attention to details.
Visual Memory 283

3. Description: concepts dealing with language *elaboration* with special emphasis on adjectives and adverbs.
Descriptive words and phrases help make meanings clear.
"Circus Horses" 55
"Terquain" 56
"Cinquains" 61
"Diamantes" 64
"So Nosey Was His Name" 75
Writing Cinquains 82

Numerals are symbols of how many and how much.

Colors of things are described with words.

Sizes of things are described with words.

Shapes of things are described with words.

(*continued*)

Table 1.1 *continued*

Smells of things are described with words.	
Sense Books	93
"Popcorn Pops"	228
Tasting Fruit	237
Popcorn	238
Pancakes	239
Tastes of things are described with words.	
Sense Books	93
"Popcorn Pops"	228
"Tongue Tinglers"	231
Tasting Fruit	237
Popcorn	238
Pancakes	239
Applesauce	240
Quickie Doughnuts	240
A Feast for Birds	241
The feel of things is described with words.	
Fashion Parade	86
What a Character!	87
Sense Books	93
"Popcorn Pops"	228
Quickie Doughnuts	240
Feelings of people and animals are described with words.	
Writing Cinquains	82
"Click! Click! Click!"	137
My "Said" List	149
What Did They Say?	149
Doodle-dee-doo!	208
Special Occasion Mobiles	213
Show Me	256
Many Moods	259
Sounds are imitated and described with words.	
What Did I Hear?	89
Sense Books	93
Communicating Animals	214
"Popcorn Pops"	228
A Clown Act	258
Bird Calls	274

Imagination promotes picturesque speech.

We can describe things without telling their names.

Numerals and number names tell the rank order of things.

Many descriptive words that compare two or more things end in *-er* and *-est*.

People use similes and metaphors to compare and contrast things and ideas.

4. Movement: concepts dealing with words describing *movement*, with special emphasis on *verbs*.

There are words for the many movements of people, animals, and things.

(*continued*)

Table 1.1 *continued*

Movements of people, animals, and things can be acted out.

Most sentences have at least one verb or a form of *be* or *have* in them.

Most verbs have different forms to express the meaning of time.

Most verbs have different forms to express the meaning of number.

5. Names: concepts dealing with names of people, places, and things, with special emphasis on words as *nouns*.

Everything has a name.

Every person has a name.

Most nouns have different forms to express number.

(*continued*)

Table 1.1 *continued*

Numerals and numbers have word names.	
Big Numbers	85
Words that Tell How Many	151
Number Posters	154
"School for the Animals"	162
"Five Somethings"	169
Count Them	171
Imaginary creatures can have names.	
Who Lives in the Mountains?	151
"Mongon Wears Shoes"	202
My Own Thing	220
"Mongon Helps"	248
Some things have several names.	
Friends Finding Things	187
Classification Games	287
Some nouns are common and some are proper.	
Words I Can Read	145
Proper nouns begin with a capital letter.	
Characters Only	148
Who's on My Family Tree?	189
I Like Music	272
Initials can stand for names.	
Who's on My Family Tree?	189
Groovy Initials	219
Cook Some Clay	219
Time concepts have specific names.	
Time Words	176
Words that are used as nouns in sentences can be used in other ways.	
More Syllable Synonyms	83
Words I Can Read	145
Incomplete Sentence Strips	148
Discovering Sentences	185

6. Phonics: concepts dealing with *analysis* and *synthesis* of sound-symbol relationships.

Many words begin with the same sound and symbol.

Many words end with the same sound and symbol.

Any sound that can be spoken can be represented with letters of the alphabet.

Changing one letter in a word can change its pronunciation and meaning.

A consonant or consonant cluster usually represents the same sound at the beginning of a word.

A vowel can represent a variety of sounds at the beginning of a word.

(*continued*)

Table 1.1 *continued*

Some syllables appear over and over in the language.
"The Twelve Jugglers" 128
Decoding 294
Syllabication 295

Consonants are sometimes blended together to represent a sound different from that of any of the single letters.
"More and More Clowns" 129
"Flight Attendant" 131
Blending 289

Many words rhyme with other words.
"Quick Couplets" 59
I Like Couplets 78
Rhyming Words 78
"Let Me Ride" 126
"School for the Animals" 162
Rhyming Names 179
Rhyming Friends 259
Listening for Rhyming Words 277
Matching Games 285

7. Reading: concepts dealing with the *decoding of meanings* in language and the ability to *reconstruct printed forms of language.*
Oral reading can bring an audience pleasure and information.
"Sijo" 71
Moving Stories 92
"Enough Friends" 139
Words I Can Read 145
Everybody Show 146
"Mongon Wears Shoes" 202

Punctuation and capitalization are aids to oral reading.
"Lickety! Splickety! Boom!" 134
Incomplete Sentence Strips 148
My "Said" List 149

Understanding and following directions helps one solve problems.
Guessing Last Lines 153
Discovering Synonyms 193

Paper Sack Pets 217
Trifold Treasures 218
Recipe Exchange 235
Pancakes 239
Applesauce 240
Comprehension I 297

A few words in a story can carry most of the meaning.
Mystery Stories 144
Everybody Show 146
Comprehension II 300

Locating facts requires one to look in many kinds of materials.
"Green Desert" 141
Who Lives in the Mountains? 151
Three Kinds of Reading 152
What's in a Tree? 155
Fact or Fantasy? 155
Where in the World Did That Word Come From? 156
Where in the World? 237

Alphabetical arrangements help one locate information.
Cinquains from A to Z 83
Who Lives in the Mountains? 151
Three Kinds of Reading 152
What's in a Tree? 155
Fact or Fantasy? 155
Where in the World Did That Word Come From? 156
"The Amorous Octopus" 160
Compound Words in Dictionary 178
Where in the World? 237

Knowing about phonics is an aid to oral and silent reading.
Comprehension II 300

A reader can enjoy the way an author says things as much as what the author says.
"Lanterne" 58
"Let Me Ride" 126
"Lickety! Splickety! Boom!" 134
Figures of Speech 149

(*continued*)

Table 1.1 *continued*

Three Kinds of Reading 152
Guessing Last Lines 153
Trifold Treasures 218
Newspaper Costumes 218

Readers use recognition skills to confirm or deny their predictions.
"Let Me Ride" 126
"The Twelve Jugglers" 128
"More and More Clowns" 129
"Flight Attendant" 131
"Lickety! Splickety! Boom!" 134
"School for the Animals" 162

8. Words: concepts dealing with the *acquisition* and *recognition* of vocabularies for language communication.
Words can be used for pleasure only.
Modern Mother Goose 84
"The Zingitty Zangetty Zoo" 204
Paper Sack Plays 257
Mother Goose in My Town 272
I Heard Music 273

Words help form pictures in the mind.
"Haiku" 66
Find Five and Seven 81
"Enough Friends" 139
What Did They Say? 149
Trifold Stories 153
"Comparisons Using As . . . As" 164
Two-faced Words 173
Paper Sack Pets 217

Some words occur frequently in our language.
"Circus Horses" 55
Fifteen Words 90
"The Twelve Jugglers" 128
Compound Word List 152
Score Five 154
"Put Togethers" 168

Compound Words in Dictionary 178
Discovering Sentences 185
Word Detail—Matching 284
Matching in Context 284
Classification Games 287
High-Frequency Vocabulary 290

Many words have more than one meaning.
More Syllable Synonyms 83
Color Talk 172
Two-faced Words 173
Sports Words 179
You're My Opposite 191
Discovering Synonyms 193
"Beauty Is Blue Sky" 205
Matching Games 285

Words have a different number of syllables or beats.
"Lanterne" 58
"Cinquains" 61
"Haiku" 66
"Tanka" 69
"Limericks" 74
Writing Limericks 79
Writing Haiku 80
Find Five and Seven 81
Writing Cinquains 82
Cinquains from A to Z 83
More Syllable Synonyms 83
Name Chant 172
Syllabication 295

Compound words are two or more words combined into one.
Compounds in My World 85
Compound Word List 152
"Put Togethers" 168
Compound Words in Dictionary 178
New Put Togethers 186
Compounds 292

(*continued*)

Table 1.1 *continued*

Contractions are two or more words shortened and joined with an apostrophe to show that the sounds and letters are missing.

I'm a Contractor 182
I Don't Like Blanks 183
Finding Contractions 188
Contractions 292

Synonyms are words that have similar meanings.

"Cinquains" 61
"Tanka" 69
Writing Haiku 80
Find Five and Seven 81
Writing Cinquains 82
More Syllable Synonyms 83
Kangaroo Words 178
That's the Size of It! 180
Discovering Synonyms 193

Abbreviations are used in places where whole words are not needed.

Can You Name It? 150
I'm Abbreviated 180
Recipe Exchange 235

Antonyms are words that have opposite meanings.

"Diamantes" 64
Collecting Antonyms 89
Guess What? 89
"At the Circus" 165
Antonym Train 184
The Opposite Pocket 185
You're My Opposite 191
Foods Change 236
Popcorn 238
What a Contrast! 274

Homonyms are words that sound alike but have different meanings.

Homonym Hunt 190

Onomatopoeic words are those whose sounds suggest their meanings.

Palindromes are words that read the same forward and backward.

New words can be created by anyone.

Words used today come from many sources.

The same words are spelled the same way wherever they appear.

9. Writing: concepts dealing with language *encoding* and with *self-expression* through language.

Stories and poems can be written with words and pictures or with words only.

(*continued*)

Table 1.1 *continued*

Stories and poems can grow out of real experiences.	
"So Nosey Was His Name"	75
Writing a Sijo	81
The Missing Person	88
"Green Desert"	141
Where Are My Friends?	156
Paper Sack Pets	217
My Own Clicks	278
Stories and poems can grow out of imagination.	
"Limericks"	74
Writing Limericks	79
Push the Button	87
The Missing Person	88
Paper Sack Pets	217
My Own Thing	220
My Own Clicks	278
Titles are used to tell the main idea of a production.	
"So Nosey Was His Name"	75
Writing a Sijo	81
"Click! Click! Click!"	137
Moving Pictures	209
I Like Music	272
What's the Title?	278
The same language patterns are used over and over in writing.	
"Circus Horses"	55
Modern Mother Goose	84
"Let Me Ride"	126
"The Twelve Jugglers"	128
"But I Smell Good Morning"	132
"Enough Friends"	139
Join Us	177
"We Are Making Soup at School"	226
"When Can I Eat?"	268
Mother Goose in My Town	272
Folk Songs	275

Alliteration is the use of two or more words together that begin with the same sound.

Rhyming is the use of two or more words that end with the same sound.

Simple statements can be extended and elaborated.

Simple stories have a beginning, an elaboration of the beginning, and an ending.

Authors describe settings in ways that let readers form mental images of them.

(continued)

Table 1.1 *continued*

Authors describe characters in ways that let readers form mental images of them.
"So Nosey Was His Name" 75
What a Character! 87
"Click! Click! Click!" 137
Characters Only 148
My Own Thing 220
"Bill Henley and the Magic Bus" 269

Authors improve writing by editing it.
"Lanterne" 58
"Diamantes" 64
"Tanka" 69
"Sijo" 71
Moving Stories 92
Editing Manuscripts for Publication 97

Many poets use unusual language to describe something usual.
"Haiku" 66
"Sijo" 71
Writing Haiku 80
Writing a Sijo 81
Three Kinds of Reading 152
Mother Goose in My Town 272

Use with Basal Readers

Language Experience Activities is a useful resource for teachers who use basal reader instruction on a daily, systematic schedule. The concepts that each activity develops support and extend the language concepts presented in basal reader teacher guides.

Teachers can use Table 1.1 as a reference to select group activities that introduce the basic language concepts that are to be developed in the reading instructional program or in one or more reading groups. These selections, with related activities, bring unity to the class. They repeat and review concepts that might not be internalized in the direct teaching. They give poor oral readers opportunities to grasp basic concepts through activities that do not require the use of usual recognition skills. They give good oral readers an opportunity to apply what they know through a variety of language experiences.

Table 1.1 can be used as a reference for selecting independent activities that have subconcepts that match those stated in the reading curriculum. These can be placed in learning centers for assigned or choice activities. The sharing and presentation of results permits all students to profit from what others learn regardless of their level of reading proficiency.

In implementing basal reader programs, there is no need to match the stated concepts of lessons one-to-one with the subconcepts listed in Table 1.1. Each subconcept is basic to literacy and will appear in basal reader teacher guides from time to time. Activities can be chosen in terms of pupil and teacher interest, in terms of learning centers that are operational at any given time, and in terms of the need to repeat and review basic understandings in new settings and with new materials.

The following tables will help the teacher to further implement a program that integrates basal reader instruction with *Language Experience Activities.*

Table 1.2, "Correlating Basal Readers and Learning Center Concepts," below, identifies some of the major emphases of a basal

Table 1.2 Correlating Basal Reader and Learning Center Concepts

BASAL READER EMPHASIS	APPROPRIATE CENTER ACTIVITIES
1. Acquisition of a sight vocabulary of high-frequency words.	1. Emphasis on the acquisition of form-class words—nouns, verbs, adjectives, adverbs—that are in the student's vocabulary. This emphasis is in all learning centers.
2. Word-analysis techniques in predetermined strategies.	2. Emphasis on an understanding of the details of printed words through the writing and spelling of familiar words and sentences in the Writing Center.

(continued on p. 25)

Table 1.2 *continued*

3. Comprehension of what others have written during student oral-silent reading.	3. Materials that give students opportunities to interact with the ideas of others in the Listening/Viewing Center and to respond in Art, Drama, and Writing.
4. "Readers" as the major material, with follow-up activities on the same content.	4. Self-produced books from the Publishing Center, recorded materials in the Listening/Viewing Center, and choice of books in the Reading Center.
5. Production of conventional language as a readiness base for success in reading at all levels of instruction.	5. Strategies for using home-rooted language in dictated and written materials that are useful in the learning environment and that show students that their language is honored.
6. Like-ability groups formed for direct instruction in reading.	6. Ways to establish a learning center organization that values and uses heterogeneous along with basal reader ability groups.
7. Convergent-type responses as requirements for success in reading.	7. Many activities with divergent responses—Art, Drama, Publishing, Writing.
8. Cognitive skills as the main feature in the direct instruction program.	8. Activities with added dimensions of affective and psychomotor skills in all the centers.
9. Evaluation of progress as judged by informal and formal instruments.	9. Suggestions for displaying evidence of progress and achievement with completed activities shared through the Appraisal of Pupil Progress procedures on pp. 37–44.

reader program. The table correlates these emphases with the major concepts behind the activities in each learning center.

Table 1.3, "Classroom Organization: Basal Reader Ability Groups," below, includes a suggested schedule for daily instruction and procedures for using activities to support and extend the major language/reading concepts in the basal reader program.

Table 1.3 Classroom Organization: Basal Reader Ability Groups

DAILY SCHEDULE

9:00–9:30	Large-Group Activities Read selections with group for unison and/or choral response. Introduce learning center activities. Demonstrate reading strategies. Use patterned language activities. Sing songs to practice language that is not home-rooted. View filmstrips that are to be placed in the Viewing/Listening Center with activities.
9:30–10:00	Group 1—Basal reader ability-group instruction Group 2—Reader workbook or learning center activities Group 3—Learning center activities
10:00–10:30	Recess
10:30–11:00	Group 1—Reader workbook or learning center activities Group 2—Learning center activities Group 3—Basal reader ability-group instruction
11:00–11:30	Group 1—Learning center activities Group 2—Basal reader ability-group instruction Group 3—Reader workbook or learning center activities

(*continued*)

Table 1.3 *continued*

11:30–12:00	Large-Group Activities Sharing of learning center activities. Assessment in terms of stated objectives. Display of pupil-produced materials.

PROCEDURE

1. Identify major language-reading concepts in the teacher's guide of the basal reader series being used with the three groups.
2. Find the concepts related to them in Table 1.1, "Language Concepts," pages 2–22.
3. Use the activities as they are presented in *Language Experience Activities* or develop others to extend the concepts into multiple learning centers.
4. Balance the types of activities by offering those with divergent responses along with those with convergent responses, those that require reading/writing abilities along with those that do not, and a variety of levels of difficulty so that every pupil has a chance to be successful. See "Why Learning Centers," pages 35–36.
5. Arrange the learning environment so that there are quiet areas away from those with noise. See "How to Organize Learning Center Environments," pages 36–37.
6. Share learning center activities with a direct focus on the language/reading concepts being developed.
7. Keep records of pupil participation in learning center activities that related to the stated objectives of the reading instructional program. See "Appraisal of Pupil Progress," pages 37–44.

9–9:30		9:30–10	10–10:30	10:30–11	11–11:30	11:30–12
Large-Group Activity	Direct Instruction Workbook or L.C.'s Learning Centers Other	Group 1 Group 2 Group 3 Choice	Recess	Group 3 Group 1 Group 2 Choice	Group 2 Group 3 Group 1 Choice	Sharing/ Assessment

FIGURE 1.1 Ability Group Organization with Basal Readers

Table 1.4, "Classroom Organization: Learning Centers," below, includes a one-week schedule based on learning centers as the major organizational pattern, with basal readers as the direct instruction component. The table also includes procedures for using the resources in *Language Experience Activities*.

Table 1.4 Classroom Organization: Learning Centers

DAILY SCHEDULE

9:00–9:30 Large-Group Activities

- Read selections with group for unison and/or choral response.
- Introduce learning center activities.
- Demonstrate reading strategies.
- Use patterned language activities.
- Sing songs to practice language that is not home-rooted.
- View filmstrips that are to be placed in the Viewing/Listening Center.
- Invite student authors to read original manuscripts.
- Demonstrate editing procedures with manuscripts that are to be published.
- Involve students in test-taking strategies.

9:30–10:00 Students in Learning Centers

	M	T	W	Th	F
Group 1	DI	WP	RR	LS	AC
Group 2	AC	DI	WP	RR	LS
Group 3	LS	AC	DI	WP	RR
Group 4	RR	LS	AC	DI	WP
Group 5	WP	RR	LS	AC	DI

(*continued*)

Table 1.4 *continued*

	Code DI—Direct Instruction in reading WP—Writing/Publishing activities RR—Reading/Research activities LS—Language Study games and activities AC—Arts and Crafts activities
10:00–10:30	Recess
10:30–11:00	Assigned skill materials that relate to selected concepts. Workbooks that accompany reading texts. Choosing time for learning center activities for students who have completed assigned work.
11:00–11:30	Sharing of learning center activities and assessment in terms of objectives. Discussion of responses to skill materials. Reading of pupil-produced materials.

Identification of Language/Reading Concepts that Need Special Emphasis in Instruction and in Learning Centers

PLANNING FOR SMOOTH OPERATION OF THE LEARNING CENTERS.

Procedure

1. Organize the class into four heterogeneous ability groups to work in learning centers. The fifth group will be students that the teacher calls out from the heterogeneous groups for direct instruction in reading. This group may be made up of students with approximately the same reading ability, or it may be a group of mixed ability. Make certain that at least one member of each of the learning center groups can carry out instructions.
2. Select language/reading concepts to be emphasized over a period of at least a week. Find those concepts in the teacher's guide of the basal reader series being used. After identifying five or more major concepts, use Table 1.1 to find matching concepts for learning centers. Activate those centers for which there are activities that relate. Also, make adaptations of activities to fit concepts.

3. Work in direct instruction with one group each day during a week. Other learning center groups work independently on assigned activities during the 9:30–10:00 period. All the assigned activities should relate to the major objectives selected for the week or to those that have been developed in previous weeks. Other activities can be in the centers for students who complete their assigned tasks early.
4. Balance the types of activities by offering those with divergent responses along with those with convergent responses, those that require reading/writing ability along with those that do not, and a variety of levels of difficulty so every student has a chance to be successful. See Why Learning Centers, pages 35–36.
5. Add learning centers other than the assigned ones for the 10:30–11:00 period. At times engage all the students in an activity from one of the centers, such as drama or cooking. At other times use one of the literature selections as a whole-group activity.
6. Share learning center activities with a direct focus on the language/reading concepts being developed. Help each student to be aware that the concept comes from communication of many types—not just from reading.
7. Keep records of pupil participation in learning center activities that relate to the stated objectives of the instructional program. See Appraisal of Pupil Progress, pages 37–44.

Use to Develop Authorship by Students

Most of the learning center chapters have selections that can serve as models for students to use with their own vocabulary and their own ideas. They furnish models for writing that use language like that which students will find when they read literature. The process of authorship—developing manuscripts; editing, paging, illustrating, and binding them; and using them as curriculum materials in the classroom—assures each child some understanding of the *reading process* that is not inherent in typical instructional programs. It is an essential experience for easy entry into literacy. Specific activities are suggested for studying the style and form of the selections, but there are some basic steps that can be followed in getting most of the selections from the *listening to* stage to the production of personal books to be used at school and in the home.

9–9:30	9:30–10	M	T	W	Th	F	10:00–10:30	10:30–11:00	11:00–11:30	11:30–12:00N
✓ Introduce L.C. activities ✓ Unison & choral reading ✓ Demonstrate reading strategies ✓ Sing songs ✓ View filmstrips ✓ Authors read manuscripts ✓ Demonstrate editing procedures	Group 1 Group 2 Group 3 Group 4 Group 5	DI AC LS RR WP	WP DI AC LS RR	RR WP DI AC LS	LS RR WP DI AC	AC LS RR WP DI	Recess	✓ Assigned skill materials ✓ Workbooks with readers ✓ Choice activities	Sharing/Assessment from learning centers Responses to skill materials Reading of pupil-produced stories and poems	Lunch

Code: DI—Direct Instruction
WP—Writing/Publishing
RR—Reading/Research
LS—Language Study Games
AC—Arts and Crafts

FIGURE 1.2 Learning Center Organization with Basal Readers

STEP 1. INPUT OF PATTERNS

Teacher reads orally.
Students read selection in the learning center.
Students listen to tape of selection.
Teacher leads discussions to identify and illustrate the constraints of the pattern.

STEP 2. REPETITION OF PATTERN

Unison reading of the selection.
Choral response by students without seeing the print.
Examining pattern for dependable visual clues.
Anchoring pattern in ears of pupils.

STEP 3. SUBSTITUTION IN PATTERN

Substitute nouns to change meanings.
Substitute verbs to go with nouns.
Choose appropriate descriptive words.
Alter other vocabulary to make sense.

STEP 4. ELABORATION OF PATTERN

Paint pictures to illustrate new version.
Dramatize new version when appropriate.
Record new version on tape for the Viewing/Listening Center
Make games with the vocabulary of the new pattern for the Language Study Center.

STEP 5. OUTPUT OF PATTERN

Edit new manuscript in the Publishing Center.
Bind material into a book in the Publishing Center.
Read new pattern orally to the class.
Read new pattern to other classes.
Place book in the Reading Center.

STEP 6. RECYCLING OF NEW PATTERNS

Publish new versions in multiple copies.
Add books to libraries.
Add books to home collections.
Make more versions from the same basic linguistic pattern.

Example 1. Read "The Twelve Jugglers," p. 128, until students can join in without seeing the print.

2. Make copies of the selection and read it in unison, noticing the progression from *first* through *fourth.* Notice the use of alliteration. Talk about the fourth line, which is shortened for effect.
3. Ask students to suggest substitutions. Try to get them to substitute nouns for which they can furnish a verb and another noun that is alliterative.

   The first batter batted one ball.
   The first cook cooked one cookie.

   Encourage children to add description that is not in the original selection.

   The first batter batted one beautiful baseball.
   The first cook cooked one chocolate chip cookie.

4. Make illustrations for each line of the selection. Act out the concept of ordinal and cardinal numbers. Talk about the difference. Make games for the Language Study Center.
5. Select some of the manuscripts for publishing. Edit the original manuscripts using suggestions from the Publishing Center. Page the manuscripts and put them in a form for binding. Share the new book with other classes. Place a copy in the Reading Center for classmates to choose as recreational reading.
6. Make additional copies of popular books. Select about one book a month to publish in a sturdy binding for the school library. Select about one book a week to be duplicated for home collections. Try to duplicate at least one book from each student during a school year.

Organization of This Book

The group and independent activities in this book are arranged in the following chapters:

Writing Center
Publishing Center
Reading/Research Center
Language Study Center

Arts and Crafts Center
Cooking Center
Dramatization Center
Viewing/Listening Center
Test-Taking Center

A language development program that is intended to increase awareness and understanding of language concepts will necessarily include many resources other than the language concept activities found in this book. For this reason, each chapter includes

A statement of purposes for the learning center chapters
Suggestions for basic materials
General suggestions for organizing and operating the center
A list of language skills inherent in the operation of the center

Many of the suggestions above do not relate directly to the activities included, but they are ongoing and general in nature. They embrace the use of such practices as

Reading with children every day
Singing songs and playing games
Discussing topics of interest
Showing films and filmstrips
Recording dictated stories
Using resource persons

Chapter 2

Language Growth in Learning Centers

In learning center environments, children are dispersed to do their work. There is a level of planning that permits independent and individual work. Resources are multiplied. Such a learning environment is useful for language growth. Theoretically, the more places a child encounters a basic concept in the learning environment, the more chances that child has to make that concept operational in personal communication through listening, speaking, reading, and writing.

Language Experience Activities offers teachers and children models for developing language activities for learning centers. Most of the book illustrates how activities that develop language concepts can be made available in many places in the classroom. Before these illustrations are presented, however, two questions need attention:

Why use learning centers for language growth?
How is the learning environment organized—room arrangement? record keeping? appraisal of progress? necessary resources?

Why Learning Centers?

Learning center environments permit language growth in multiple ways. Many children who make little, if any, progress in conventional classroom environments experience a measure of success in learning centers. These centers are particularly useful for the following reasons.

1. *Basic language concepts are available for study and review in multiple places in the learning environment.* Once a language concept is selected for emphasis, it can be illustrated in enough learning centers that it makes little difference which a child chooses. There will always be some activity that will help the child grasp that particular concept.
2. *Many of the activities permit divergent thinking and invite divergent responses.* These creative and personal responses from children are valued and are used along with convergent or "right-answer" responses.
3. *Much direct instruction is planned for individuals and small groups* because students are dispersed for independent work. The majority of students will be gainfully employed, allowing the teacher to concentrate on directly teaching a few or on counseling those who need only a little help.
4. *Language activities in each learning center represent a variety of levels of difficulty.* Some are simple and some are challenging. Children respond in terms of their interests, abilities, and needs.
5. *A high level of independent work and of student self-evaluation, not typical of conventionally organized classes, is in operation for most individuals.* Teachers help children plan their programs and record their own participation and progress. Students develop a basis for determining their own skill development and for increasing their ability to express their ideas in many different ways.
6. *Different levels of the cognitive domain are represented in learning center activities.* Some students develop abilities at the rote memory level. Others require some application of personal experience. Many require some degree of evaluation of information and past experience.
7. *The affective domain is developed in an environment in which human interaction is central to successful operation.* The personal valuing inherent in the development of the various activities builds ego strength for language growth that permits and promotes communication abilities.

8. *The movement and self-discipline necessary for the smooth operation of learning centers is recognized as basic education.* Children discipline themselves as they select tasks, carry them out, and report on them in multiple ways.
9. *Personal commitment is made to self-selected tasks.* This commitment is usually conducive to some type of self-evaluation. Individuals learn *how* to learn at the same time that they learn something.

How to Organize Learning Center Environments

The operation of a learning center environment requires careful attention to such topics as room arrangement, pupil-teacher record keeping, appraisal of pupils' progress, and resources that continue through the program. These topics are developed in the sections that follow.

Room Arrangement

Learning center room arrangements should be highly individualized for each teacher and each class group. Local resources dictate some limitations, but they also offer possibilities that are unique to each situation.

The diagrams on pages 38–39 serve only as examples of possible selections and arrangements of furnishings and materials.

Although room arrangements have no set requirements, most have some common characteristics:

1. The atmosphere is informal, with no assigned seats. The whole room is a "home" for the children.
2. Storage space or a tote tray is assigned to each student when desks are removed.
3. Open shelves are used for storage and display.
4. Display space is available for pupils' productions.
5. Privacy is provided by equipment such as shelf dividers, movable bulletin boards, large, decorated cardboard boxes (used to display children's work or as resources for a center), and see-through materials, such as netting or clear plastic sheets, that can serve as display space.

6. Homelike furnishings are included when available, such as couches, rocking chairs, lamps, floor pillows, and area rugs.
7. Space is provided for the total class group to meet for planning and discussion. A large area rug is enough, and it requires a minimum of space compared with any arrangement of chairs or desks. Table arrangements can also be used.
8. The teacher's desk is situated so that it can serve as a place for individual conferences away from most of the group activity. It is angled so that the teacher can maintain visual contact with all centers when working with individuals and small groups.
9. The Discussion Center is usually near a chalkboard. If not, an easel with a pad of paper is available for planning and record keeping.
10. The room arrangement changes at the suggestion of students and with the changing curriculum emphases.

Appraisal of Pupils' Progress

A learning center environment permits teachers to visit and plan with pupils on an individual basis. At conference time the teacher and pupil can agree on areas where progress has been made. They can plan the next stages for the pupil and identify materials in the learning laboratory that will be useful in achieving goals.

Skills and abilities identified as important are checked in some manner. Informal discussions introduce topics of interest and concern. Formal records furnish evidence of achievement. Some attempt is made to appraise each pupil on language concepts, such as those listed in How to Use This Book. The list of concepts can be used as a guide for developing conference check lists on topics being emphasized. Other language concepts not included here can be added to the program.

The following Pupil Appraisal Check Lists serve as models for those to be developed for specific learning situations: Figure 2.3, "Pupil Appraisal Check List 1" illustrates the use of the concepts at the least demanding level; Figure 2.4, "Pupil Appraisal Check List 2" illustrates the use of the concepts at an advanced level; and Figure 2.5, "Pupil Appraisal Check List 3" illustrates the use of skills and abilities highlighted in the group activities of various chapters.

There should be no secrets about the basic ideas and purposes of the individual appraisal forms. Points from the lists being used at any

(continued on p. 43)

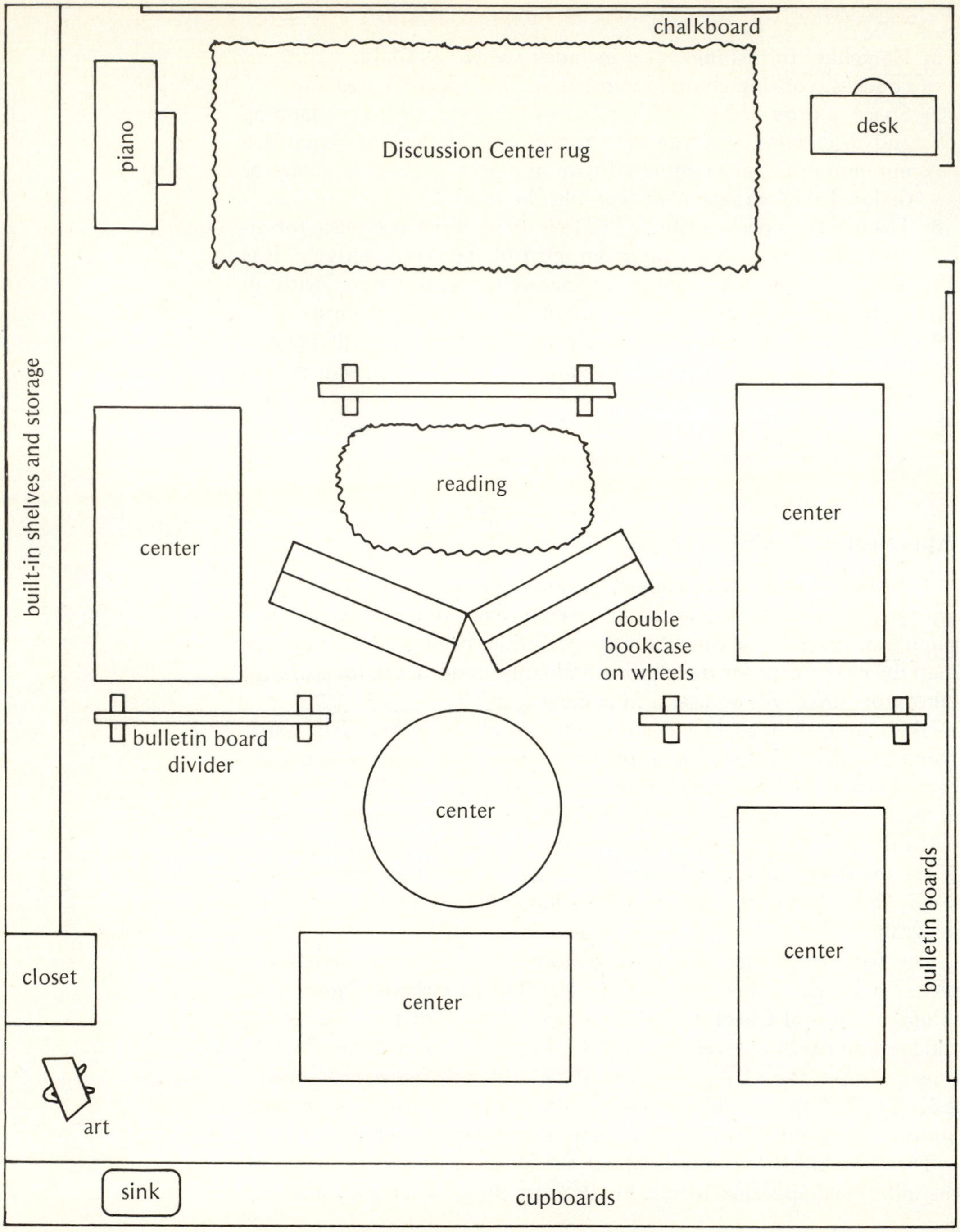

FIGURE 2.1 Suggested Floor Plan Utilizing Learning Centers

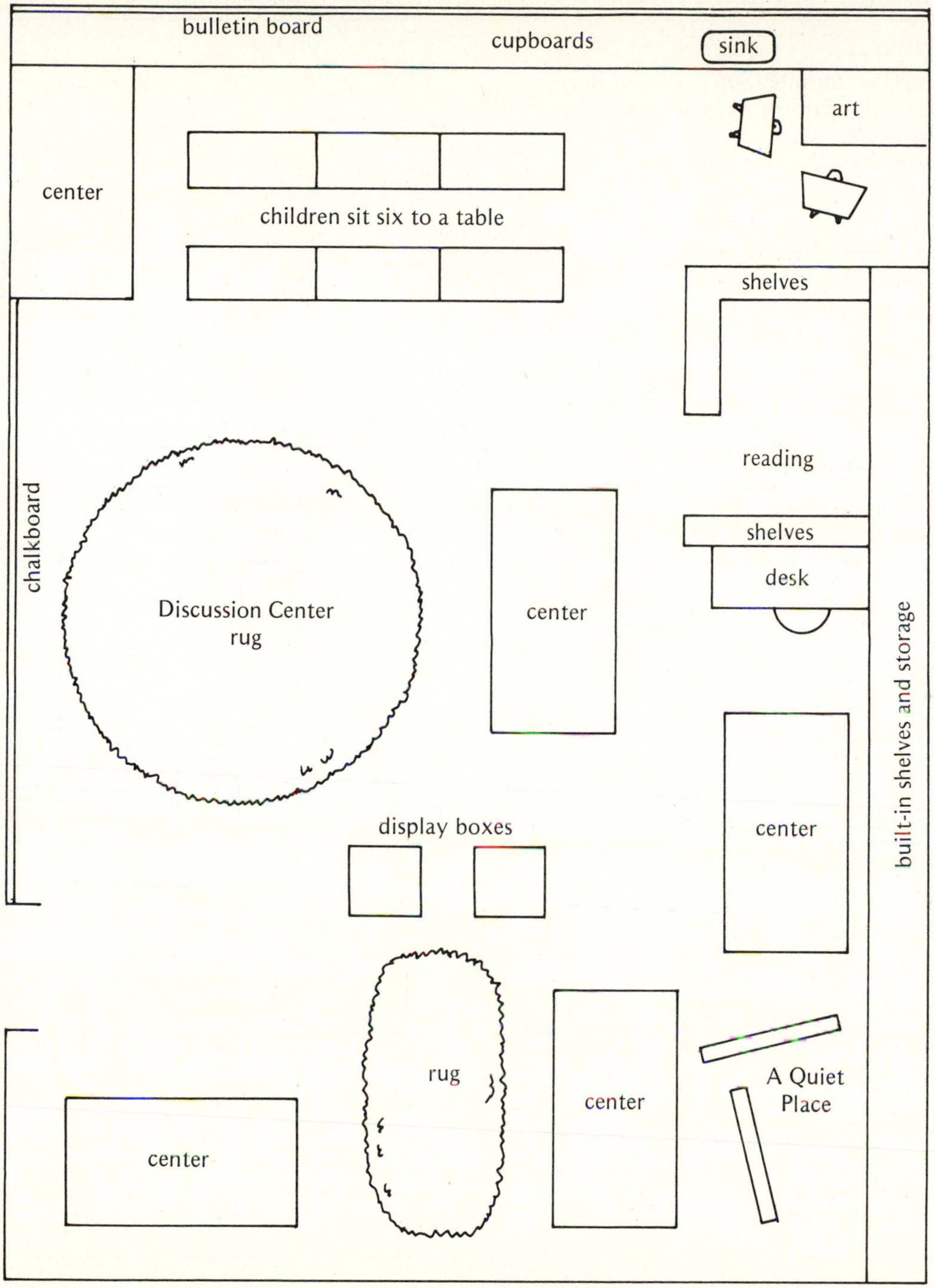

FIGURE 2.2 Suggested Floor Plan Utilizing Learning Centers

NAME ______________________________

Key:
1 *(Independent,* no need for follow-up at present time.
2 *Progress since last conference,* needs guidance.
3 *Low-level understanding,* needs specific instruction.
4 *Does not understand,* needs extension of experience.
5 *Other* (use Comments)

Concepts Developed	Date	Appraisal				
		1	2	3	4	5
Each letter of the alphabet has a name.						
A sequence of pictures can tell a story without words.						
Colors of things are described with words.						
There are words for the many movements of people, animals, and things.						
Everything has a name.						
Many words begin with the same sound and symbol.						
Punctuation and capitalization are aids to oral reading.						
Words can be used simply for pleasure.						
Some words occur frequently in our language.						
Stories and poems can grow out of real experiences.						

Teacher's and Pupil's Comments: ______________________________

____

____

____

FIGURE 2.3 Pupil Appraisal Check List 1

NAME ______________________________

Key:
1 *Independent*, no need for follow-up at present time.
2 *Progress since last conference,* needs guidance.
3 *Low-level understanding,* needs specific instruction.
4 *Does not understand,* needs extension of experience.
5 *Other* (Use Comments)

Concepts Developed	Date	Appraisal				
		1	2	3	4	5
Some letters are called consonants and some are called vowels.						
Language can be expressed in rhythmic patterns.						
Imagination promotes picturesque speech.						
Most verbs have different forms to express time.						
Words that are used as nouns in sentences can be used in other ways.						
Beginning vowels represent a variety of sounds.						
Knowing about phrases is an aid to oral and silent reading.						
New words can be created by anyone.						
Authors improve writing by editing it.						

Teacher's and Pupil's Comments: ______________________________

____

____

____

FIGURE 2.4 Pupil Appraisal Check List 2

*NAME*______________________________

Key
1 *Independent,* no need for follow-up at present time.
2 *Progress since last conference,* needs guidance.
3 *Low-level understanding,* needs specific instruction.
4 *Does not understand,* needs extension of experience.
5 *Other* (Use Comments)

Skills and Abilities	Date	Appraisal				
		1	2	3	4	5
Selects stories and poems with repeating language patterns.						
Substitutes form class words (such as nouns or verbs) to change content but not language patterns.						
Writes poetry with syllabic control.						
Writes poetry with word class restraints.						
Writes poetry with rhyming patterns.						
Predicts words and phrases when reading.						
Interprets with voice when reading orally.						
Edits manuscripts for publication.						
Produces books for others to read.						

Teacher's and Pupil's Comments:______________________________

FIGURE 2.5 Pupil Appraisal Check List 3

given time should be clarified and elaborated in group seminars. They should be illustrated with pupil and teacher demonstrations. Pupils who seem to understand should express their ideas in their own words. Those who do not should be free to ask questions.

Seminar sessions should be summarized so that children understand the relationships of specific language concepts to the broad base of communication that is being developed. The children should have opportunities to discover that they are developing a language base that permits them to read and write with increasing efficiency and effectiveness.

The following are some specific suggestions for using the appraisal forms.

1. Duplicate enough copies to have two for each pupil—one for the pupil and one to be kept in a notebook for the teacher's use at conference time.
2. Begin by covering only two or three items at a conference. Be sure the pupil can indicate some success in at least one area. If this is not possible, then that check list should not be used for that conference.
3. If a pupil receives a check in column 1 on the first conference, do not appraise in this area again until other areas have also been appraised. Checks in columns 2 and 3 indicate a need for follow-up. Checks in column 4 indicate a need for more input and more background experiences.
4. Before planning follow-up conferences, scan the pupil sheet from the previous conference. Have on hand, or ask pupils to bring, materials that will enable you to assess certain abilities.
5. Scan the record book occasionally to see if three or four pupils have similar needs. If so, plan small-group instructional sessions.
6. Involve each pupil in making a self-evaluation of language abilities and progress. Record some of the most significant comments under Teacher's and Pupil's Comments.
7. Record materials used if this information is helpful. For instance, follow-up would be different depending on whether a pupil read fluently something self-produced or something from another source with language patterns unlike those used by the pupil.
8. Record different conferences with different color inks so that progress can be judged at a glance.
9. Appraise in all areas for the most advanced pupils only. There is no need to try to record progress in areas where little, if any, awareness or skill has developed.

10. Locate topics that are feasible for the individuals to discuss and illustrate. Do not embarrass pupils with failure. Rather, use different topics to help pupils participate in planning their next steps, using the resources in the language laboratory.
11. Use the appraisal forms as a basis for pupil-parent-teacher conferences. Lead the pupils to discuss with parents some of the things they have learned and to demonstrate some of the activities on which the evaluation was based.
12. Invite parents to respond to the appraisals. Is the child progressing as expected? Are there areas of learning that parents would like to see strengthened? Are there resources at home that the parents might volunteer for classroom use?

Pupil-Teacher Record Keeping

Pupils should participate with the teacher in designing schemes for keeping records of their participation and progress in the study program. They should know that when they have the freedom to choose, they have a responsibility to account for what they do and what they think they learn.

The Language Center Learning Log is presented as an example of how pupils and teachers can develop an accounting system for the language tasks in the independent activities sections of the chapters. The logs provide pupils and teachers with an informal record of language skills development as the activities are completed.

Following are some suggestions for designing and using the Language Center Learning Log:

1. Design and duplicate blank forms to be filled in with the names of activities actually in the learning centers.
2. List the activities on the blank forms you design.
3. List skills that are basic to the completion of each activity.
4. Number the learning logs in order so that students have a record of continuous skill development over the school year.
5. Duplicate enough of the logs for each pupil.
6. Demonstrate and discuss ways of using the logs both with pupils who can work independently and with those who will need conferences to fill in the logs.
7. Schedule periodic conferences with pupils who have filled in their learning logs. Discuss the skills and attitudes they are developing and write comments. Help those who are unable to work in-

continued on page 46

Language Center Learning Log	Name		
Learning Center and Language Experience Activity	*I chose*	*I completed*	*Things I Learned (Write skill numbers)*
GAME CENTER			
Stepping Stones			
Definition Puzzles			
My Car Race			
Crosswords			
READING/RESEARCH CENTER			
Clip Cards			
Everybody Show			
Trifold Stories			
Number Posters			
WRITING CENTER			
Fifteen Words			
Comic Stories			
Feet Riddles			
Modern Mother Goose			
Teacher's Comments:	My Own Comments:		

Continue comments on back side of this sheet.

Choose from This List and Add Your Own at the Bottom

(Skill names should be selected to match the activity for each learning log.)

Skills

1. Alphabet
2. Descriptive words
3. Following directions
4. Meaning
5. Names
6. Numerals
7. Rhyming words
8. Sentence sense
9. Sequence
10. Sight vocabulary
11. Spelling
12. Summarizing
13. Verbs
14. Vocabulary (new)
15. Word Recognition
16. Writing (creative)
17. Writing (handwriting)
18.
19.
20.
21.
22.
23.
24.
25.

dependently by reviewing with them their completed activity cards.

8. Include on the learning logs space for new activities designed by pupils during the period the logs are being kept.
9. Use the Comments sections to reflect a continuing dialogue between pupil and teacher relative to language skill development.
10. Study the learning logs before developing criterion-referenced tests. Estimate "reasonable expectations" from the information on individual learning logs plus teacher observation.

Resources that Continue through the Program

A program of activities that increases awareness and understanding of language concepts is based on the assumption that the learning center environment will include many resources other than the language concept activities found in this book. For this reason, there is a presentation for each center that includes a statement of purpose, suggestions for basic materials, general suggestions for organizing and operating the center, and a list of language skills inherent in its operation.

Many of the suggestions do not relate directly to the activities included, but are ongoing and general in nature. They embrace such practices as reading to children every day, singing songs and playing games, discussing topics of interest, showing films and filmstrips, recording dictated stories, using repeating language pattern selections, and using resource persons.

Group activities for the centers are initiated with selections that highlight some characteristic of language that is frequently found in reading materials used in elementary and secondary schools. The activities relating to the selections can be used as they are, or they can serve as models for teachers and pupils to develop their own activities with other selections that have similar language characteristics.

The ability of pupils to recognize and use available reading materials to extend the language activities for the classroom multiplies the resources in ways that are not possible when the pupils read one story after another and then answer questions related directly to those stories. A well-written story or poem with language that has a dependable pattern can be multiplied into many resources.

A dozen or more stories or books might be written by imaginative children who use the pattern to write on their own topics. The children learn that by substituting new nouns they can change many stories. By substituting new nouns and verbs, they can produce stories quite different from the original. And by substituting new descriptive words as well, they create a story that differs from the original in everything but structure. The content becomes personal to the new author.

"Names for Games" (Appendix B) and "Words Used Frequently" (Appendix C) are lists of words found frequently in the language. The two lists combined total five hundred and fifty words. These words include approximately 65 to 70 percent of the words children will find in elementary-school texts and standardized tests—exclusive of proper names. They should be mastered for sight vocabulary and spelling by as many children as possible. This goal is continually emphasized in the language laboratory because these words are essential for independent reading and writing.

The words on the two lists should be available in the learning environment in many places and in many forms, such as those illustrated in the activities provided in this book. They can be used for games that repeat, review, and reinforce. They can be reproduced on wall charts for ready references for spelling and reading games. They can be duplicated, and copies can be laminated for frequent use as individual spelling references when pupils are writing. They can be available in various learning centers as resources for students making their own learning center activities for others to use.

Resources such as those provided in the Appendixes are used along with ideas from teachers and pupils. They illustrate the kinds of materials that allow for and promote personalized language activities at the same time that language learnings are extended and enriched.

In summary, learning center environments promote

efficient use of materials and equipment
self-selection by pupils of learning tasks and materials
personal commitment on the part of pupils to complete tasks selected
independent work by pupils
independent record keeping by pupils
individualization of study programs
movement on the basis of individual need
pupil-pupil interaction
pupil-teacher interaction on a personal basis
creative responses by pupils to learning situations
pupil participation in changing the learning environment
learning how to learn

Chapter 3

The Writing Center

What Is a Writing Center?

The Writing Center is a place

for exploring self-expression through writing in many forms
for writing as a recreational activity
for developing the skills necessary to encode one's ideas in language
for using already produced selections as models for literary-level writing
for using a variety of poetry forms to express ideas
for extending language for writing beyond home-rooted language and the language of conversation
for refining written language so it is useful in the school curriculum

The Writing Center is a place where children find resources and motivation that promote self-expression through writing. It must be stocked with supplies that children can use for first-draft copies as well as finished copies. Some essentials are

Paper

variety of qualities, sizes, and colors
handwriting paper to practice writing skills

newsprint for first drafts
blank sides of already used paper
computer printout paper
printer's scraps

Markers

different kinds and colors of pencils
different kinds and colors of felt-tipped pens
crayons

Writing models

several configurations of capital and lower-case letters suitable for titles, posters, and other special publications
standard models for general handwriting improvement
calligraphy for students who use artful handwriting in their publications

Spelling aids

lists of high-frequency words, found in Appendixes C and D.
lists of name words used frequently, found in Appendix B.
lists of words of movement that are used as verbs in sentences, found in Appendix C.
lists of descriptive words, found in Appendix C.
proper names useful for special projects and seasons
picture dictionaries
school dictionaries

A Word Wall can be established to hold the lists. During periods of considerable writing activity, a Word Wall Monitor can be appointed to identify words for spelling. This can be a young student who can read all the words or an older student who is assigned as an aide. The teacher does not need to provide much help in spelling when these ready resources are available.

Story stimulators and motivators

sentences and phrases to begin stories collected from many sources, written on cards, and filed in random order model stories with noun, verb, adjective, and adverb slots left blank for the authors to fill in

story beginnings copied on cards with just enough story to suggest characters, setting, and a hint of plot

story middles, copied on cards, that can be developed in both directions to tell a story

story endings, copied on cards, that give a hint of what might have happened in the entire story

story pictures for personal interpretation by authors

collections of pictures, in envelopes, that include people, places, transportation, food, entertainment, accidents, and special occasions that can be arranged in an endless number of stories

headlines from newspapers, mounted on cards, that can be used as ideas for stories and poems

riddles and jokes that can be used as models

publications such as school newspapers, magazines, classbooks, and individual books that might furnish ideas and format

Vocabulary enrichment

figurative language files with examples of similes, metaphors, and personification as used by other authors

lists of synonyms and antonyms—especially words of two, three, and four syllables that are useful in writing poetry with controlled syllabic patterns

alliteration aids, such as lists of words beginning with the same sound or symbols, including nouns, verbs, adjectives, and adverbs

rhyming aids, including groups of two, three, and four words with like rhymes

how to say "said" in many ways as an aid to writing conversation that emphasizes characterization: cried, shouted, whispered, moaned

nonsense words that can be used or can serve as examples for making up words for nonsense writing

Children who paint at the easel or make crayon drawings are encouraged to take their pictures to the Writing Center to add stories or captions. Children who are not able to do their own writing schedule a time for the teacher to record their story as they present it through dictation. While recording the dictation, the teacher can talk informally about the requirements of spelling and writing—about words that are alike, words that begin alike, words that are not the same, and words that are spelled like they sound, and about letter formation, punctuation, and capitalization. At times when a teacher or another adult is not present, a cassette recorder can be used to record the child's language.

Enjoyment is a key goal for the Writing Center. The mechanics of writing should never overshadow the pleasure of recording ideas in creative and clever ways. The publishing emphasis provides the motivation to edit manuscripts that are to be published in multiple copies for others to read. The raw writing of children is to be valued and encouraged at all times.

A Writing Center is essential for a teacher who is sensitive to the creative spirit within every child. Writing is one of the many channels through which this creative ability becomes visible. This visibility permits authors to see themselves as creators of beautiful things.

Language Skills Developed and Practiced

The child develops creative ways to express ideas through writing—poetry forms, poetry patterns, stories, comic strips, posters, plays, and games.

The child practices handwriting skills and learns multiple ways of representing the letters of the alphabet.

The child learns to use simple punctuation when writing.

The child learns to use capital and lower-case letters when writing and when publishing books.

The child learns to talk about spelling and writing skills.

The child enlarges expressive vocabulary.

The child participates in making story charts and class books.

The child makes individual books to express ideas and feelings.

The child writes imaginary stories.

The child writes stories with characters who use conversation.

The child writes notes and greeting cards.

The child writes plays and produces them with classmates.

The child learns to write words in more than one language.

Suggestions for Taking Dictation

Relationships between talking and writing exist, but writing is always an imperfect representation of talking. It lacks *pitch, tone, emphasis, pause,* and *juncture.* But writing is highly useful and can be learned early along with reading. Whereas talk is highly perishable, written records have a degree of permanence. They hold thoughts for long periods of time and can be used over and over. Refined writing represents communication with word order and patterns that are not characteristic of spontaneous expression. It can raise language to a literary level.

Procedures vary in instructional programs that help children bridge from talk to writing, but a few basic steps are required.

STEP 1

Visit with children in ways that cause them to tell names for things, how things move, and descriptive categories such as color, size, shape, texture, sound, taste, smell, number, and emotions or other feelings. *Do not write anything until there has been some talk!*

STEP 2

Use your judgment as to whether you use labels or try to elicit a story of some kind that includes syntactical structure. If a story is the goal, let the child tell the whole story before beginning to write anything. *Communicate!* Then decide whether to write the whole story or a portion of it. Usually the goals of taking dictation can be achieved by writing only one or two things the child has said.

As you write, talk to yourself audibly so the children can hear. Let it be known through your talk that

- the alphabet symbols you are using represent sounds people make when they talk
- the letters have names
- some words begin with capital letters
- the same letters are used over and over as the first letters of words
- the same words appear over and over
- some ending sounds appear over and over, and they may tell "how many" and "when"

STEP 3

Read back what you have written to check with the child that what you have written is what was said. If appropriate, ask the child to read with you. When the time is right, ask the child to call some words alone, then move on to the time when the child can repeat whole sentences.

STEP 4

Display paintings with dictation strips attached. Invite authors to tell about or "read" for the group. Read some of the sentences in unison.

Model reading with good phrasing rather than word calling as most young children do.

Ask children to use crayons or Magic Markers to identify language characteristics that are obvious in the display of four or five selections.

words that are the same
words that begin alike
words that end alike
words with capital letters
punctuation that is the same
rhyming words
words that are names
words that tell how things move
words that describe
other words that are appropriate for what is displayed

Children mark each category with a different color. Usually two, and not more than three, categories will be used with any set of dictated stories.

STEP 5

Invite children to read words, phrases, and sentences from the material displayed. Involvement is more important at this stage than correctness. Continue to model good reading and unison reading so that every child can participate. *Do not try to identify poor readers!*

STEP 6

Words that appear five or more times in the stories are collected for a chart, Words We All Use. This chart becomes a major spelling resource in the Writing Center. It is used as a source of words for games that develop a sight vocabulary of high-frequency words for reading.

It is only when most of the words on the chart are found in the "reader" that children are ready for direct instruction in that book. If children are not using the words of highest frequency that are scheduled into instructional material, they are not ready for that reading program.

STEP 7

Copy dictated words and sentences and ask children to make drawings for ditto masters. Duplicate stories for books for every child. Make attractive bindings. Use eight to ten stories for each book. Continue until every child has a contribution in at least one book.

STEP 8

When a child indicates an interest in writing, record the dictation very lightly; the child then traces over the letters. A model alphabet that shows the direction of strokes for letters is appropriate at this point.

STEP 9

After a child can trace, record dictation with space beneath each line for copying. Use writing that is large enough so children have no difficulty copying beneath what the teacher has written.

STEP 10

When a child can copy directly beneath, move to copying on another sheet of paper. This is a more mature skill and is solid evidence that the child is almost ready to do independent writing without dictation.

STEP 11

Attach two or more paintings (or fine art prints) to the top of the chalkboard for children who are ready to compose their own stories. Leave space below for writing. The children compose on the chalkboard.

STEP 12

A small group or the whole class listens to the reading of the chalkboard story and then makes suggestions for editing it—capitalization, punctuation, spelling, and the improvement of statements by adding descriptive words. Children begin to use the *language of writing* that was introduced in Step 2. The author copies the edited version on a story strip and attaches it to the painting. Other children may copy the edited story.

STEP 13

Children are on their own to write, using the resources that have been developing on charts and on cards in the Writing Center. At this point it is important that the Writing Center include activities for those who cannot write independently—short poems to copy, names of children to copy, sentence strips to trace, and alphabet cards to copy and/or trace.

STEP 14

Provide blank books with substantial covers for children to use for their stories after they are edited. Parents, aides, and older children can help by typing and by making the blank books into which the edited stories are pasted. This process assures young children access to individual authorship. This authorship serves as a launching pad to successful reading.

Group Activities

Circus Horses

The black horses prance in one by one.
The black horses prance in one by one.
The black horses prance in one by one.
They look like they're having lots of fun!

The white horses dance in two by two.
The white horses dance in two by two.
The white horses dance in two by two.
Tra-la-la-la! How do you do!

The brown horses gallop in three by three.
The brown horses gallop in three by three.
The brown horses gallop in three by three.
Tra-la-la-la! They're a sight to see!

The gray horses run in four by four.
The gray horses run in four by four.
The gray horses run in four by four.
Tra-la-la-la! Do you want more?

The spotted horses walk in five by five.
The spotted horses walk in five by five.
The spotted horses walk in five by five.
Followed by clowns very much alive!

LANGUAGE CONCEPTS

Some words occur frequently in our language.
The same language patterns are used over and over in writing.
Rhyming is the use of two or more words that end with the same sound.
Everything has a name.
There are words for the many movements of people, animals, and things.
Descriptive words and phrases help make meanings clear.

1. Read "Circus Horses" and ask children to join in as soon as they know the repeating pattern. After a while let them say the lines by themselves.
2. Copy the selection on a chart and look at the repetition. Make sure that the words that are alike in lines 1, 2, and 3 are directly beneath each other.
3. Talk about the verbs in the selection.

   prance
   dance
   gallop
   run
   walk

   Ask children to demonstrate the differences.
4. Let some children act out the selection as class members not acting say it in chorus. Substitute words in the pattern to write other selections. Let children make suggestions like

   I eat my strawberries one by one.
   I eat my strawberries one by one.
   I eat my strawberries one by one.
   My, I'm having lots of fun!

   White rabbits hop in one by one.

   Black rabbits jump in two by two.

6. Make the student productions into books. Duplicate copies for students to read and take home. Space can be left for personal illustrations.
7. Talk about words that are the same, words that rhyme, words that are names, and words that describe.

Terquain

Puppy
Wiggly, waggly
Mine

Rope
Loop and lasso
Cowboy

Cereal
Crisp, sweet
Grain

Squirrel
Frisking, frolicking
Robber

Woodpecker
Hammering and drilling
Carpenter

Basketball
Jump and turn
Fun

LANGUAGE CONCEPTS

Everything has a name.
Descriptive words and phrases help make meanings clear.
People express feelings and emotions through creative activities.
Simple statements can be extended and elaborated.

1. Read examples of terquains. Use expression that illustrates the simplicity and feeling in this terse verse. It is a simplified form of the cinquain, originated by Geraldine E. Miller in 1970.
2. Copy one or two examples for students to look at while you explain the pattern

Line 1:	One word	the subject
Line 2:	Two or 3 words	describe the subject
Line 3:	One word	a feeling about or a synonym for the subject

3. Compose some terquains with children making suggestions. Take dictation on a chart or on the chalkboard.
4. Ask for individual contributions by dictation or in writing.
5. Collect terquains for a display and for unison reading.

6. Duplicate a collection and make it into books for children to read and take home.
7. Talk about names of things and descriptions of them.

Lanterne

Plant
In my
Hanging pot
Hides three young finch
Eggs

Queen
Of all
Lovely birds
Regal is white
Swan

Brave
Tortoise
Lumbers by
Giving child a
Treat

LANGUAGE CONCEPTS

Words have a different number of syllables or beats.
A reader can enjoy the way an author says things as much as what the author says.
Simple statements can be extended and elaborated.
Authors improve writing by editing it.

1. Read examples of lanternes. Give poetic expression to the reading of this verse form from Ruth Kearny Carlson's *Sparkling Words*, Geneva, Ill.: Paladin House Publishers, 1979, pp. 167–168.
2. Copy one or two examples for students to look at as they read with you.
3. Explain the pattern of this five-line syllabic verse form.

Line 1:	one syllable	—
Line 2:	two syllables	— —
Line 3:	three syllables	— — —

Line 4:	four syllables	— — — —
Line 5:	one syllable	—

Notice the shape that results from the spacing. It may be a lantern or it may be a tree.

At Christmas time students might make tree-shaped lanterne books.

Toys
Awaited
Gifts of love
From my family
Treats

4. Compose some lanternes with children making suggestions. Edit the suggestions in terms of the form. Beat out the syllables. Display the lanternes.
5. Invite students to write their own lanternes. Authors can read theirs and then display them on a special bulletin board.
6. Collect the lanternes into a book. Duplicate copies for each student to read and take home.

Quick Couplets

Monkeys swing
Ring to ring.

Seagulls glide
With the tide.

Sheep sleep
In a heap.

Rabbits run
In the sun.

Horses neigh—
Out of hay.

Ducks quack
Back to back.

Dogs bark
In the park.

Birds sing
On the wing.

Lions roar
Four-by-four.

Camels chew
Two-by-two.

Kangaroos jump
Bumpety-bump.

Elephants spray
As they play.

Tigers growl
After a prowl.

Bells ring
Ding-a-ling!

Racers zing
Around the ring!

LANGUAGE CONCEPTS

Stories and poems can be written with words and pictures or with words only.
There are words for the many movements of people, animals, and things.
Everything has a name.
Many words rhyme with other words.

1. Read two or three quick couplets to illustrate the pattern. After that, pause before the rhyming word and let children predict what it will be. Note their responses. If no one guesses the word printed, tell them the initial consonant as a clue.
2. Talk about the meaning of *couplet*. Think of a synonym that most of the children will know.
3. Duplicate copies of "Quick Couplets" for reading. Have one child read the first line of the couplet and let others take turns reading the second line. The process can be reversed.
4. List all the words used as names in the first lines.
5. List all the words used as verbs in the first lines.
6. Choose rhyming endings from the couplets and let children think of other words they know with the same endings. Write the lists

on cards and place them in other learning centers.

7. Collect quick couplets from the children for a bulletin board. Later, bind them into books for the children to read.

Cinquains

A lone
Male cardinal
Brightens dull morning scene
Like a royal gem among the
Gray birds.

From plane—
Tall mountain peak
Pushes through cloud patterns
Like a sea of giant snowballs—
Mt. Hood.

Summer:
Tall grass sparkles
Shimmers as sun beams down
Dancing many grass routines led
By wind.

Comics
Satirical, humorous
To be enjoyed
Read and quickly forgotten
Funnies.

J. Smith

Rodeo
Competitive, rough
Riding, roping, challenging
Determined cowboys in the
Event.

P. J. Belous

Squirrel
Quiet charmer
Darts for peanuts
Sits nervously—an entertaining
Rodent.

Double Cinquain

Gradually
The bright light reflections at dawn
Change almost altogether to shapes of objects—
Houses, churches, trees, monuments all share their own shapes upside down
With the river.

LANGUAGE CONCEPTS

Descriptive words and phrases help make meanings clear.
There are words for the many movements of people, animals, and things.
Everything has a name.
Words have a different number of syllables or beats.
Synonyms are words that have similar meanings.

1. Talk about cinquains as a poetry form. The first ones were written by Adelaide Crapsey in the 1920s. The cinquain is an American form. The original version had five lines with twenty-two syllables.

   Original version:

Line 1:	two syllables
Line 2:	four syllables
Line 3:	six syllables
Line 4:	eight syllables
Line 5:	two syllables

   The cinquain began to be used in schools for writing simple verse from the experience and imagination of students. For young children a simplified version was developed.

Simplified version:

Line 1:	one word, a title
Line 2:	two words to describe the title
Line 3:	three words to tell an action
Line 4:	four words to tell a feeling
Line 5:	one word to refer to the title

Students enjoyed writing cinquains and began to expand the pattern into double cinquains. They learned that by doubling the number of syllables in each line, they produced beautiful poetry.

Double cinquain	Line 1:	four syllables
	Line 2:	eight syllables
	Line 3:	twelve syllables
	Line 4:	sixteen syllables
	Line 5:	four syllables

The cinquain emphasizes the use of form class words. Children using the simplified version have to differentiate between words that pattern in sentences as nouns, verbs, adjectives, and adverbs. The skill of elaboration is exercised also as they take one topic and use ten other words to describe it. Syllabication is optional, but when used, it yields a more rhythmic production.

2. Read the selections to illustrate the different forms of cinquains. The first three illustrate the original version, and the next three illustrate the simplified version. There is one example of a double cinquain.
3. Talk about synonyms used in lines one and five of the simplified version. Make lists of synonyms to use in writing cinquains. Use a thesaurus for this activity. Place the lists in centers where they will be useful to authors.
4. Create group cinquains. One person writes a title on the chalkboard. Others add lines until the five have been completed. Edit the group cinquains to conform to one of the patterns.
5. Find pictures that suggest cinquains. Write several cinquains from the same picture. Students in the upper grades might wish to try writing double cinquains.
6. Copy cinquains on construction paper in writing large enough to be read across the room. Illustrate them with pictures or designs. Display them on walls or on a bulletin board.

Diamantes

Night
Dark quiet
Resting relaxing sleeping
Moon stars sun clouds
Working playing eating
Bright busy
Day

Sun
Bright direct
Shining warming shimmering
Heat light cool dark
Shifting shortening lengthening
Muted cool
Shadow

Hills
Eroded rugged
Rolling repeating patterning
Peaks promontories meadows fields
Recreating replenishing providing
Pleasant peaceful
Vales

Boulders
Huge towering
Resisting wearing remaining
Castles caravans beaches beds
Shifting changing remaining
Tiny endless
Sand

Spring
Yellow green
Bursting blossoming refreshing
Flowers leaves twigs seeds
Coloring shedding dying
Brown vermillion
Fall

LANGUAGE CONCEPTS

Antonyms are words that have opposite meanings.
Descriptive words and phrases help make meanings clear.
There are words for the many movements of people, animals, and things.
Everything has a name.
Authors improve writing by editing it.

1. Explain that the diamante is an exercise in developing contrasting ideas. Usually one begins by selecting antonyms. These become the first and last lines of the diamante. Then descriptive materials are arranged, with half describing the top word and half describing the bottom word. The words are arranged in the following diamond-shaped pattern:

    noun
    adjective adjective
    participle participle participle
    noun noun / noun noun
    participle participle participle
    adjective adjective
    noun

    Lines 1 and 7 are always antonyms.
    Line 2 adjectives describe line 1.
    Line 6 adjectives describe line 7.
    Line 3 participles describe line 1.
    Line 5 participles describe line 7.
    The first two nouns of line 4 refer to line 1 and the next two nouns refer to line 7.

    Although there is no syllabic control, words that bring rhythm to the reading can be selected. Alliteration is a common characteristic. Words can be selected at random for the different slots. A diamante is seldom written from line 1 through to line 7.
2. Discuss the meaning of the word *diamante.* It will not be in most dictionaries because it is a special word made up for a poetry form. It is related to the definition of the word *diamond,* when that word means a four-sided figure with two acute and two obtuse angles.

3. Write one or two diamantes on the chalkboard or on a chart. Space the words so that they fit into a diamond shape. Draw the diamond shape around the writing.
4. Talk about antonyms and how they form the key meaning of a diamante. Ask children to list words of opposite meaning. Any pair of name words that are antonyms can be used as the first and last lines of a diamante.
5. Talk about participles. Lead children to see that the roots of the participles in the diamantes are words usually found in verb slots in sentences. As participles they describe nouns and function as adjectives. They have a common *-ing* ending.
6. Choose a pair of antonyms for a group-composed diamante. Illustrate the writing technique by writing the first and last lines before writing anything in between. Put the slash mark (/) in the center and then choose words at random to put into the other places in the pattern. Read the diamante orally to determine the rhythm of the language.
7. Edit the diamante.

   Check to see that the descriptive words change in direction at the slash mark.
   Arrange the words in each line so that they create a rhythmic flow. In lines 2, 3, 5, and 6, try placing the word with the fewest syllables first and then increasing the number of syllables in some of the words that follow.
   Select words that are alliterative for some of the lines.
   Use alliteration to connect one line with the following line.

8. Duplicate or make transparencies of some diamantes for choral reading.

   Male voices can read to the slash mark in the pattern. Female voices read the other half.
   Divide into three choirs. One choir reads the nouns, one reads the adjectives, and one reads the participles.

Haiku

Only a light touch.
Only a flutter of bright wings.
A butterfly feeds.

Six anxious finches
crowd the swaying bird feeder.
Winter wind howling.

Tall yucca candles
lighted by sun's rays. Lizard
slithers from dark hole.

Senryu

Screeching and screaming,
Huge bird rises into sky,
Belching jets of flame.

Ruffled edges dance
In steaming, bubbling butter.
Eggs over easy.

Nicki Quinn

Ghostly faces pass,
Peering through my window pane,
Shouting "Trick or treat!"

Patricia Mortimer

LANGUAGE CONCEPTS

Words have a different number of syllables or beats.
Words help form pictures in the mind.
Many poets use unusual language to describe something usual.

Haiku, according to classic Japanese poets, expresses an overall mood or emotion produced by a simple description. It is a plain statement of fact that makes a picture. Two parts make up the whole. They are compared, not by simile or metaphor, but by two phenomena that exist in their own right. Differences are just as important as likenesses.

Haiku and senryu reflect one's sensitivity to feelings, observations, and reflections. The rhythm that makes the statements poetry is the syllabic control. The author must be selective with words to get the idea across in the right number of syllables.

1. Explain the haiku and senryu pattern.

   Haiku and senryu are Oriental verse forms with the same language pattern. Frequently the term *haiku* is used to identify both. Each one has the following characteristics:

   Three lines with a total of seventeen syllables
   Line 1 has five syllables
   Line 2 has seven syllables
   Line 3 has five syllables
   There is no rhyme
   Rhythm is internal

   Haiku always refer to nature, whereas senryu refer to other topics.
2. Read haiku and senryu. Use your voice to emphasize the rhythm of the syllabic pattern.
3. Talk about topics such as

   beauty all around us
   reflections and contemplations
   saying things with few words
   observing patterns in nature

4. Duplicate copies of the selections. Use them to study the structure of each haiku and senryu. Count syllables, and talk about the simplicity of each haiku and senryu. Look for key words in each line.
5. Write some haiku and senryu as a group project. Look outside, listen, view a painting or photograph, or reflect on a beautiful spot. Write three or more quick thoughts on the topic selected. Use names, color, motion, shape, texture, and feelings as starting ideas. Compare and contrast. Ask questions. Use the chalkboard so the editing is easy.

   Don't pay any attention to the number of syllables when jotting down first thoughts.

   Check the syllables in what you wrote. Some of your thoughts will be in lines of five or seven syllables naturally. This may be a surprise, but it is true.

   Edit to get the five-seven-five pattern.

omit structure words or add them
use synonyms
change tenses
add descriptive words with nouns

Test the haiku or senryu for structure. When one is finished, read it with a voice that conveys the sensitive feeling described in the poem.

6. Ask pupils to try writing on their own. Some will succeed very quickly; others will need time. Haiku and senryu cannot be forced.
   Always have a place for beautiful statements that do not fit the pattern.
7. Plan to decorate the classroom with illustrated haiku and senryu as they come from the authors.
8. Plan at least one illustrated book of haiku and one of senryu. Do special things with leaves, flowers, feathers, and twigs for illustrations.

Tanka

Cardinal flies down
To find a sunflower seed
On cold, winter ground.
The welcome red visitor
Brightens a cold New Year's Day.

Rows of cottonwoods
Pointing the way to the town
Vibrant with new leaves.
Dozens of black dots fly down.
Starlings! searching for breakfast.

Streaking cloud deforms
Rosy early morning ball
Shining through blue mist.
Two black birds knife through the view
Bringing life into the morn.

Even in dying
The giant saguaro cactus
Delights boys and girls
Becoming a freakish clown
As it sheds its coat of life.

Falling rain splatters
Against the closed windowpane.
Young faces peer out
Waiting for the sun to come
After a summer shower.

Lynn Waters

LANGUAGE CONCEPTS

Language can be expressed in rhythmic patterns.
People express feelings and emotions through creative activities.
Words have a different number of syllables or beats.
Synonyms are words that have similar meanings.
Authors improve writing by editing it.

1. Explain the tanka pattern. It has five lines or thought parts and thirty-one syllables.

   Line 1—five syllables
   Line 2—seven syllables
   Line 3—five syllables
   Line 4—seven syllables
   Line 5—seven syllables

   If you know about haiku, you will observe that tanka begins with a haiku form and then adds two thoughts in two lines of seven syllables each.

   An important thing to keep in mind when writing is that tanka is real and sincere. It comes from the heart. The images must be clear enough for the reader to associate personal meanings. The author compares, questions, and makes statements, but never preaches.
2. Read some tanka selections to illustrate the language rhythm of the pattern. As you read, notice that the author usually expresses five thoughts on one topic. These may include

the name of something.
its actions.
its location.
its usefulness.
its beauty.
something distinctive.
something unusual.
a comparison.
the color, size, shape, texture, or sound.

3. Write some tanka as a group project. Use as a topic something you can observe, like the weather, an animal, an insect, a plant, or a person.

   Some hints

   Write what you think first and then count the syllables.
   As you count, delete words not required for the meaning.
   Change words to get more or fewer syllables in a line.
   Change tense to change the number of syllables.
   Add one-syllable descriptive words to nouns. Experiment with new words.
   Use a thesaurus to find new words with the same meanings.
   Consider the five lines as one or two sentences. Even though you want five thoughts, you can make sentences continuous and achieve this.

4. Plan displays and publications so students will know their productions are useful and needed.
5. Collect tanka from other authors if they are available. Copy them and illustrate them for a book.

Sijo

For a fleeting moment
the winter dawn watercolors
a mountain of tall buildings
blending them with city's backdrop
of rugged desert mountains.
Study in grays, orange accents.

On a cloudy winter day
Woodpeckers, finches, and quail
Join in a Thank-you Chorus
As I return to the house
After tossing them bread and seed
And filling their water bowl.

An artful, graceful skater
ballets across the smooth ice
to classical music
like a flower growing
and swaying in the breeze—
hair flowing, long arms expressive.

Pistachio fudge and pumpkin pie
Chimichangas, chicken chow mein
Popcorn, pizza, and pasta
Two thousand calorie fun
Mere moments of wicked delight
Better to write it than eat it!

Peggy Goldman

Swings ascending higher, higher,
Children tumbling, intertwining,
Chasing flies and low bounces,
Stoop-tag, touch-tag, calling, "You're it!"
Follow the leader, choo-choo trains,
Fun on the playground at school.

Patricia Mortimer

In the garden was a surprise.
Popcorn was on the apple tree.
I ran out to take a handful,
A popcorn ball to make and eat.
Looking closer I soon saw
Popcorn was a fragrant blossom.

Lorelyn Thomas

LANGUAGE CONCEPTS

Many poets use unusual language to describe something usual.
People express feelings and emotions through creative activities.
Alliteration is the use of two or more words together that begin with the same sound.
Oral reading can bring an audience pleasure and information.
Authors improve writing by editing it.

1. Duplicate copies of some of the sijos, but do not describe the pattern. Have students follow along as they listen to the reading. Then ask them to figure out the pattern. Because the syllable pattern varies, this will be difficult.

   Listen for statements regarding six lines, alliteration, repetition, and varied number of syllables per line. Lead a discussion on the variety of possibilities inherent in this form.

   (Some students will be interested in knowing that sijo was developed during the Yi Dynasty in Korea in the fourteenth century. Some of it was translated into English and explained by Peter H. Lee, in his book *Korean Literature, Themes and Topics,* when Dr. Lee was a visiting scholar at the University of Arizona in Tucson. The book was published in 1965 by the University of Arizona Press.)

   School use of sijo was introduced in an article, "Sijo," by Lee Bennett Hopkins in *Instructor Magazine* in March 1969. (It is a new verse form for school use.)
2. Explain the sijo pattern.
   Sijo, pronounced "shee-djo," is a Korean form.
   The pattern

six lines
six to eight syllables in each line
forty-two to forty-eight syllables total
a statement or question for each line
no rhyming pattern, but internal rhyming and alliteration are common characteristics of Korean verse
no limitation of topics

The sijo is based on syllabication, but it is not as strict a pattern as haiku and tanka. The thoughts are arranged in six lines of six, seven, or eight syllables each.

This pattern highlights elaboration abilities. Authors must say six things about one thing. The form is akin to outlining but is more artistic and challenging.

3. Have students practice writing sijo individually and in small groups. Use hints from tanka for those who need help. Read the sijos orally as they are finished.
4. Transfer some student sijos to transparencies for group editing. They can be projected on the chalkboard for ease of editing. Edit for alliteration and internal rhyming where appropriate.
5. Plan some uses for the productions that come from students. A special bulletin board can be developed for the writing and accompanying art. Selected sijos can be published for a book for the library.

Limericks

A daring young woman from Lockey
Would often like to play hockey,
    But when she got hit,
    She'd most have a fit,
And what she said then would shockee.

Tyrone just out of the Navy,
Grew hair that was long and wavy.
    He grew him a beard,
    But just as he feared,
He couldn't keep it out of his gravy.

Ohjojo, a very strong batter,
Hit baseballs so hard they did shatter.
    One day he hit one
    Clear into the sun,
And caused quite an earth-shaking clatter.

There is a young lizard named Lyle,
Reputed by all for his smile.
    With flies for his dinner
    He feels like a winner
Just grinning away all the while.

Joseph Ullman

LANGUAGE CONCEPTS

We can use language for fun and nonsense.
New words can be created by anyone.
Words have a different number of syllables or beats.
Any sound that can be spoken can be represented with the letters of the alphabet.
Rhyming is the use of two or more words that end with the same sound.
Stories and poems can grow out of imagination.
The words we say are written with the letters of the alphabet.

1. Explain the limerick pattern.

   Limericks are anecdotes in five-line verses. They have a syllable structure that varies. Some common ones are

   99669 99559 88558

   Some variations in this structure result in good limericks.
   They have a rhyming structure that does not vary. It is:

   aabba

   This is a triplet broken by a couplet. Writers need three words that rhyme plus two other words that rhyme to make a limerick. Unusual pronunciations are allowed in limericks, both to make the words rhyme and to give them the required number of syllables.
2. Read limericks with one reader taking the first, second, and fifth lines and the other one taking the third and fourth lines.
3. Write limericks as group compositions. Edit them for syllable structure, rhythm, and rhyming pattern. Create new words if needed for rhyming.
4. Publish some of the limericks for the classroom library.
5. Talk about the fun of writing nonsense words. Make lists of nonsense words that students produce.
6. Practice changing words slightly to make them fit into patterns.

So Nosey Was His Name

"Look at that busy little nose! My new hamster is smelling the roses you put on the table, Mother. Oh, look now! He smells the candy in that box. His nose is busy, busy, busy!" exclaimed Susan, cupping her small hands about the tiny, wiggly animal.

Susan tossed her long ponytail into place and sat down on the bright red carpet. Her big brown eyes twinkled with delight as she stroked the nervous, furry ball who was not yet accustomed to his new mistress. "My hamster is so-o-o-o pretty! He's just the color of cinnamon and sugar. What can we name him, Mother?"

"Let's watch him a day or two, then I'm sure you will think of the right name."

Just then the tiny slick hamster escaped between Susan's fingers and scampered away to explore his new home.

Following closely, she scolded him in her high-pitched voice as he tried to gnaw on the furniture. She saw his busy nose twitch excitedly as he dashed from her white bed to the bright red toy chest, from the toy chest to the shiny blue wastebasket, from the wastebasket to her big fuzzy teddy bear standing beside the closet. The tiny pet nosed up close to the teddy bear, then climbed upon its cuddly shoulders.

Susan, seeing that her pet had found a stopping place, turned to pick up her favorite doll to introduce it to the newest member of the household. But the tiny animal was not ready to stay still. He took a quiet slide down the teddy bear's back, and found himself at the closet door. Flattening his body in a magic sort of way, the hamster disappeared under the door just as Susan turned to speak to him.

"Where's my hamster?" she called with a quavering voice. "He was here on teddy bear's shoulder just a minute ago."

"I'm sure he'll show up soon. Don't cry, Susan. Just look around for him and don't forget to listen," suggested Mrs. Carlson.

Susan looked under her table. She looked in her doll buggy. She looked under her bed. She looked in her doll house. But no hamster!

She listened for him. She heard a bird singing. She heard a plane fly above the house. She heard a car whizz by. Then—she heard a faint rattling sound. "Where can that noise be coming from?" she thought. "It isn't inside the room. It isn't from outside. Then it must be from the closet."

Quietly she opened the closet door. She looked on the floor, but no hamster was there. She looked in the doll bed, but no hamster was there.

Again she heard the faint rattling sound.

As she stood up, she looked at the line of clean clothes hung on wire hangers. One hanger was moving slightly and tapping the next one. A small head with beady red eyes and a wiggly nose peeked up from the collar of her long fuzzy bathrobe that reached almost to the floor. Quickly Susan cupped her hand over the soft, silky ball of fur and exclaimed,

"You're nosey!
You're nosey!"
So, NOSEY WAS HIS NAME!!!

LANGUAGE CONCEPTS

Authors describe characters in ways that let readers form mental images of them.
Titles are used to tell the main idea of a production.
Stories and poems can grow out of real experiences.
Descriptive words and phrases help make meanings clear.
Simple stories have a beginning, an elaboration of the beginning, and an ending.

1. Read the story aloud to the class, but stop just before the ending, after the words ". . . and exclaimed." Ask children to predict what Susan exclaimed. Jot down some of the predictions, then read the real ending. Was it a good ending for the story? Do some of the predictions give clues for names for the hamster? Do some names and nicknames come from what we see and hear?
2. Read stories about other animals. Where did they get their names? Do their names have anything to do with their traits?
3. Compare Nosey as a character with other main characters in stories. How did the authors help you understand the characters? Did certain key descriptive words help you make up your mind? Did the actions of the characters reveal anything?
4. Duplicate copies of "So Nosey Was His Name" for children to use. They can mark words that help them understand Nosy with one color and those for Susan with another.
5. Do a critique of the story in terms of its beginning. Did it introduce the main characters and the setting? Was the problem stated early in the story? Did the action that followed complicate the problem or clarify it? Was the problem solved as the climax was reached? Was the ending sharp and satisfying?
6. Talk about topics such as

   where names come from
   meanings of some names
   story ideas that might come from names

7. Try some new names, such as Scamper, Nibbles, Twitter, and others. Make the character fit the new name.
8. Copy the story about Nosey, but use the new name and the new ending that will go with it. Make a new story title and bind your pages into a book.

Independent Activities

I Like Couplets

LANGUAGE CONCEPTS

Many words rhyme with other words.
Stories and poems can be written with words and pictures or with words only.
Rhyming is the use of two or more words that end with the same sound.

You can't eat couplets, but they are fun to write.

1. List some names of food you like.
2. Choose one or two other words that rhyme.

Examples cake: wake/bake/take
bread: said/red/thread
coke: joke/poke/soak

3. Make rhyming couplets. Use one food word and one other word for the rhyme.

Examples

When I wake	Butter and bread	It's no joke
I want cake	Is what I said.	That I like coke.

4. Illustrate your couplets with magazine pictures or your own drawings. Put one couplet to a page.
5. Put the pages together and you will have your own "I Like" book.

Rhyming Words

LANGUAGE CONCEPTS

There are words for the many movements of people, animals, and things.

Many words end with the same sound and symbol.
Many words rhyme with other words.

1. Make a list of rhyming words.
2. Try to rhyme a word of movement with the name of something.

Examples glide/tide run/sun

3. Put your list in the Writing Center for someone to use to write couplets.

Writing Limericks

LANGUAGE CONCEPTS

Words have a different number of syllables or beats.
New words can be created by anyone.
Stories and poems can grow out of imagination.
Rhyming is the use of two or more words that end with the same sound.

1. Try writing a limerick on your own.
Remember the syllabic and rhyming patterns.

There are several syllabic patterns.

9	9	8
9	9	8
6	5	5
6	5	5
9	9	8

There is only one rhyming pattern. a
a
b
b
a

2. Change the pronunciations of words to make them rhyme or to give them the right number of syllables. Make up nonsense words. Have fun writing.

Example A waitress in Fundy made sundaes,
But would serve them only on Mondays.
To order one then,
You crowed like a hen,
To make Monday in Fundy fun days.

Writing Haiku

LANGUAGE CONCEPTS

Words have a different number of syllables or beats.
Synonyms are words that have similar meanings.
Many poets use unusual language to describe something usual.

Birds fly over me
In the afternoon sunlight.
I watch them go by.

1. Haiku is a short nature poem that originated in Japan. A haiku describes or tells of a specific thing at a specific time and place. If you wish to write good haiku, look for some of the poems of the Japanese masters of this form: Basho, Moritake, Kakaku, Shiki, and Buson. Notice how they say things. These men worked many years to perfect the form.
2. Haiku in its Japanese form is written in three lines.

Line 1:	five syllables
Line 2:	seven syllables
Line 3:	five syllables

   To start with, this is a good plan to follow.
3. If you read Japanese haiku, you will notice that the translated poems usually do not follow the 5-7-5 pattern. This is because it is impossible to change the Japanese words and meanings into English words and still keep that form. Therefore, many American scholars of haiku use only a short line/long line/short line style. You may wish to try this as well as the 5-7-5 form.
4. When writing haiku, be specific with your wording. Do not say *flower*, but tell the kind—rose, pansy, daisy. Do not say *bird*, but say *wren, lark, woodpecker.*
5. Do not make your haiku a simile or a metaphor. These are Western forms, not Oriental.
6. Take a walk and watch for nature happenings that interest you. Look out your window. These are ways to find material for haiku. Jot down words or phrases that will help you recreate the sight—the moment in time.

   A haiku usually has an interplay of two objects. This can be an implied contrast or comparison.

Example Seagull on red sun
Reflecting motions on waves
Barefoot boy watching.

Find Five and Seven

LANGUAGE CONCEPTS

Words help form pictures in the mind.
Words have a different number of syllables or beats.
Synonyms are words that have similar meanings.

Could it be that tanka is easy to write because much of what we say and write comes out in gushes of five and seven syllables? Check your own language.

1. Look around you at any scene or object—real or in a picture.
2. Write random thoughts as you observe and think.

Examples autos whizzing by
smoke and smog are choking me
a bird tries to sing
it flies away
tries to find fresh air
I wish I could fly away

3. Count the syllables in each of your written random thoughts.
4. Adjust lines by striking out structure words, by changing tense, or by using a synonym.
5. You may have a tanka or another poem.

Writing a Sijo

LANGUAGE CONCEPTS

Stories and poems can grow out of real experiences.
Titles are used to tell the main idea of a production.
Simple statements can be extended and elaborated.
Many poets use unusual language to describe something usual.

1. Choose topics for your own sijo. Try topics that you know something about, such as

classmates	teachers	airplanes
yards	shops	collections
boats	books	cars

2. For each topic you choose, make a list of descriptive words, phrases, and sentences.

3. Extend or reduce each of your ideas into a statement of six, seven, or eight syllables.
4. Choose six of the statements that describe, contrast, or compare and arrange them into a sijo.
5. Check your poem to see that it is in the sijo form of

   six lines
   six to eight syllables in each line
   forty-two to forty-eight syllables total

6. Read your sijo orally. Make changes to get a rhythm you like.
7. When you have written several sijos, illustrate them and make them into a book. You may ask some of your friends to write with you and make a book together.

Writing Cinquains

LANGUAGE CONCEPTS

Descriptive words and phrases help make meanings clear.
Feelings of people and animals are described with words.
There are words for the many movements of people, animals, and things.
Words have a different number of syllables or beats.
Synonyms are words that have similar meanings.

Write some cinquains.

1. Remember

   They have five lines.
   There is no rhyme.
   There is a thought pattern.
   There is a syllable pattern.

   When you use the thought pattern only, you will write

   Line 1—one word—the title
   Line 2—two words—describes the title
   Line 3—three words—expresses an action
   Line 4—four words—expresses a feeling
   Line 5—one word—another word for the title

Example **Thought Pattern**

Mannequin
People model

Stares at shoppers
Watches for prospective buyers
Sentinel

When you use the thought pattern and the syllable pattern, you will write

Line 1—two syllables
Line 2—four syllables
Line 3—six syllables
Line 4—eight syllables
Line 5—two syllables

Example **Syllable Pattern**

Buildings
Tall, elegant
Mushrooming from desert
Filling with lonely retirees
Highrise

2. Display your finished cinquains and then collect them into a book.

Cinquains from A to Z

LANGUAGE CONCEPTS

The English alphabet has twenty-six letters.
Alphabetical arrangements help one locate information.
Words have a different number of syllables or beats.

Syllable-pattern cinquains need two-syllable words for lines 1 and 5.

1. As you read and browse in books, list two-syllable words that would make good cinquain topics.
2. Alphabetize your list. Try to find words beginning with each letter of the alphabet.
3. Put your list on the Ideas Board to help others with writing cinquains.

More Syllable Synonyms

LANGUAGE CONCEPTS

Words that are used as nouns in sentences can be used in other ways.

Many words have more than one meaning.
Words have a different number of syllables or beats.
Synonyms are words that have similar meanings.

When you write, you can use a collection of synonyms with different numbers of syllables.

1. Begin a list of words that can be used in writing haiku and senryu. To each word add synonyms that have more or fewer syllables. For example:

One	**Two**	**Three**	**Four**
old	ancient	archaic	prehistoric
big	monstrous	gigantic	
wet		watery	

2. Trade lists with your friends and help each other.
3. Use your list when you write poetry patterns with an exact number of syllables in each line.

Feet Riddles

LANGUAGE CONCEPTS

Some symbols other than our alphabet communicate meaning.
We can describe things without telling their names.

Now you can make your own riddles.

1. Find a picture of an animal or person with feet in the picture.
2. Paste the picture on a piece of paper so there is room for a flap to cover all of the picture except the feet.
3. Fold the flap over and write a riddle on it.
4. Display your riddles for others to solve.

Modern Mother Goose

LANGUAGE CONCEPTS

Language can be expressed in rhythmic patterns.
Words can be used for pleasure only.
The same language patterns are used over and over in writing.

Old Mother Goose
When she wants to fly
Gets in her jet
And climbs eight miles high.

1. Copy some of your favorite Mother Goose rhymes.
2. Use the language pattern of the rhymes for a modern poem.

Example

Little Miss Muffet
Sat on a tuffet
Eating her curds and whey.
Along came a spider
And sat down beside her
And frightened Miss Muffet away.

Little Miss Snooter
Sat on a scooter
Eating an ice cream cone.
There came a drug peddler
And tried some to sell her
And frightened Miss Snooter away.

3. Illustrate your modern Mother Goose and make the pages into a book.

Compounds in My World

LANGUAGE CONCEPT

Compound words are two or more words combined into one.

1. Look around you for compound words.

Classroom	**Food**	**Self**
chalkboard	applesauce	fingernail
bookcase	peanut	eyeball
Insects	**Clothing**	**Flowers**
ladybug	buttonhole	paintbrush
housefly	undershirt	larkspur

2. Make lists of compound words you find.
3. Copy your longest list and mount it on construction paper.
4. Put it on the display board in the Writing Center.

Big Numbers

LANGUAGE CONCEPTS

Some symbols other than our alphabet communicate meaning.
Numerals are symbols of how many and how much.
Numerals and numbers have word names.

1. Make a book of big numbers.
2. Try writing millions, billions, and trillions.
3. Can you think of a number that is as big as a zillion?
4. Ask your friends to try to read your big numbers.
5. Write the biggest number you can read and put it on the Big Numbers bulletin board.

Comic Stories

LANGUAGE CONCEPTS

The same picture suggests different words and ideas to different people.
We perceive our own meanings from our experiences.
Stories and poems can be written with words and pictures or with words only.

1. Cut the "talk" out of some comic strip frames.
2. Paste each frame on a piece of paper.
3. Write your own "talk" on the frames.
4. Staple your pages together for a comic book.
5. Edit your book and put it in the Reading/Research Center.

Fashion Parade

LANGUAGE CONCEPTS

Colors of things are described with words.
Sizes of things are described with words.
Shapes of things are described with words.
The feel of things is described with words.

1. Cut pages from fashion sections of magazines.
2. Write the script for a fashion show to go with the pictures.
3. Describe the pictures. Tell something about what each person is wearing—its texture, design, color, highlights, and other outstanding characteristics. Don't forget the accessories.
4. Record the show on tape and place it in the Viewing/Listening Center for others to enjoy.

Why That Name?

LANGUAGE CONCEPTS

Imagination promotes picturesque speech.
Everything has a name.
Some nouns are common and some are proper.

1. Collect pictures of cars with animal names.
2. For each one write something about the animal.
3. Give your reasons why the name is a good one or not a good one for that car.
4. Notice that you use both capital letters and small letters to begin the same words.
5. Find pictures or make sketches of the animals to go with the cars.
6. Collect your illustrations and information into a display.

Push the Button

LANGUAGE CONCEPTS

People communicate some information in sequence.
Stories and poems can grow out of imagination.

1. Make believe that you can push three buttons and make three wishes come true.
2. Write the three wishes.
3. Make up a story about the three wishes and how they come true.
4. Illustrate your story and make it into a book for the Reading/Research Center.

What a Character!

LANGUAGE CONCEPTS

Colors of things are described with words.
Sizes of things are described with words.
The feel of things is described with words.
There are words for the many movements of people, animals, and things.
Authors describe characters in ways that let readers form mental images of them.

Authors tell about characters by describing them. You, too, can describe characters.

1. Make a chart to keep track of words you find to describe characters.

Example

Words that Describe	Color	Size	Actions	Texture
Nosey	cinnamon and sugar	tiny	wiggly smells scampered	furry

Your character:

2. Read stories with characters in them.
3. Write the names of the characters on your chart.
4. List the words the authors use to tell color, size, action, and texture.
5. Keep a list for writing your own stories.

The Missing Person

LANGUAGE CONCEPTS

We perceive our own meanings from our experiences.
Imagination promotes picturesque speech.
Stories and poems can grow out of real experiences.
Stories and poems can grow out of imagination.

1. Choose a picture with a "missing person" in it.*
2. Pretend you are the person missing from the picture.
3. Write a story about how and why you got to the place where the picture was taken.
4. What were you doing at the time the camera clicked?
5. What else happened that is not shown in the picture?

---

* *To the teacher:* Find pictures that have several people or people and animals in them. Cut out one person. Mount the pictures for children to use in writing stories.

What Did I Hear?

LANGUAGE CONCEPTS

Sounds are imitated and described with words.
Onomatopoeic words are those whose sounds suggest their meanings.
New words can be created by anyone.

1. Here are some made-up words to show sounds we hear: ssszp, nreet.
2. Find pictures for which you can make up sound words.
3. Try to write a sentence or a poem using your sound words.

Example Swing, swing,
Ereek-erawk!
Back and forth
Like a pendulum clock.

Collecting Antonyms

LANGUAGE CONCEPTS

Antonyms are words that have opposite meanings.

1. Collect antonyms from all around you by looking and listening.

Examples music—loud/soft
weather—hot/cold
traffic—fast/slow
food—sweet/sour
clothing—dark/light

2. Write the pairs of words on cards. Put them in the Writing Center to use as a resource when writing diamantes or other poetry.

Guess What

LANGUAGE CONCEPTS

We can describe things without telling their names.
Antonyms are words that have opposite meanings.

1. Cut colorful pictures from magazines.
2. Paste each picture on one-half of a card.
3. Fold the other half of the card over the picture to make a covering flap.
4. Cut a hole about 1/2 in. in diameter so just a little of the picture shows through when the flap is down.
5. Write a riddle, using an antonym as a clue. The answer to the riddle will be the picture itself.
6. Make a collection of the Guess What cards for the Reading/Research Center.

Fifteen Words

LANGUAGE CONCEPTS

People communicate by speaking and writing in sentences.
Most sentences have at least one verb or a form of *be* or *have* in them.
Some words occur frequently in our language.

1. Choose fifteen words that you know how to spell.
2. Write as many complete sentences as you can using just the fifteen words. You can use each one as many times as you need it.
3. Invite a classmate to write with you to see who can write the most sentences from the fifteen words.

Fifteen Words

John	in	the
run	walk	to
can	by	Mary
around	myself	house
your	I	and

Here are some starters.

John can run.
John can run and walk.
John can run and walk around the house.
I walk by myself to the house.

4. Take it from here. Can you get one hundred sentences?

Take a Pill

LANGUAGE CONCEPTS

We can use language for fun and nonsense.
Greeting cards and letters are special ways of saying things.

1. Write cheerful or nonsense notes on strips of paper.
2. Roll the strips to make pills.
3. Paste the rolls or tie them with thread.
4. Put the pills in a box.
5. Send them or give them to a friend who is ill.

Stories from Classified Ads

LANGUAGE CONCEPTS

People communicate in many ways through many media.
People express feelings and emotions through creative activities.

1. Look in the Classified Ad section of a newspaper and select some ads that suggest stories to you.
2. Clip out the ads and paste them at the heading of the story that you write from the ad.

Examples

Lost and Found: LOST: Female skunk. Descented. Casas Adobes area. Reward. Call 779-1467.

FOUND: Collie, male, approx. 4 years old, sable & white. Call 435-4118.

Free: FREE KITTENS. Three. 8 weeks old. Mother Himalayan. Call 411–7186.
For Sale: WEDDING GOWN. New. White with lace. Never used. Size 10. Call 543–9876.

3. Write and illustrate your story from the viewpoint of the thing that was advertised.
4. Collect a book of Classified Ad stories and bind them into a book for the Reading/Research Center.

Moving Stories

LANGUAGE CONCEPTS

Oral reading can bring an audience pleasure and information.
Stories and poems can be written with words and pictures or with words only.
Authors improve writing by editing it.

1. Write and illustrate a story on a strip of paper that is strong enough to be pulled through a cardboard frame.
2. Make a frame with an opening the right size to show one frame of the story at a time.
3. Edit your story and copy it on the back of the strip of illustrations. Make sure that what you copy is one frame ahead of what is showing.
4. Read your story and show the illustrations to a group. Use your best oral reading, because none of the audience will have a copy to follow along.

Sense Books

LANGUAGE CONCEPTS

Smells of things are described with words.
Tastes of things are described with words.
The feel of things is described with words.
Sounds are imitated and described with words.

1. Cut out pieces of cardboard in the shapes of your nose, your eyes, your ears, and your fingers.
2. Make each shape into a book with several blank pages.
3. List words in each book that describe that sense.
4. Try to write question and answer couplets in some of your books.

Example Are there smells that send you flying?
I run when I get the scent of bacon frying.

5. Put your books in the Reading/Research Center for a few days before you take them home.

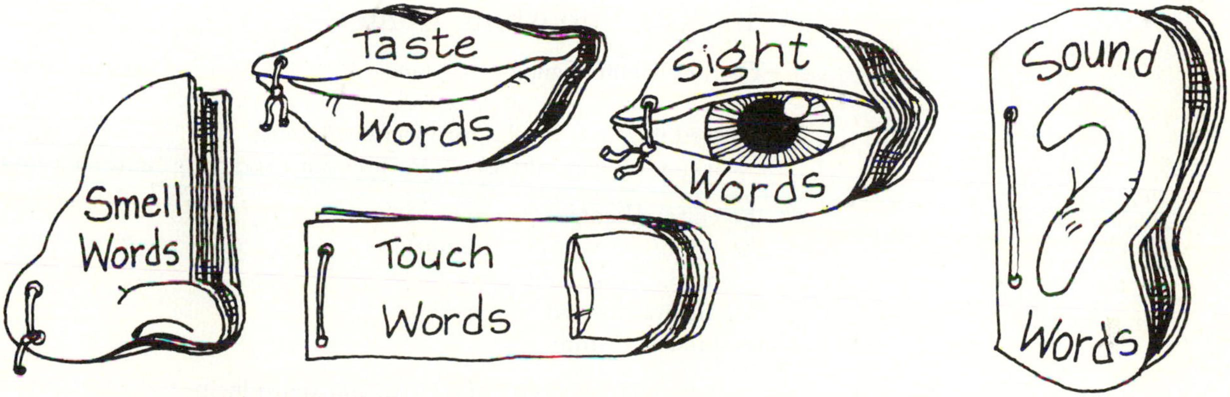

Chapter 4

The Publishing Center

What Is a Publishing Center?

The Publishing Center is a place

for self-editing at a level appropriate to ability
for working on committees responsible for producing finished books

- the editorial committee
- the typing or printing committee
- the duplicating committee
- the illustrating committee
- the bindery committee

to page manuscripts for illustrating and reproducing
for using spelling resources in editing personal manuscripts
for checking capitalization and punctuation before publishing individual books
for adding descriptive categories to elaborate simple language constructions
for reducing length and difficulty of sentences without destroying meaning when publishing for young children

The Publishing Center is an area in a classroom or a designated area in another part of the school building where children process their original manuscripts. They may edit them or leave them for an editorial committee. They may illustrate them or find an illustrator to work with them. They page the manuscript and copy it for binding. They bind the completed manuscript or use a blank book from the collection in the Publishing Center. Usually, when blank books are used, the text and illustrations are glued into the blank books. This prevents mistakes in copying into the already bound pages.

Some schools with many authors maintain one central Publishing Center for the whole school and invite parents to assist in the operation by supplying materials, typing manuscripts, and helping with binding. In these schools simple bindings are made in classrooms, and only manuscripts selected for production in multiple copies go to the Publishing Center for processing.

Not everything that children write needs to be published. Single, original copies are enough for most of what is written. These can be read by the author and enjoyed by classmates. If children take the original manuscripts home, the teacher might have a stamp, ORIGINAL MANUSCRIPT, to indicate that the story or poem has not been corrected. This gives parents and other adults an opportunity to see the child's real performance. It also relieves the teacher of much unnecessary work of reading and correcting materials that are not to be used in the school curriculum. Another stamp, EDITED MANUSCRIPT, should be used for selections that have been processed by the teacher and/or the editorial committee.

Publishing of manuscripts produced by students is a peak experience in the language arts/reading curriculum.

It truly integrates writing with other communication abilities.
It brings into sharp focus the mechanics of language.
It draws on influences from many authors and publishers.
It uses graphics as an essential ingredient in the language arts.
It can be extended and interpreted through dramatization and choral reading.

Supplies and aids that are not typical of other language arts/reading programs are needed. Some of them are

1. Paper in a variety of sizes and qualities
2. Typewriters for children and adults to use
3. Scraps of cardboard, cloth, wallpaper, adhesive paper, and other materials for covers and illustrations
4. Sewing equipment for hand and machine sewing

5. Lettering guides and pens
6. Paper cutter
7. Paper punch to cut holes for some bindings
8. Heavy-duty stapler
9. Iron to use with laminating paper
10. Art supplies if the Publishing Center is far removed from the Arts and Crafts Center

The Publishing Center is a place where children can participate in the process of seeing their own ideas and their own language become useful reading materials for recreation and for information. Adult volunteers and older children can work with younger children, but authors must participate in the processes and procedures if the inherent value of a Publishing Center is to be realized. Materials and guides for typing and binding books should be in diagram form whenever possible so that authors can use them independently. Older children can participate by making blank books for young children to use. They can also serve as co-authors and as illustrators.

Samples of commercially produced children's magazines should be in the Publishing Center to give children ideas on different sections they might produce, how they might illustrate their own work, and how they might gather pages into attractive publications. Samples of books produced by children should be in the collection to give other children ideas for binding and illustrating their own books.

Language Skills Developed and Practiced

The child develops the ability to read copy for spelling errors.

The child develops the ability to read copy for punctuation and capitalization errors.

The child develops a sensitivity to clear and meaningful ways of saying things.

The child increases ability to discuss errors as an author.

The child recognizes appropriate formats for publishing newspaper and magazine articles.

The child develops ability to organize many items into an attractive and readable publication.

The child learns to make stencils for multiple copies.

The child learns to use publishing equipment—typewriter, carbon paper, paper cutter, laminator, and sewing machine.

The child learns to scan printed materials for errors.

The child increases ability to plan publications with a group of editors.
The child is interested in and influenced by the format of published books.

Editing Manuscripts for Publication

An editorial committee for a Publishing Center can operate informally in a classroom, or it may have scheduled times to function in an all-school Publishing Center. Its major function is to raise the level of awareness of its members. The committee might divide responsibility by assigning each member a specialty, such as

spelling
capitalization
punctuation
sentence sense
paragraphing
syllabication for some forms of poetry

Editing Seminars

Preparation for editing responsibilities can be fostered by editing seminars led by the teacher. Two or three stories per week can be written on chalkboards. The whole class can be included in the editing procedures. Suggestions can be made in terms of style and form as well as mechanics. Descriptive categories can be added for clarification. If the story has been written to go with a painting, the painting can be removed to see if the story stands alone. After the seminar the author and others may choose to copy the edited composition.

Two or three stories per week can be transferred to transparencies. These should always be submitted by volunteers. The transparencies can be projected on the chalkboard for the whole class to view during the editing seminar. The teacher leads the class in the major strategies editors use to prepare manuscripts for publication. They might be

mechanics of spelling, capitalization, and punctuation
characterization

settings
use of conversation
active and passive voice
sentence form and meaning
paragraph form and meaning
use of descriptive words and phrases

Students participate by going to the chalkboard to make changes and corrections. After suggestions have been made, the teacher leads the group in re-reading the manuscript. Then the author is asked to accept or reject the suggestions. Too many changes may alter the purpose of the original manuscript, and the author has the right to reject some of the suggestions. Occasionally the use of "invented spelling" adds to the charm of a story; in this case, it should remain in its original form. The editing seminar gives the teacher an opportunity to teach in a real setting.

Individual Books

Authors may leave rough draft manuscripts in a designated place for the editorial committee to process. Each "specialist" reads a manuscript and notes suggestions. When all members have read the

manuscript, the committee calls for a conference with the author to review the suggestions.

The author accepts or rejects the suggestions of the committee in terms of the purpose of the manuscript. When there is disagreement between author and editors, the author takes the manuscript to the editor-in-chief, who is usually the teacher. After review by the editor-in-chief, necessary revisions are made. The manuscript is then ready for paging, illustrating, and binding.

The teacher may function as the editor for the author. Such editing should always be done *with* the author. It is never a procedure for grading a composition but for helping the author get the material ready for publication. The relationship established by the teacher is one of supporting the student rather than evaluating a composition.

Class Books

Some of the books published for classroom use contain selections from different authors. The selections may be on the same topic, or they may be a collection of poems using the same pattern, such as haiku or sijo.

Editing for class books should be, first of all, self-editing. Discussions of expectancies are appropriate. Models can be furnished. Beyond that, a committee might be appointed to read manuscripts before final copying on uniform paper. The editorial committee should represent a range of "specialists."

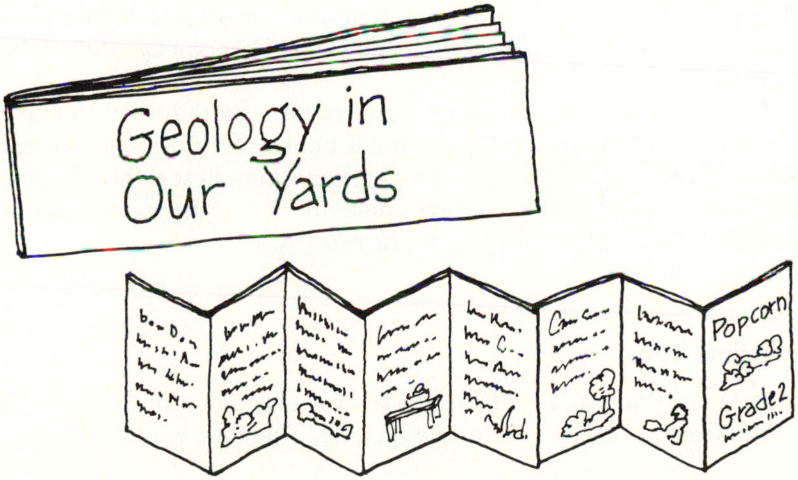

Class books can be made in single copies to be used in the classroom, or they may be prepared for duplication so that every student will have a copy for a home library. Duplicated books need careful editing by the editor-in-chief, whereas single-copy books may reflect the level of expertise of student editors.

Newspapers and Magazines

The publication of class newspapers and magazines will involve several editors for special sections, such as

stories
reports
comics
sports
fashions
entertainment
editorials
interviews
puzzles

Each editor should have an envelope or a box where contributors can place their rough drafts. Contributors should know that all contributions will have to be edited for the final production.

At publishing time, each editor is assigned space in the final production. Selections are made, and editing is done with authors. Manuscripts may need to be rewritten and refined to fit space constraints. Some may need to be lengthened. Others may need to be shortened.

Editors for magazines and newspapers have more liberty to make changes than do editors of individual books of stories and poems. They have to work as a team to make everything fit together. Editing has to be careful and consistent, since the publications will be distributed widely after they are duplicated.

Spelling Aids

A Word Wall can be established to hold lists of words that student editors need to check most of the spelling. These are words for which

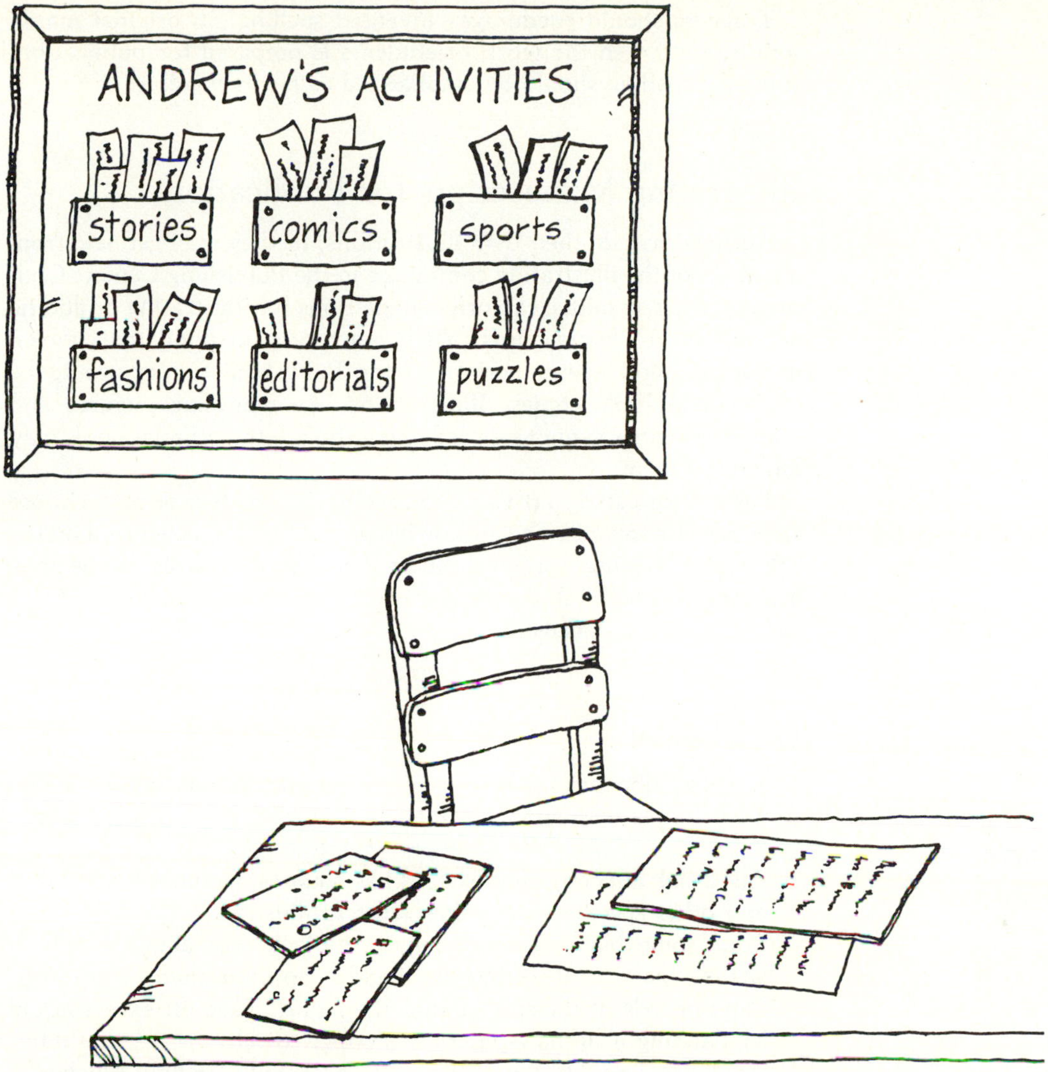

editors do not need meanings and therefore do not need to take time to look up in a dictionary. Some of them are

lists of high-frequency words that all authors use. See Appendix C
lists of name words that are used frequently. See Appendix B
proper names and other words for special seasons and projects

Teachers should encourage "invented spelling" in original manuscripts, but when the work of students is prepared for publication, standard spelling should be emphasized as far as possible.

Illustrating Manuscripts for Publication

Authors may do their own illustrations, or they may get help from members of the illustrating committee in the Publishing Center. Children on the committee can offer suggestions for illustrating or adding art support to manuscripts. They must keep in mind that books, magazines, and newspapers from the Publishing Center are to be made in multiple copies. Illustrations like magazine pictures and crayon drawings cannot be used, even though the original book may have used them.

The author can do art work to accompany the text or may choose someone else to do it. The author-illustrator team is recognized on the title page as having worked together. The illustrations should be done in pencil or black ink for heat-process duplicating machines. Pencil can be used for stencils.

Sponge Prints

Borders, silhouettes, and other informal decorations can be added to manuscripts with sponge prints.

1. Cut a slab of sponge into shapes like squares, rectangles, triangles, and other specific shapes that serve to illustrate.
2. Pour some black tempera paint or black washable ink into a shallow pan or lid so that the liquid is no more than ¼ in. deep.
3. Dip one side of the sponge into the liquid. Take off excess liquid by daubing it on newspaper or a paper towel.
4. Apply the liquid to the paper to be decorated with light touches of the sponge. Press hard for dark images and lightly for light images.
5. Sponge shapes can be cut to make specific illustrations. Overlapping light and dark prints adds texture to title pages. Sponge prints can be added after the printing or typing has been done. In this way the print or type can be boxed in.

Note: Sponge printing can be done in multiple colors for original manuscripts that are not to be reproduced.

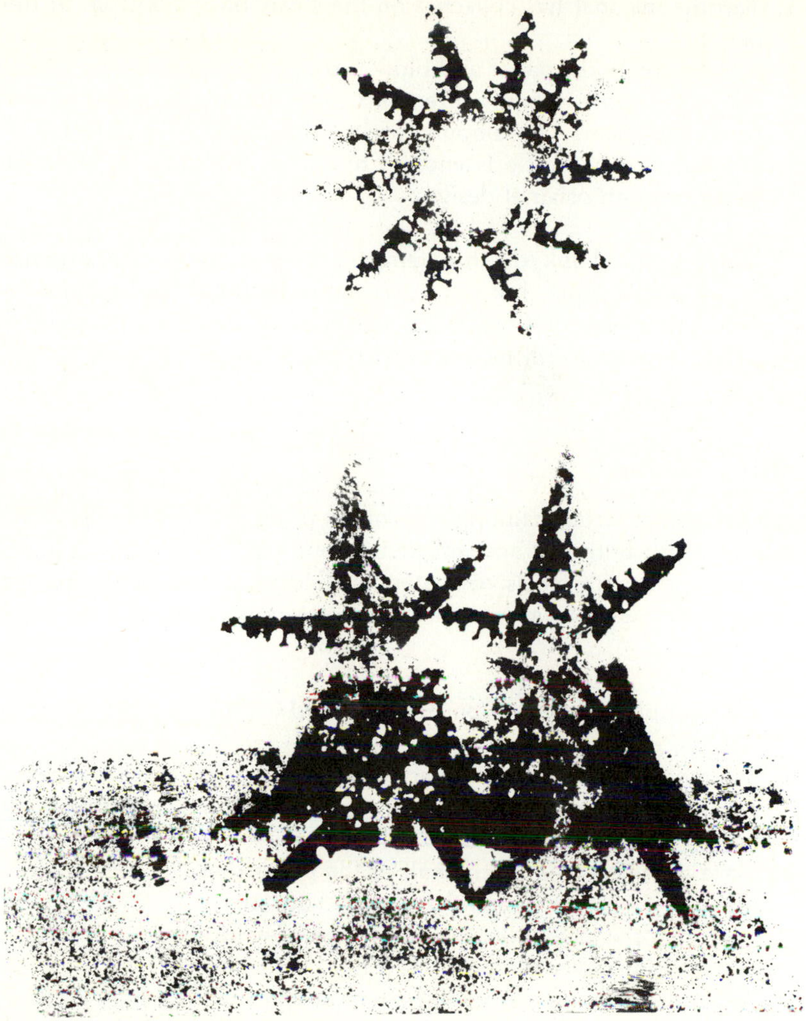

Blown Ink

Oriental poetry, such as haiku and tanka, can be supported with blown ink art work.

1. Place the piece of paper for the illustration on a flat surface that has been covered by a newspaper.
2. Dip a drinking straw into black washable ink or thin tempera paint. *Do not suck up on the straw!*

3. Tap the ink that has collected on the straw on the bottom of the page.
4. Get level with the paper and blow through the straw to spread the ink. It will flow in many directions. Keep following the wet spots to spread them. The amount of ink the straw holds when it is dipped into the bottle is enough to fill an 8½ x 11 in. sheet of paper with an original design.

Note: Colored ink or thin tempera can be used with original manuscripts. Ink pen or crayon additions can be made in the form of flowers on the ends of branches or colored mosaics to fill in spaces with boundaries.

String Painting

Many times string paintings are made prior to writing. They furnish ideas for both real and imaginary compositions. Young children can use them with labels or sentences. Older children can compose stories and poems to accompany the abstract painting they will get with the string.

1. Fold double the piece of paper to be used for the art work. Unfold and place on a flat surface.
2. Dip most of a piece of string about 18 in. long into black washable ink or black tempera. Hold it so that excess liquid can drain back into the container.
3. Place the wet string on the half of the paper that has been folded. Make any kind of design that comes naturally.
4. Fold the other half over the string and press down.
5. Place a book over the paper and hold it firmly.
6. Pull out the string. You will have a design that you may or may not want to use. Practice until you get a satisfying design.

Note: Multicolored string paintings can be used with original manuscripts.

Crayon Rubbings

One of the simplest ways to develop artistic support for manuscripts is to use crayon rubbings.

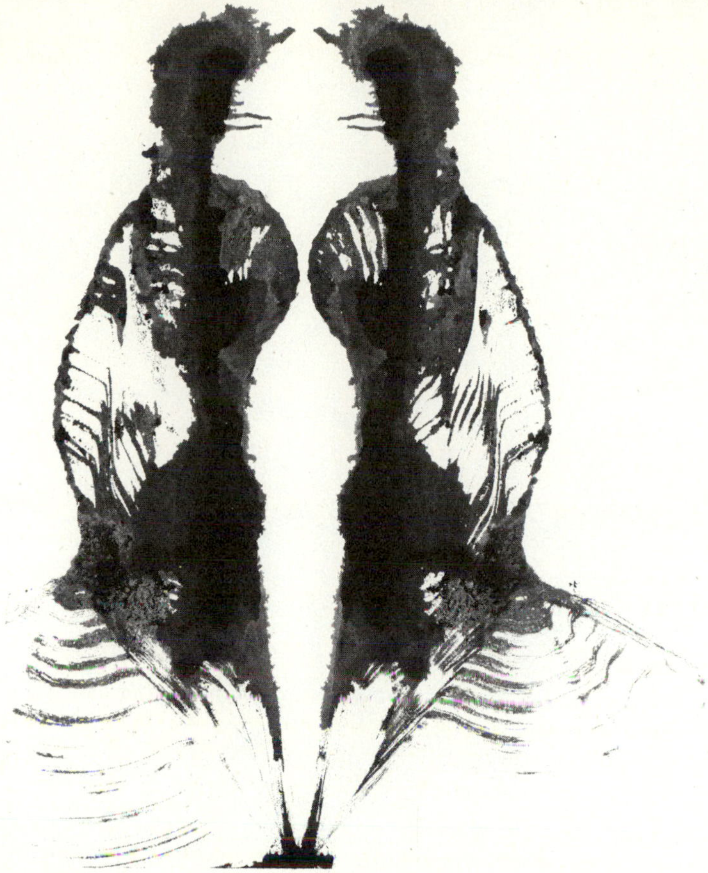

1. Find a leaf, a flat flower, or shapes cut out of tagboard to illustrate your manuscript.
2. Place the flat object on a flat surface.
3. Place your paper for illustrations over the object.
4. Hold the paper in place while you rub across the object firmly with a black crayon. The design will come through. It can be trimmed, mounted, and used as an illustration.
5. A variation is to draw a simple outline and then lay roving yarn around it. The outline can be covered with white glue, or the string can be dipped in diluted white glue. When the string dries, lay paper over the string and rub firmly with crayons.

Blottoes

Blottoes are easy forms of expression for any age. They are easy to do and result in abstract productions for interpretation. They are especially useful in developing basic reading abilities because they exercise the ability to see reality in abstractions. Blottoes are good for displays that reflect variety in experience.

1. Fold double the piece of paper to be used for the art work. Unfold and place on a flat surface.
2. Dip a brush in the ink or thin tempera to be used. Black ink can be used for illustrations for multiple copies, but children usually enjoy a combination of colors.
3. Fold the piece of paper back on top of the paint. Smooth out and rub vigorously until all the paint has been spread evenly.
4. Unfold carefully and spread out to dry.
5. Use for labeling, for descriptive sentences, or as the basic idea for a poem or story.

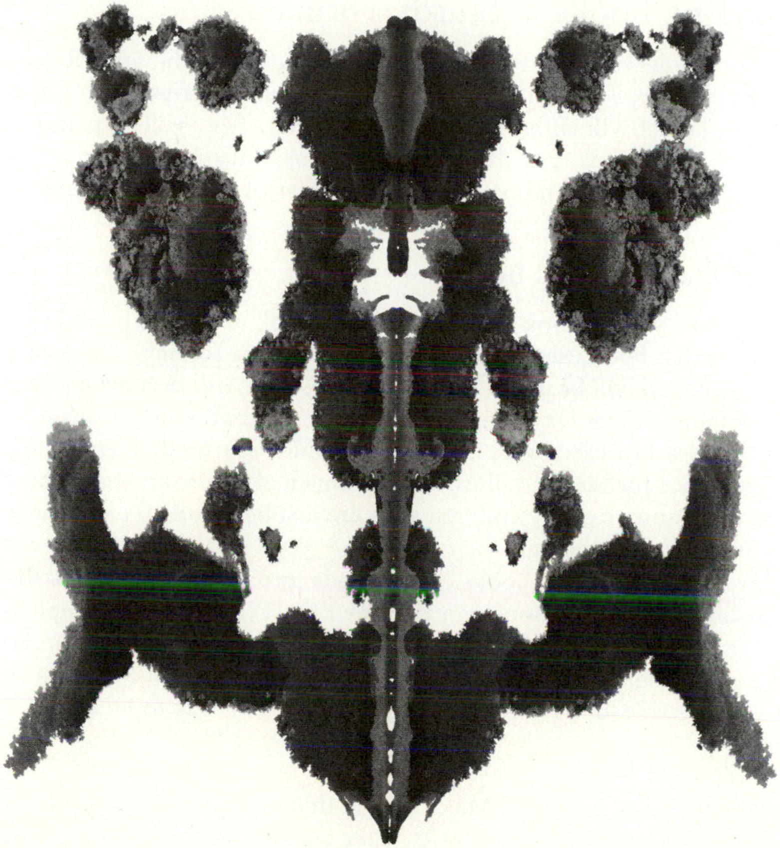

Blanks for Illustrations

Frequently children like to have illustrations more colorful than those the duplicating processes available to them can reproduce. For this reason, many teachers encourage children to leave blank spaces for the illustrations and let each child fill in the space for his or her book. Sometimes simple outlines are duplicated so that the illustrator can add color and detail. Occasionally a child will take home a book with blank spaces for illustrations and get the father or mother to do the illustrations.

Copies of duplicated books that go to libraries are usually illustrated by the author or by members of the illustrating committee. Original art used with duplicated text makes an interesting variation for the collection of books by student authors.

Binding Books in Sturdy Formats

The bindery committee is made up of volunteers who are willing to learn the steps and strategies for binding manuscripts into sturdy bindings that will withstand a lot of handling. They will help authors bind single copies, but their major responsibility is to organize and work through the binding of multiple copies of selected manuscripts.

Folded and Stitched Books

A twenty-page book is about as big a book as can be folded to lie flat. Such a book uses five sheets of paper before folding. The outside sheet, which will be at the bottom of the stack, will become a part of the binding. That leaves sixteen pages for text and illustrations when both sides are used. When only front sides are used, there will be eight pages for text and illustrations. This makes a neat, sturdy binding for manuscripts by children who are just beginning the experience of individual authorship.

Folded and stitched books can be made into blank books first, then the text and illustrations can be glued in. When text is completed prior to binding, authors need to consult with the bindery committee or the teacher about the order of pages as they will appear when the pages are folded. This is especially true if the text is to be typed.

STEP 1

Stack the pages in order. Make certain that there is at least one blank sheet at the bottom of the stack. Make a trial fold to check the book.

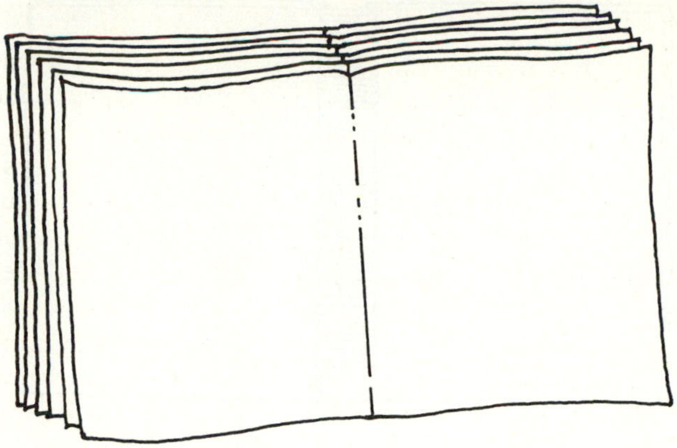

STEP 2

Sew on the fold. Use hand stitching with heavy thread or machine stitching with the longest stitch on a household sewing machine. Make the stitching tight and secure the ends of the thread so that they will not come loose.

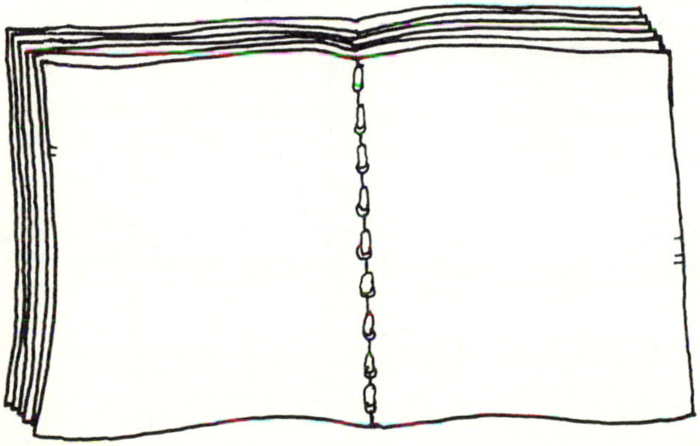

STEP 3

Cut two pieces of cardboard ¼ to ½ in. larger than the folded book.

STEP 4

Tape the cardboard together with masking tape. Leave at least a 1/2-in. space between the pieces of cardboard. The space may need to be wider if heavy cardboard is used. This makes the cover flexible.

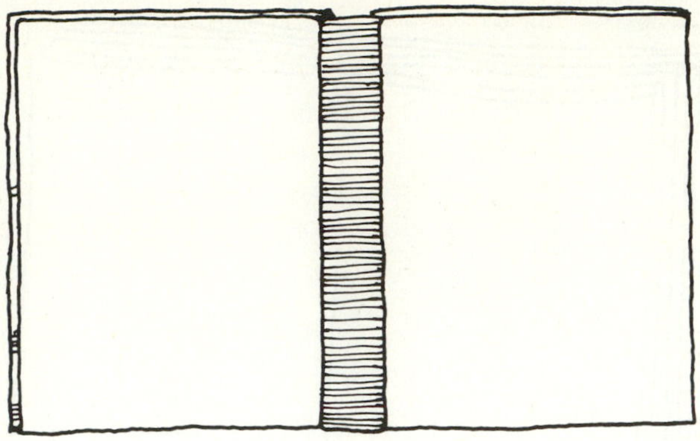

STEP 5

Cover the cardboard with adhesive paper, cloth, wallpaper, used wrapping paper, or some other appropriate material. Lay the cardboard on a covering that is 2 in. wider all around. Apply glue as needed.

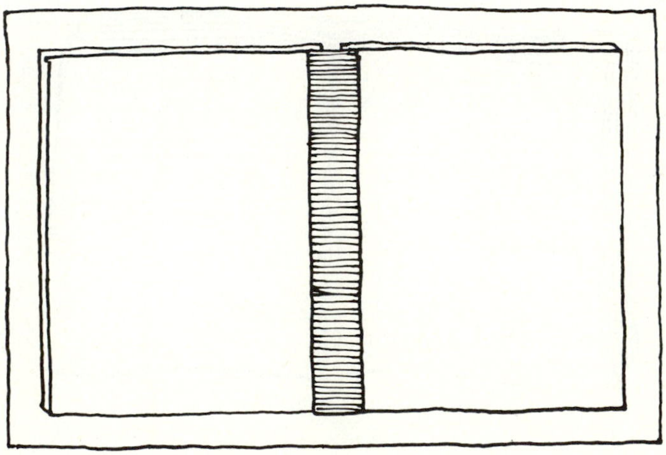

STEP 6

Fold the edges over, beginning at the corners and then going along the length and width. If very heavy covering material is used, the corners may need to be trimmed off rather than folded over.

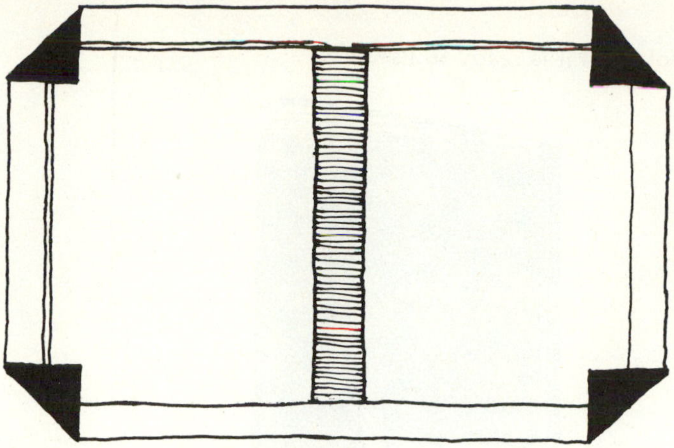

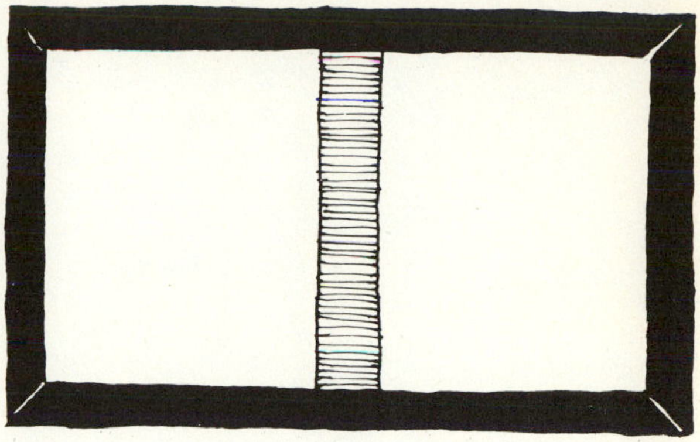

STEP 7

Apply rubber cement or glue to the unfinished side of the cover.

STEP 8

Place the center of the book along the center of the cover. Press down the blank pages and let dry. If rubber cement is used, apply it to both surfaces and let dry until "tacky." Adhere the two surfaces. Rub off the excess rubber cement from around the edges.

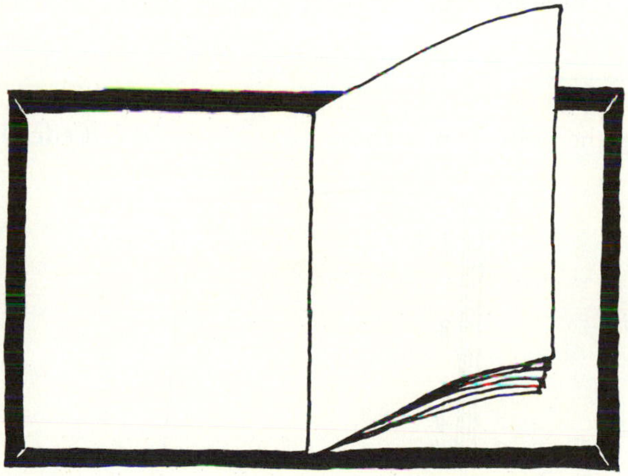

STEP 9

Fold the book, and it is ready to use.

Stapled Edge Books

Both thick and thin books can be stitched with staples on the left edge. A heavy-duty stapler is needed for thick books.

STEP 1

Stack pages in order. Add one blank page on top and one on the bottom.

STEP 2

Stitch together with staples about ¼ in. from the left edge.

STEP 3

Cut two pieces of cardboard ¼ to ½ in. larger than the stack to be bound.

STEP 4

Tape the cardboard together with masking tape. Leave a space of at least ½ in. between. Make the space larger for thick cardboard and thick books.

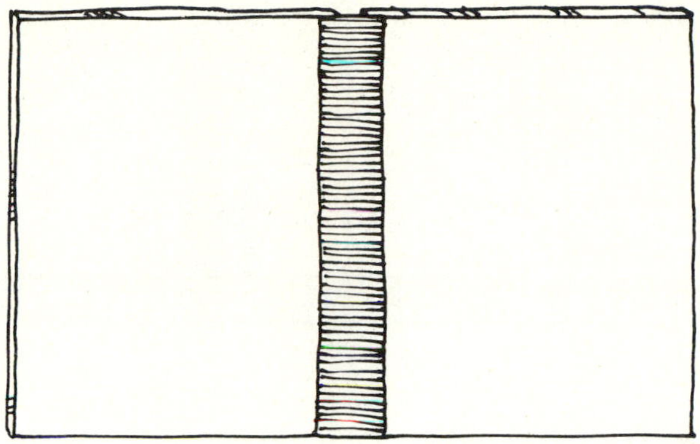

STEP 5

Cover the cardboard with adhesive paper, cloth, wallpaper, used wrapping paper, or some other appropriate material. Apply glue as needed. Make the covering material at least 2 in. wider all around than the cardboard.

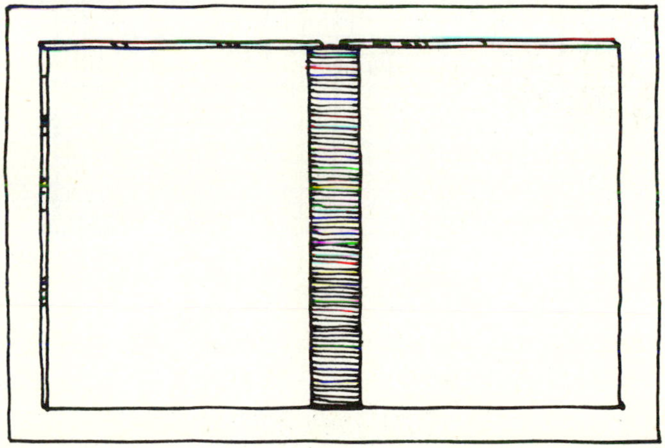

STEP 6

Fold the edges over, beginning at the corners and then going along the length and width. If very heavy covering material is used, the corners may need to be trimmed off rather than folded over.

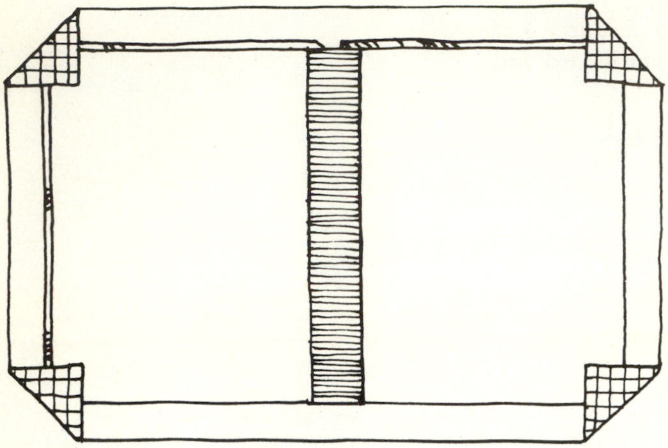

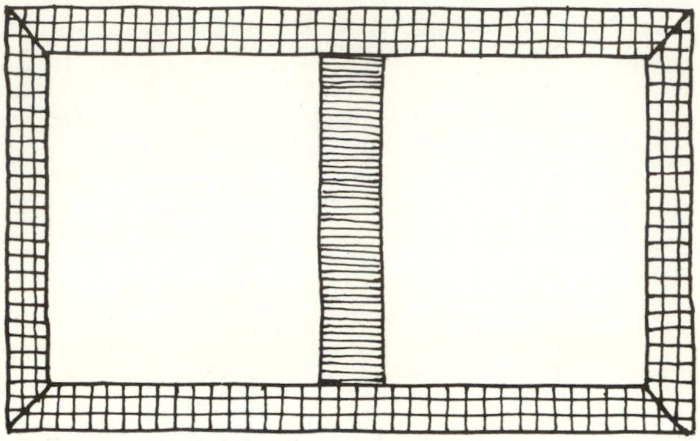

STEP 7

Cover the unfinished side with a piece of material like that used for the outside. Cut the piece about ¼ in. smaller than the cover.

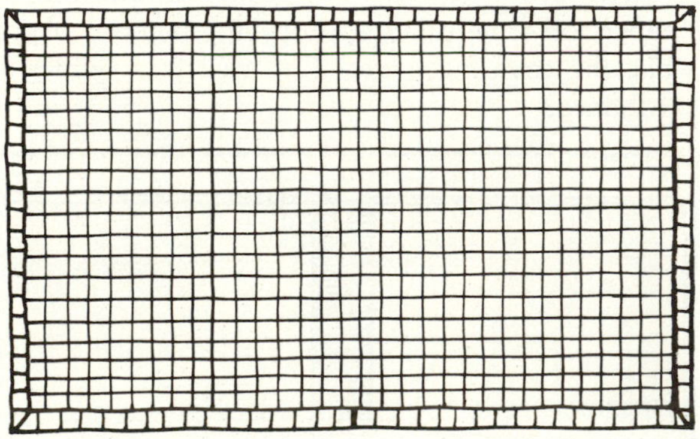

STEP 8

Place the stapled text inside the cover. Fold the cover over so that the placement is right inside the cover.

STEP 9

Open the front lid carefully and tape the text to the cover with a strip of tape going lengthwise. If adhesive paper is used, a strip of the paper about 4 in. wide is good to use as the tape.

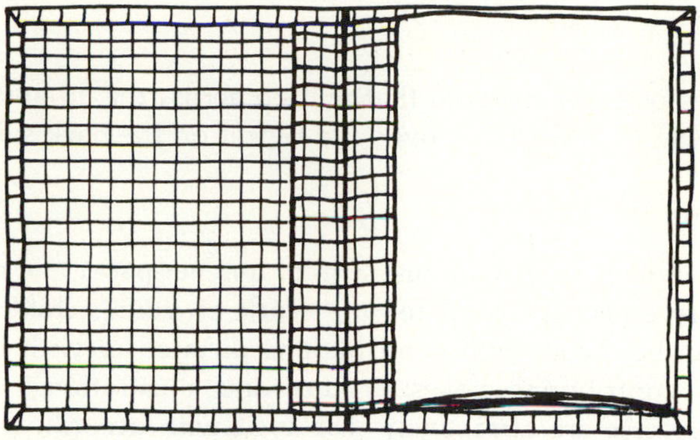

STEP 10

Close the front lid. Turn the book over and open the back lid. Tape the book as in Step 9.

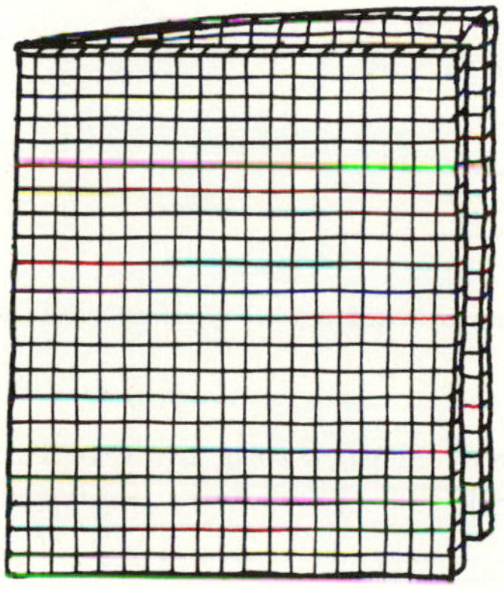

STEP 11

The book is ready for use.

Alternative Steps 9 and 10.

STEP 9

Open the lid carefully and fasten the text to the cover with strips of masking tape going crosswise.

STEP 10

Cut pieces of cover material that will go across the lid and the text. Glue down. Turn the book over and repeat on the back side.

Accordion Books

Book bindings made with one strip of butcher paper and no glue or staples are especially good for the work of young children. Class books can be made, with contributions dictated or with individual members contributing pages of text and illustrations. Books of children's verse are attractively displayed with accordion bindings. The books can be stretched out on top of a bookshelf, on a window sill, or on the floor. Those made with butcher paper are durable.

STEP 1

Cut a piece of butcher paper about 6 feet long. Use white, brown, or colored butcher paper.

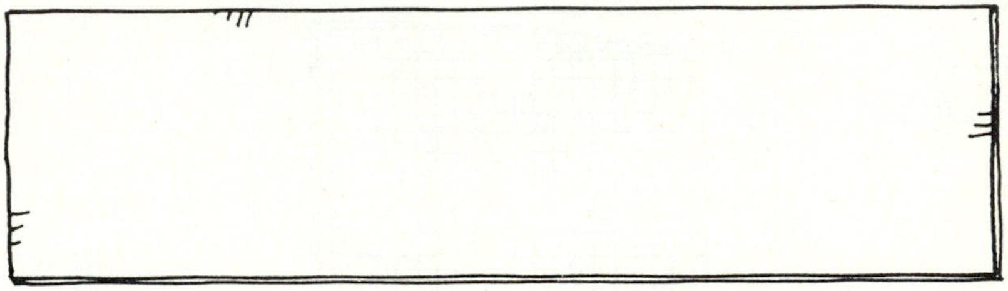

STEP 2

Lay the butcher paper flat on a long table or on the floor. Fold it in about 2 in. all around.

STEP 3

Fold the edges together to make the paper half as wide as the original. Crease.

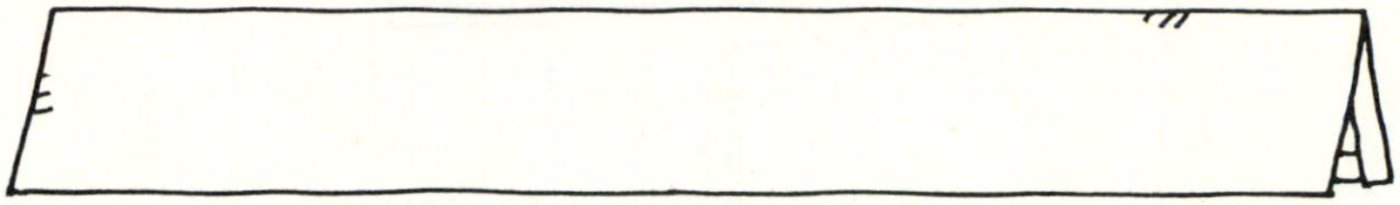

STEP 4

Fold the ends together to make the paper half as long as the original.

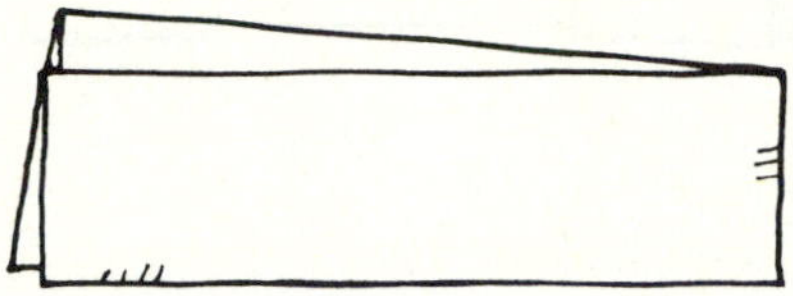

STEP 5

Open up lengthwise with the crease showing in the middle.

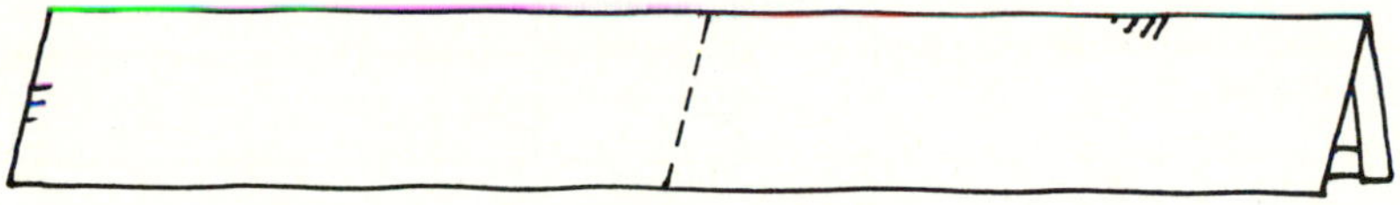

STEP 6

Fold one end from the outside to the center crease. Fold the other end from the outside to the center crease. Crease the outside edges.

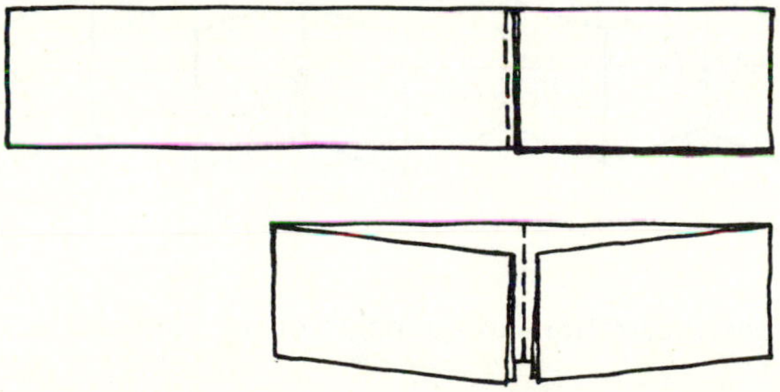

STEP 7

Fold both sides from the inside crease to the outside. Crease the newly folded edges.

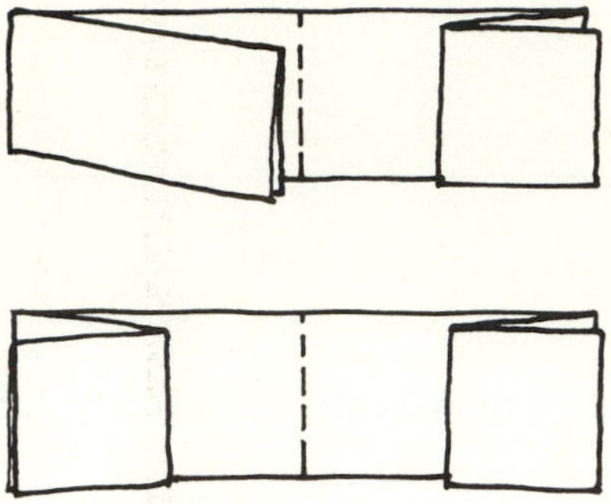

STEP 8

Flip the paper over.

STEP 9

Fold both sides from the outside edges to the center crease.

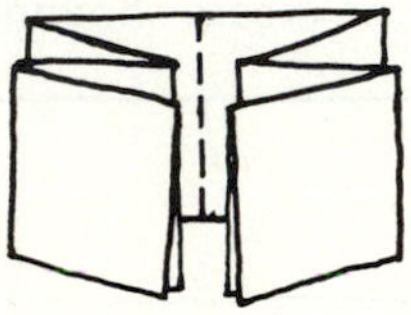

STEP 10

Pick up. You will have a sixteen-page blank book for young authors in the classroom.

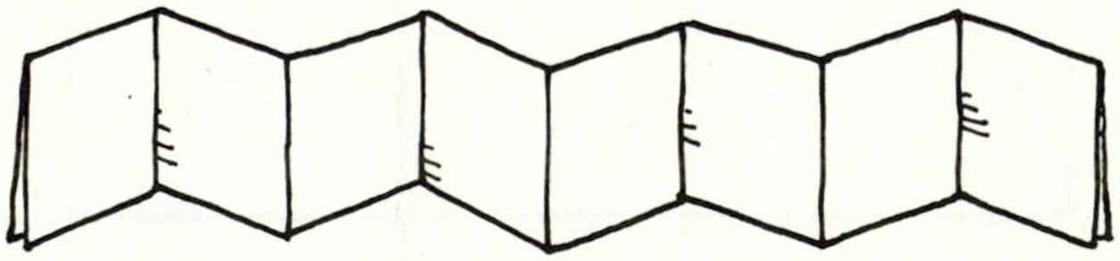

STEP 11

Glue text and illustrations to the pages of the blank book.

STEP 12

Read and display.

Shape Books

Some books are effective when the pages and the cover are cut in the shape of something that has to do with the topic of the book. Usually they have soft, flexible covers made from construction paper or tagboard. These can be fastened by sewing, with brads, by being stapled, or with rings.

Producing Multiple Copies

The production committee should be composed of volunteers who help authors produce multiple copies of their manuscripts. Parent volunteers can be committee members. Each committee should have at least one member who can use a typewriter (not necessarily a typist). All members should be familiar with the options for type of book, type of reproduction, and schedules for reproducing the material.

Type of Book

Production committee members help authors select the type of book to be produced. They could have samples available to show books such as

folded and stitched
stapled flat
accordion
shape books
held with ring binders
text and illustrations glued into a blank book

Authors are responsible for paging the manuscript, but production committee members know how to arrange materials so paging is consecutive in folded and stitched books. They can also recommend the type of binding to use in terms of the thickness of the finished manuscript.

Type of Reproduction

Production committee members help the authors decide on the type of reproduction. For two or three copies, carbon paper is used. For more than three, a master copy can be made for heat-process reproduction. A stencil can be cut for duplication on a spirit-master duplicator.

The author may do the typing or printing or may choose a member of the production committee to do it. When heat-process machines are to be used, typing or pencil copy duplicates best. Most children like to try to do some of their own typing, even though they type with only one finger. The editor-in-chief may require that all manuscripts be reviewed for correctness before they are typed. If pencil copies for duplicating stencils are to be made for the work of young children, an adult or older student can print lightly and the author can trace over the printing with bold strokes.

Schedules for Reproduction of Manuscripts

Multiple-copy productions should not be made more than once a month. Single-copy manuscripts will serve other needs. For producing selected manuscripts, children or adults can learn to operate the duplicating equipment. If teachers or parents are in charge of the machines, the author or authors whose work is being duplicated should be able to observe the process at least once during the school year. This is the most exciting part of the production for some children.

Books by Older Students for Young Readers

Students in upper grades and secondary schools can produce books to be used by young readers. This activity gives meaning to writing with a "sense of story," and it provides much-needed materials in many schools. In preparation for the writing, students can read many books for young readers to observe what authors have done to make them easy.

Procedures for the production of the reading materials might be as follows:

1. Students write original manuscript in full language.
2. Manuscripts are revised to reduce the difficulty load for young readers.

   Increase the percentage of words of highest frequency. See Appendix C.
   Increase the percentage of nouns of highest frequency. See Appendix B.
   Decrease the length of long, involved sentences.
   Transpose passive voice to active voice.
   Eliminate some of the adjectives and adverbs and move the meaning they carry to illustrations.

Use predictive lines and repeating patterns like those in selections found in this book.

3. Bind the books into sturdy bindings.
4. Make copies of the books and distribute them to classrooms and libraries. Authors should be invited to read the books before they leave them for the young readers.

Chapter 5

The Reading/Research Center

What Is a Reading/Research Center?

A Reading/Research Center is a place

for guided practice in silent and oral reading
for developing specific assignments that lead to reading improvement
for independent skill-building activities in reading
for browsing through a variety of books and magazines
for making choices of reading materials
for children to contrast and compare their own books with those of other authors
for building awareness of repeating patterns in language
for predicting language found in reading without seeing the print
for participating in unison and choral reading

The Reading/Research Center has two major purposes: to furnish a variety of materials for children to browse through and read on a self-selection basis, and to provide stimulating activities for children to use for practice and review of basic reading skills.

The pupil-teacher reading conference plays an important role in the Reading/Research Center. Through this conference, the child's general abilities in silent and oral reading are assessed. Activities are designed so that at conference time the child can demonstrate these abilities or lack of them in a friendly, personal setting and can then plan with the teacher some things to do to improve reading skills or to explore new ones. Over a period of time the teacher will suggest activities that give practice in

choosing books for different purposes
increasing speed in silent reading
improving effectiveness of oral reading
adjusting reading speed to the purpose and type of reading material being used
using multiple sources—tables of contents, chapter headings, and indexes and other alphabetical arrangements—to locate answers to questions
extending ideas by reading between the lines
recognizing different literary forms and styles through their physical appearance and content
projecting interest and reasoning beyond what is actually stated in the reading
sensing the humor of a passage, determining the feeling and tone, and selecting passages of high sensitivity

The Reading/Research Center should have available activities, and materials for developing activities, that review reading skills already introduced: vocabulary skills, comprehension skills, study skills, word recognition skills, silent reading skills, and oral reading skills.

The Reading/Research Center is also a place where children go to browse, either for recreation or for study. It should contain a wide variety of books in a minimum of four categories.

1. *Books for recreational reading and for browsing*—picture books, story books, story books with recordings, books older children or aides might read to children, books the teacher has read to the class, comic books, books that two or more children might read together orally (jokes, riddles, poetry), and books written in other languages.
2. *Books for locating information*—factual picture books, picture dictionaries, other dictionaries, encyclopedias, science books,

history and geography books, books on how to make things, and vocabulary books for foreign languages.

3. *Books dealing with language understanding*—alphabet books, books with definite story sequences (picture books, comic strips), basal readers, supplementary readers, patterned poetry books (haiku, cinquains, rhymes), a thesaurus, and language activity books.

4. *Books authored by children in the class and in the school*—alphabet books, story collections, poetry collections, individually authored and illustrated books. Some collections include books co-authored by parents and children and books co-authored by older children and younger children who work as writing "buddies."

The Reading/Research Center should be a comfortable place, with rugs and mats so children can sit on the floor while browsing and reading. The books should be arranged so that the covers, not just the spines, make an attractive display with colorful illustrations and inviting titles. Tables and chairs are useful but not necessary.

Language Skills Developed

The child reads silently with comprehension and with increased independence and speed.
The child distinguishes fact from fantasy.
The child asks relevant questions.
The child draws conclusions from evidence.
The child reads to find answers to questions.
The child relates stories to personal experience.
The child uses dictionaries and other word-study books.
The child uses reference books and other informational sources.
The child uses tables of contents and indexes to locate information.
The child understands the main idea after reading.
The child reads stories with a natural voice.
The child uses punctuation marks effectively in oral reading.
The child participates in simple dramatization of stories.
The child listens to and enjoys poems and stories.
The child participates in choral reading.
The child develops wide interests through reading experiences.
The child chooses reading for recreation.

The child increases in the ability to tell a story in sequence.

The child learns to look at pictures and words for details of color, size, shape, texture, and character.

The child distinguishes differences between books written for recreational reading and those written for information and the development of language skills.

The child identifies differences between poetry and prose from the printed format.

The child uses language clues and picture clues to predict what a story is about or what word is printed.

The child studies words independently.

The child distinguishes language written in a language form other than English.

The child produces new kinds of personal writing through studying the writing of others.

The child increases interest in personal authorship.

Group Activities

Let Me Ride

Big bus! big bus!
I loudly cried.
Big bus! big bus!
Let me ride.

Pony! pony!
I loudly cried.
Pony! pony!
Let me ride.

Taxi! taxi!
I loudly cried.
Taxi! taxi!
Let me ride.

Airplane! airplane!
I loudly cried.
Airplane! airplane!
Let me ride.

LANGUAGE CONCEPTS

The same language patterns are used over and over in writing.
Everything has a name.
Many words rhyme with other words.
Readers use recognition skills to confirm or deny their predictions.
A reader can enjoy the way an author says things as much as what the author says.

1. Read the first stanza of "Let Me Ride." Read it again and ask students to join in.
2. When students can say the first stanza, begin the second one, "Pony! pony!" Expect some students to say the remainder of the stanza.
3. Continue with the selection, adding

   bicycle
   motorbike
   silver train
   race horse
   elephant

4. Copy "Let Me Ride" on a chart or project it on a transparency. Let the students see that they can read language that has been anchored in their ears.
5. Look at the printed stanzas. Notice that the only change from stanza to stanza is in the name. Talk about the importance of recognizing the names in reading.
6. Make a chart of a stanza with blanks for the names.

   ____________ ! ____________ !
   I loudly cried.
   ____________ ! ____________ !
   Let me ride.

   Ask children to fill in the blanks orally. Keep a list.
7. Make a "shuffle book." Put each stanza on a separate card. Children shuffle the cards, and in groups of three or four take the top card off and read it in turn. A child who reads the stanza correctly gets to keep it. If not, the card goes to the bottom of the stack. The game is over when all the cards are gone. The winner is the one with the most cards.

8. Duplicate, or let students copy, the stanzas of "Let Me Ride" plus those the students have added. Make one stanza for each page. Assemble the pages into books for each student. Bind the books in the Publishing Center and let students take them home to read in the family setting.
9. Each student can make illustrations to give clues as to the topic of each page. Stencils can be made for children to use as crayon rubbings or silhouettes.

The Twelve Jugglers

The first juggler juggles one pan.
The second juggler juggles two pans.
The third juggler juggles three pans.
The fourth juggler juggles four.

The first juggler juggles one ball.
The second juggler juggles two balls.
The third juggler juggles three balls.
The fourth juggler juggles four.

The first juggler juggles one ball and one pan.
The second juggler juggles two balls and two pans.
The third juggler juggles three balls and three pans.
The fourth juggler juggles four.

The fifth juggler juggles five pans and five rings.
The sixth juggler juggles six pans and six rings.
The seventh juggler juggles seven pans and seven rings.
The eighth juggler juggles more.

The ninth juggler juggles nine rings.
The tenth juggler juggles ten rings.
The eleventh juggler juggles eleven rings.
The twelfth juggler drops them

ALL ON THE FLOOR!

LANGUAGE CONCEPTS

Readers use recognition skills to confirm or deny their predictions.
Most nouns have different forms to express number.
Many words end with the same sound and symbol.

Alliteration is the use of two or more words together that begin with the same sound.
Some words occur frequently in our language.
The same language patterns are used over and over in writing.
Some syllables appear over and over in the language.

1. Read the first stanza of "The Twelve Jugglers" to introduce the language pattern. Invite children to join in if they think they can. Call attention to the "clipped end" of the pattern in line four. Practice saying it before going on to other stanzas.
2. Duplicate copies or make transparencies for children to use in following along. Give close attention to recognition skills needed for line four in each stanza. Look for words that repeat over and over.
3. Dramatize the stanzas, using real or imaginary items to juggle. Let the whole class say a stanza in chorus as selected students do the acting.
4. Add other words that can be juggled. Create new stanzas with alliterative words, such as

   ____________ batter batted ____________ ball
   ____________ cook cooked ____________ cookie
   ____________ runner ran ____________ race

5. Make books with the new characters students suggest. Put them in the Reading/Research Center. They will be books that students can and will read.
6. Make word cards of the words in "The Twelve Jugglers" for sight recognition activities for the Language Study Center.

More and More Clowns

A tall clown climbs out of the car at the circus.
A taller clown climbs out of the car at the circus.
The tallest clown climbs out of the car at the circus.
Look! There come more and more!

A short clown climbs out of the car at the circus.
A shorter clown climbs out of the car at the circus.
The shortest clown climbs out of the car at the circus.
Look! There come more and more!

A fat clown climbs out of the car at the circus.
A fatter clown climbs out of the car at the circus.
The fattest clown climbs out of the car at the circus.
Look! There come more and more!

A thin clown climbs out of the car at the circus.
A thinner clown climbs out of the car at the circus.
The thinnest clown climbs out of the car at the circus.
Look! There is something more!

What can that be in the car at the circus?
What's coming out of the car at the circus?
A GIRAFFE COMING OUT OF THE CAR AT THE CIRCUS?
IS THE GIRAFFE A CLOWN?

LANGUAGE CONCEPTS

Many descriptive words that compare two or more things end in *-er* and *-est*.

Many words begin with the same sound and symbol.

Consonants are sometimes blended together to represent a sound different from that of any of the single letters.

Readers use recognition skills to confirm or deny their predictions.

1. Read the first stanza while children listen carefully.
2. Read "A short" in the second stanza. Let children predict what will follow. Do the same for the other stanzas.
3. Prepare a chart or a transparency to show children how they can check out their predictions with recognition skills.
4. Read the selection in unison.
5. Ask for volunteers to read it or to identify known words.
6. Identify words that are used frequently.
7. Talk about words that compare size, stressing *-er* and *-est* endings.
8. List all the words that begin with the letter *c* and say them in unison. Listen for the initial sounds. Are they all the same? Pronounce them carefully. Are there any clues to the differences? How can one learn to pronounce them?
9. Plan to publish some clown books for the Reading/Research Center.

Flight Attendant

Sing to the tune of "Row, Row, Row Your Boat."

Fix, fix, fix the meal
While we fly along.
Busily
Busily
Busily
Busily
Fixing for the throng.

Serve, serve, serve the meal
While we fly along.
Busily
Busily
Busily
Busily
Serving all the throng.

Walk, walk, walk the aisle
While we fly along.
Busily
Busily
Busily
Busily
Waiting on the throng.

Talk, talk, talk to folks
While we fly along.
Busily
Busily
Busily
Busily
Talking to the throng.

Take, take, take the trays
While we fly along.
Busily
Busily
Busily
Busily
Taking from the throng.

LANGUAGE CONCEPTS

There are words for the many movements of people, animals, and things.

Everything has a name.

Readers use recognition skills to confirm or deny their predictions.

Consonants are sometimes blended together to represent a sound different from that of any of the single letters.

1. Ask children if any of them have made a flight on an airplane. Was a meal served? Who served it? Did they call the person a flight attendant?
2. Tell the children that you are going to sing a song about the work of the flight attendant.
3. Sing "Flight Attendant" to the tune of "Row, Row, Row Your Boat."
4. Arrange the seats in the classroom in a passenger plane configuration. Select children to be flight attendants to act out the song. Sing one verse at a time and let children act it out.
5. Duplicate the song or copy it on a chart for group reading. Sing while you follow along the print.
6. Ask for volunteers to sing different stanzas and then point to words they recognize.
7. Look at words that begin with the letter *t*.

   throng
   trays
   take
   taking
   talk
   talking

   Say them in chorus. Are the beginning sounds the same? Which ones are alike? Which ones are different? Talk about blends.
8. Look at the slots in the sentences that change from stanza to stanza. They are names and verbs. To change them changes the meaning.

But I Smell Good Morning

The rising sun peeks out. It sends out flashes of reds, yellows, and sparkling clean blues to shatter the gray of the sleepy sky. That's the way the sun says,

GOOD MORNING!

Our paper boy whizzes by fast on his new bike. He throws the paper against the house with a loud thud. That's how he says,

GOOD MORNING!

A big fluffy cat alone at the break of day swishes past my window. It scratches it as if to tell me, "It's time to get up and play." That's his

GOOD MORNING!

My dog pulls at the covers on my bed and barks a friendly "Yip! Yip!" That's his way to say,

GOOD MORNING!

Brr-rr-rr-rung! Brr-rr-rr-rung! Brr-rr-rr-rung! goes the alarm clock by big brother's bed. That's a loud way to say,

GOOD MORNING!

The smells of bacon frying and good brown toast cooking come into my room. I know that's mother's way to say,

GOOD MORNING!

IT'S GREAT TO SMELL

GOOD MORNING!

LANGUAGE CONCEPTS

Greeting cards and letters are special ways of expressing ideas and feelings.

Meanings change by voice inflection, rate of speaking, and other oral characteristics that do not show in print.

The same language patterns are used over and over in writing.

1. Read three or four sections of "But I Smell Good Morning," then stop to let children tell ways they hear, see, smell, and taste "good morning."
2. List on the chalkboard some of the ways suggested. Then read the remainder of the selection.
3. Talk about greetings of all kinds and what they mean. Share some ways that people greet one another.

4. Say and write "good morning" in different languages, such as

   Hawaiian
   Spanish
   French
   German
   Navajo

   Look in a large dictionary or a foreign language dictionary for other greetings. Plan books using greetings in different languages.
5. Make a "shuffle book." Copy each section of "But I Smell Good Morning" on a separate card. Shuffle the cards and let children draw them one at a time and read them orally. The order will change with each shuffle.
6. Read "good morning" with different voice inflections to represent different feelings.

   happy
   sad
   angry
   sleepy
   indifferent
   enthusiastic

   Talk about how the same words convey different meanings and feelings by the way they are said.
7. Read stories that have conversation in them. Make a list of words or phrases of greetings.

Lickety! Splickety! Boom!

Lickety! Splickety!
Rickety! Reet!
The big bus hurries
Along my street.

Lickety! Splickety!
Rickety! Right!
The big bus hurries
To dodge a kite.

Lickety! Splickety!
Rickety! Rool!
The big bus hurries
To the swimming pool.

Bumpety! Humpety!
Jumpety! Too!
The big bus hurries
Along to the zoo.

Bumpety! Humpety!
Jumpety! Rack!
The big bus hurries
Across the track.

Bumpety! Humpety!
Jumpety! Hum!
The big bus hurries
To meet my chum.

Reakity! Beakity!
Squeekity! Sway!
The bus slows down.
It's going my way.

Reakity! Beakity!
Squeekity! Squeck!
The bus slows down
To prevent a wreck.

Reakity! Beakity!
Squeekity! Squee!
The bus slows down
To miss a tree.

Clackety! Rackety!
Hackety! Huck!
The big bus hurries
To pass the truck.

Clackety! Rackety!
Hackety! Zhane!
The big bus hurries
To beat the train.

Clackety! Rackety!
Hackety! Ow!
The big bus hurries
To miss a cow.

Clackety! Rackety!
Hackety! Zome!
The big bus hurries
To get me home.

LICKETY! SPLICKETY!
BUMPETY! HUMPETY!
REAKITY! BEAKITY!
CLACKETY! RACKETY!

BOOM!

LANGUAGE CONCEPTS

New words can be created by anyone.

Rhyming is the use of two or more words that end with the same sound.

A reader can enjoy the way an author says things as much as what the author says.

Readers use recognition skills to confirm or deny their predictions.

Punctuation and capitalization are aids to oral reading.

Many words end with the same sound and symbol.

1. Read the selection to the students. Read it fast enough to portray the rhythm of the noisy bus.
2. Reread the selection and ask students to say the third line and predict the fourth line.
3. Duplicate copies of "Lickety! Splickety! Boom!" Ask for volunteers to read stanzas. Enjoy the sound words as children say them.
4. Make books with one stanza for each page. Encourage each student to add at least one page to the book. As students can read them, let them take them home.
5. Make "rhyming triplets." List the two words that rhyme in each stanza and add a third.

reet	right
street	kite
treat	fight

   Students who wish to do so might change the last line of some stanzas. They can do it either orally or in writing.
6. Talk about "made up" words in the selection. Who can make up words? Try making up words not in the selection. Use them for additional stanzas.

Click! Click! Click!

Click!
Click!
Click!

Click! went the camera as the baby llama nibbled at the bright orange carrot.

Click! went the camera as the happy young elephant took the peanuts from tiny Susie.

Click! went the camera as the tortoise sat very still so that a small child could sit on his big hard-shelled back.

But no one took a picture of Spotty, the little goat. No one said anything to Spotty except "Go away!" "Get!" or "Stop!"

The runty goat with spots and splashes of black, brown, and white watched the gate. "Oh, here comes a man with a camera. Maybe he'll take my picture," thought Spotty as he went slowly toward the tall man pushing a baby carriage.

"Hmm-m, I'll bet those straps on the carriage would really taste good." Without thinking, Spotty started nibbling at the straps.

"Oh—Wha-a-a! Wha-a-a!" screamed the frightened child as he flung his arms, searching for a familiar sight to touch.

"Go away! Get!" shouted the man as he pushed the goat from the carriage. Spotty hurried for a few steps, then said, "Bah-h-h! That didn't get my picture taken, so what can I do next?"

The mischievous little goat wandered over close to the trash cans. "Maybe someone will take my picture here," he thought. Because he had nothing to do at the moment, Spotty tugged and pulled at the lid. Crash! Bang! Bang! Over went the can and off came the lid. Out tumbled candy wrappers, paper sacks, cans, boxes, milk cartons—oh, everything! There was such a loud commotion that Janet, the hefty, red-headed attendant, came running and shouting, "Stop! Go away! Get! Spotty! Won't you ever learn to behave?" she asked as she gave the startled animal a rough slap on his rumpled coat.

"Well, she really spoiled that picture," baahed Spotty as he cast a disdainful look at Janet and made a fast retreat.

"Ah, there's a little old lady with a camera. Maybe she'll like a goat picture," thought Spotty as he made his way close to her. "Hmm-m, what a nice leather purse she has. I'll bet that would taste good." Quickly he began to nibble at the long brown purse strap.

"Stop! You awful goat! Get away from me!" she cried as she jerked the strap away and whacked at the retreating animal.

No matter how hard Spotty tried to be friendly, he couldn't succeed. No one wanted him near. No one wanted to hold a camera up to him. All he could hear was "Stop!" "Get!" "Go away!"

All around him he heard Click! Click! Click! He looked up to see a small boy riding the tortoise. "That ugly old thing! Why do they take pictures of it?" he asked himself. Just then the small child fell off the tortoise and ran crying to his mother.

"Well, since no one wants to feed me, since no one loves me, and no one wants to take my picture, I might as well go take a ride on the tortoise," thought Spotty.

The big old tortoise let the tiny goat get upon his hard mosaic back, then slowly rose and ambled toward a fence where some green leaves were sticking through.

"Oh, look," cried the tall man pushing the baby carriage as he stopped to cock his camera. Click!

"Why, you clever little goat!" said the zoo attendant as she grabbed her tiny pocket camera. Click!

"Oh, what a cute picture!" said the little old lady as she quickly grabbed her camera. Click!

Never had the tiny tacky goat been so happy!

Click!
Click!
Click!

LANGUAGE CONCEPTS

Simple stories have a beginning, an elaboration of the beginning, and an ending.
Authors describe characters in ways that let readers form mental images of them.
Authors describe settings in ways that let readers form mental images of them.
Titles are used to tell the main idea of a production.
People express feelings and emotions through creative activities.
Feelings of people and animals are described with words.

1. Make pinhole cameras. Use them to look for points of interest both inside and outside the classroom. Let children talk about the imaginary pictures they take.
2. Read "Click! Click! Click!" to the children. Ask them to tell the main ideas of the story.
3. List words describing the characteristics of the main characters. Do such words actually appear in the story? If not, how was each idea

developed? Did other characters give some clues? Did their clues turn out to be right?

4. Look for other short stories with one main character. Compare them with "Click! Click! Click!" as to character development, setting, and plot. Talk about beginning, problem development, solution, climax, and ending.
5. Ask children to volunteer their own short stories for class seminars. Reproduce some of them on transparencies and project them for class discussion. After editing and copying, publish them as books for the Reading/Research Center.
6. Talk about taking pictures—how you focus on a main idea. Take sheets of paper and punch pinholes to look through until you can focus on one main idea. Take the papers on a walk around the school ground.
7. Discuss how to organize ideas for a short story—a beginning, an elaboration of the beginning, and an ending. Try to think of an idea and build an outline with the whole class participating. See what happens when several students write from the same outline. You may have enough short stories for a collection to add to the Reading/Research Center.

Enough Friends

Star moved to a new home. She was lonely, so she went to hunt for new friends.

Star went out to the big tree beside the old creek bed. As she walked around the tree, she found many old branches and many holes. "What could live here?" wondered Star, as she peeked among the branches. "What could live here?" wondered Star, as she looked at the small holes. "Oh! There's a bigger hole! I wonder what lives there?"

Suddenly Star had an idea! Quickly she ran into her new home! Just as quickly she came back!

The first morning Star put beside the big tree some bread crumbs,
an apple core,
a small bit of lettuce,
and best of all,
a bit of candy she'd saved.

What came that day? The quail came one by one.

On the second morning Star put beside the big tree some bread crumbs,
an apple core,
a small bit of lettuce,
and best of all,
a bit of candy she'd saved.

What came that day? The quail came one by one, and the lizards came two by two.

On the third morning Star put beside the big tree some bread crumbs,
an apple core,
a small bit of lettuce,
and best of all,
a bit of candy she'd saved.

What came that day? The quail came one by one, the lizards came two by two, and the worms came three by three.

On the fourth morning Star put beside the big tree some bread crumbs,
an apple core,
a small bit of lettuce,
and best of all,
a bit of candy she'd saved.

What came that day? The quail came one by one, the lizards came two by two, the worms came three by three, and the squirrels came four by four.

On the fifth morning Star put beside the big tree some bread crumbs,
an apple core,
a small bit of lettuce,
and best of all,
a bit of candy she'd saved.

What came that day? The quail came one by one, the lizards came two by two, the worms came three by three, the squirrels came four by four, and the beetles came five by five.

On the sixth morning Star put beside the big tree some bread crumbs,
an apple core,
a small bit of lettuce,
and best of all,
a bit of candy she'd saved.

What came that day? The quail came one by one, the lizards came two by two, the worms came three by three, the squirrels came four by four, the beetles came five by five, and the bunnies came six by six.

On the seventh morning Star put beside the big tree some bread crumbs,
an apple core,
a small bit of lettuce,
and best of all,
a bit of candy she'd saved.

What came that day? The quail came one by one, the lizards came two by two, the worms came three by three, the squirrels came four by four, the beetles came five by five, the bunnies came six by six, and the ants came seven by seven, and ten by ten, and
hundreds by hundreds, and
ZILLIONS BY ZILLIONS!
STAR HAS ENOUGH FRIENDS! ! !

LANGUAGE CONCEPTS

The same language patterns are used over and over in writing.
Words help form pictures in the mind.
Oral reading can bring an audience pleasure and information.

1. Read "Enough Friends" until children discover the repeating pattern. Invite them to join in the reading when they hear the repeating lines.
2. Talk about

   the setting where these animals might live
   the kind of person they think Star is
   the biggest number they know

3. Discover repeating patterns in things besides stories. Students can find them in cloth, wallpaper, wrapping paper, and music. Have a "repeating pattern" display.
4. Suggest that students try to discover other stories and poems with repeating patterns. Read them with the class and put them in the Reading/Research Center for browsing and reading.

Green Desert

The chubby nine-year-old plunged his shovel deep into the wet sand as his large, worried brown eyes looked up at his mother. "Alonzo says we're moving to the desert, Mom. Is Arizona really a desert?"

"Part of it is, Tammy."

"Is Tucson in the desert?"

"Yes. It's in a part of Arizona called a green desert."

"A green desert? What's that? Do you mean the sand's green?"

A big smile played on Mrs. Lorenzo's sun-bronzed face. "No, dear. A green desert is one that has many plants on it that have learned to live with very little water."

"Alonzo said that only a few sharp pointed plants grow on a desert and that only rattlesnakes and lizards live there. He said we would have sand hills all around us."

"Some deserts are like that, son. Other deserts are almost altogether rock—rock mountains and all kinds of strange-shaped rocks. Other deserts have plants, animals, and birds on them. Tammy, you'll love the desert around Tucson. I was just a little older than you when I spent my Easter vacation there with Aunt Grace."

"I didn't know you had been there, Mom. Tell me about it."

"Several rains had fallen during the winter months before I was there in the spring."

"You mean it rains in the desert?"

"Sure. Often when it rains the water comes suddenly and fast. At other times the rain comes slowly and soaks into the dry ground. Many of the plants have roots that spread out close to the surface of the earth. When rain comes, they greedily absorb all the moisture they can hold. After a rain many of them look full and fat."

"Gee! That sounds neat! Are the trees big like the ones in our yard?" Tammy moved closer to his mother and stretched his chubby frame over the cool wet sand.

"No, Tammy. They're quite different. I remember one called the Palo Verde tree that has a green trunk and green limbs. The tiny green leaves drop off when the weather is dry."

"They must look funny. What makes the trunk green?"

"I was told that these trees manufacture chlorophyll in their bark."

"You mean the stuff that's in flowers and in my new toothpaste?"

"That's it. They don't have to have leaves to manufacture their food. When I saw the Palo Verde trees they were covered with tiny yellow flowers. They looked like a soft yellow snow had fallen and covered them."

"Gee! They must've looked neat!"

"They did. But I'll bet you'll like seeing the giants of the desert."

"Giants?"

"Yes, they're called saguaro. Look, Tammy, it's like this." Mrs. Lorenzo sketched a tall straight shape in the sand, then added some curved arms extending from either side. "Some of them grow forty to fifty feet tall."

"Wow! That's taller than our two-story house! Say! I've seen pictures of those saguaro. They grow in Mexico."

"Yes. The Sonoran Desert, where they grow, is in both Arizona and Mexico."

"Grady brought some postcards to school with saguaro on them. One looked like it was waving to people."

"I remember some looked like hitchhikers and some looked like they were holding their hands in prayer. It was fun trying to decide what different ones were doing."

"Maybe we can grow some in our yard."

"Maybe some will be there already. I don't want to bother growing them from seeds. They grow less than one inch a year and they don't put out their first arm until they are about seventy-five years old."

"Then those giants on the postcards must have been very old. They had lots of arms."

"Some with many arms may be two hundred years old."

"Two hundred years! Wow! Do saguaro swell up when it rains?"

"Yes. On the inside of each plant is a circle of wooden ribs that extend the full height of the plant. The outside is covered with a rubber-like skin that is pleated like an accordion. The skin expands when the plant gathers water during a rain."

"Is the giant good for anything? You know—lumber, food, or something like that?"

"Oh, yes. The saguaro has a white flower crown around the top of its long arms in the spring. When the flowers dry up, the seed pods that are left in their places are a bright red fruit. Birds love to eat the fruit and the seed. Indians harvest them to make their jelly."

"But if the plants are stickery and very tall, how can they get the fruit?"

"They make long gathering poles from dead saguaro ribs. Also, I've heard that saguaro rib trim is used on the inside of some of the expensive homes in Arizona."

"Gee! They use those giants for everything! I can hardly wait to see them. When did you say we were moving?"

LANGUAGE CONCEPTS

We perceive our own meanings from our experiences.
Locating facts requires one to look in many kinds of materials.
Stories and poems can grow out of real experiences.

1. Project slides or use a filmstrip of deserts so that the children can see the different ways that deserts can look.
2. Ask children to look for information about deserts in encyclopedias and dictionaries. Provide a blank book in which they can put new facts they discover about the deserts of the world. Later, this book can be shared with the whole class.
3. Read "Green Desert" to the class. Discuss kinds of deserts and help children understand that not all deserts are just sand hills. Perhaps some children have been to various deserts and can share some of their experiences.
4. Make a bulletin board, What I Discovered about Deserts. Children can display pictures with captions, poems, and facts they have discovered.
5. Collect books about deserts from the school library. Encourage children to read them in order to discover information that is new to them.

Independent Activities

Mystery Stories

LANGUAGE CONCEPT

A few words in a story can carry most of the meaning.

1. Copy a good story or part of a story in large print.
2. Choose and mark some of the words that tell what the story is about. They might refer to the setting, the main characters, the weather, or the main action.
3. Place a piece of paper the same size as that on which the story is written over the story, hold it up to the light, and mark around the words you selected.
4. Cut out the marked sections so that the selected words will be the only ones to show through when the page is placed over the story.
5. Tape the pages together on one side to let the selected words show.
6. Ask classmates to read the words that show through and then tell you the story.
7. Lift the cover sheet and read the story together.

Once a tiger was caught in a trap. He tried to get out through the bars. He bit with rage and grief, but he failed.
tiger
caught
trap
out
bars
bit
rage
grief
failed.

Words I Can Read

LANGUAGE CONCEPTS

Some nouns are common and some are proper.
Words that are used as nouns in sentences can be used in other ways.
Oral reading can bring an audience pleasure and information.

1. Find words you can read in magazines.
2. Cut them out.
3. Paste them on sheets of paper.
4. Make a book of words you know.
5. Read your book at school and at home.
6. Read only the words that are names of things.

Everybody Show

LANGUAGE CONCEPTS

Any sound that can be spoken can be represented with letters of the alphabet.
Oral reading can bring an audience pleasure and information.
A few words in a story can carry most of the meaning.

1. Choose a story you can read and understand.
2. Choose ten to fifteen words from that story that a reader has to know to understand the story.
3. Make four sets of cards with one of the words on each card in a set.
4. Invite classmates to play a game with the cards. Each player has a set of cards on the table with the words showing. You say, "Everybody show" when you say one of the words. Each player immediately picks up the card and shows you the word.
5. You collect the right answers.
6. The player who gets rid of all the cards first wins the game.
7. The winner gets to read the story orally to the group.

Clip Cards

LANGUAGE CONCEPTS

Many words begin with the same sound and symbol.
A consonant or consonant cluster usually represents the same sound at the beginning of a word.
A vowel can represent a variety of sounds at the beginning of a word.

1. Cut words and pictures from newspapers and magazines.
2. Clip each one to the alphabet card to which it belongs.*
3. Read words and say words that go with the pictures that other children have clipped to the cards.

* *To the teacher:* Make alphabet cards in shapes or in squares. Put three or four large paper clips on each of the cards to hold words and pictures children add to the cards. Take time periodically to check the words and pictures with groups of children. Take them off and make them into alphabet books.

If I Had $100

LANGUAGE CONCEPTS

Numerals are symbols of how many and how much.
Everything has a name.

1. Read the advertisements in a newspaper.
2. Make a list of things you would like to have, but the total cost must not be more than $100.
3. Don't go into debt.
4. If you enjoyed doing this, you may spend $1,000 for things you would like to have. Keep an accurate account.
5. Put your list in the Reading/Research Center for your classmates to see.

Incomplete Sentence Strips

LANGUAGE CONCEPTS

Most sentences have at least one verb or a form of *be* or *have* in them.
Words that are used as nouns in sentences can be used in other ways.
Punctuation and capitalization are aids to oral reading.

1. Make a sentence strip with two or more blanks.
2. Make a stack of cards of words that could go in the blanks.
3. Clip different words in the blanks to make sentences.
4. Read the sentences with the new words.
5. Keep a record of all the sentences you make with each sentence strip.

Characters Only

LANGUAGE CONCEPTS

Proper nouns begin with a capital letter.
Authors describe characters in ways that let readers form mental images of them.

1. Pick a story with people or animals in it.
2. Write the names of the characters on a piece of paper.

3. Bring the list of characters with you to your reading conference.
4. Talk about the characters as you remember them in the story.

My "Said" List

LANGUAGE CONCEPTS

Feelings of people and animals are described with words.
Punctuation and capitalization are aids to oral reading.

1. Read a story or a book that has written conversation. You can tell by looking for quotation marks.
2. List different words the author used to signal the talk. The word can be "said" or any word that could go in the place of "said."
3. Begin a list of "said" words to use when you write a story using characters who talk. Did the best authors use "said" over and over, or did they use different words to help you understand the characters?

What Did They Say?

LANGUAGE CONCEPTS

Feelings of people and animals are described with words.
Words help form pictures in the mind.

1. Make a list of three or four feelings that people might write about. They might be

anger	loneliness
happiness	love

2. During one week keep a list of words authors use to describe feelings in the stories you read.

Figures of Speech

LANGUAGE CONCEPTS

People use similes and metaphors to compare and contrast things and ideas.
A reader can enjoy the way an author says things as much as what the author says.

1. Make a Figures of Speech chart to use when reading.
2. When you come to "as ________ as" or "like ________," stop to see if something is being compared. If it is, add the statement to your chart.

Figures of Speech

as ________ as ________	________ like ________
as black as coal	runs like water
as cold as ice	shines like the sun
as sharp as a tack	sounds like thunder

Now you are on your own.

3. Share your list with others who are making Figures of Speech charts.
4. Use figures of speech in your writing.

Growing Up Stories

LANGUAGE CONCEPTS

People communicate some information in sequence.
A sequence of pictures can tell a story without words.
The same picture suggests different words and ideas to different people.

1. Draw or collect pictures to show how things grow up—people, plants, animals, and so forth.
2. Dictate or write stories to follow the pictures.
3. Copy and illustrate each sequence.
4. Make the stories into books for the Reading/Research Center.

Can You Name It?

LANGUAGE CONCEPTS

Some symbols other than our alphabet communicate meaning.
We perceive our own meanings from our experiences.
Abbreviations are used in places where whole words are not needed.

? ? ?

2 c. uncooked oatmeal	3 T. cocoa
¾ c. sugar	1 T. water
⅔ c. butter	½ tsp. vanilla

Cream the butter and sugar. Add other ingredients. Blend in oatmeal. Take one tsp. of the mixture at a time and roll it in sugar. Chill and eat.

1. Here is a recipe without a name.*
2. Read it and give it a name.
3. Cut out other recipes from magazines and newspapers.
4. Cut off or fold back their names.
5. Have your friends try to figure out names for them.

Words that Tell How Many

LANGUAGE CONCEPTS

Numerals are symbols of how many and how much.
Numerals and numbers have word names.

1. Choose any book from the Reading/Research Center.
2. Copy the words and numbers that tell how many.
3. Read your list to the class.

Who Lives in the Mountains?

LANGUAGE CONCEPTS

Imagination promotes picturesque speech.
Imaginary creatures can have names.
Locating facts requires one to look in many kinds of materials.
Alphabetical arrangements help one locate information.

Look at pictures of mountains. Can you see anyone living there? Could someone be living there that you can't see in the pictures? Someone or something must be living there.

1. Ask your teacher, your parents, your librarian, or a friend if they know of any real or imaginary people who live in mountains most of the time.

* *To the teacher:* Cut recipes from magazines and newspapers. Remove the names, but keep a list of them for follow-up discussions after several students have tried to name the recipes.

2. Choose something to read about life in mountains. It can be about people who live in moutains, such as forest rangers, miners, and loggers, or it can be about animals that live in mountains, or it can be about imaginary characters like Pepe, who lives in Kilauea, Hawaii.
3. Tape a story about what you found when reading.
4. Add your tape to those in the Viewing/Listening Center.

Compound Word List

LANGUAGE CONCEPTS

Some words occur frequently in our language.
Compound words are two or more words combined into one.

1. Make a compound word list from words you find in your reading.
2. Tally the number of times you find the same word.
3. Put your list in the Language Study Center.

Three Kinds of Reading

LANGUAGE CONCEPTS

Locating facts requires one to look in many kinds of materials.
Alphabetical arrangements help one locate information.
A reader can enjoy the way an author says things as much as what the author says.
Many poets use unusual language to describe something usual.

1. Choose a topic that you are interested in, such as

buildings	birds	fairs
roads	rocks	trains
rivers	guitars	insects

2. Search for at least three forms of writing on the topic: poetry, scientific articles, true stories, imaginary stories, and others.
3. Read them all.
4. In the weekly conference with your teacher, read the selections or selected paragraphs.
5. Talk about the style of writing you like best on the topic.

Guessing Last Lines

LANGUAGE CONCEPTS

Understanding and following directions helps one solve problems.
A reader can enjoy the way an author says things as much as what the author says.
New words can be created by anyone.
Rhyming is the use of two or more words that end with the same sound.

Make a collection of limericks.

1. Copy each limerick on a three-by-five card. Omit the last line of each limerick.
2. Number each card.
3. Copy the missing last line on an answer sheet.
4. Number the missing line with the same number used on the card.
5. Read the limericks to a group of friends. Let them make up last lines. Tell them to make up words if they can't think of real ones that rhyme.
6. Read the last line of the limerick from the answer sheet to compare it with those made up by your friends.

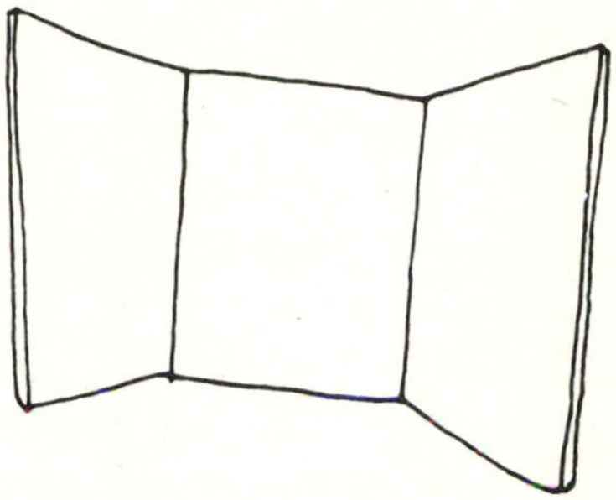

Trifold Stories

LANGUAGE CONCEPTS

People communicate by speaking and writing in sentences.
Words help form pictures in the mind.
Simple statements can be extended and elaborated.
Simple stories have a beginning, an elaboration of the beginning, and an ending.

1. Make some trifolds by taping together three pieces of heavy paper or light cardboard.
2. Choose stories you have enjoyed reading to make trifold stories for the Writing Center.
3. Copy a story beginning and a story ending on the trifold. Leave the middle space blank.
4. Ask classmates to tell on tape or to write the unfinished part of the story.

5. Listen to or read the stories together.
6. Read the original story and compare it with the stories created by your classmates.

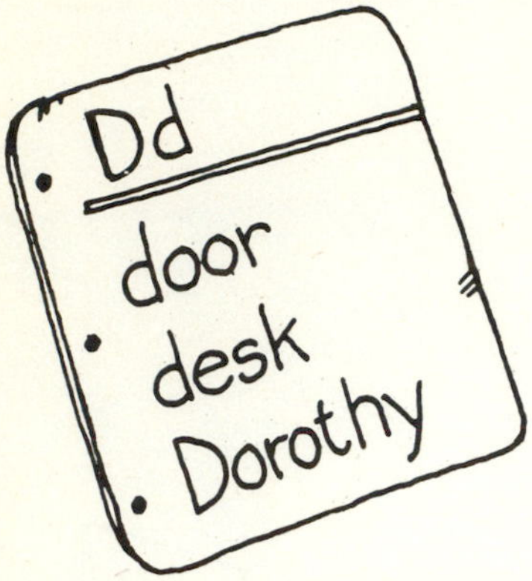

Number Posters

LANGUAGE CONCEPTS

Some symbols other than our alphabet communicate meaning.
Numerals and numbers have word names.

1. Cut different numbers from newspapers.
2. Paste them on a poster board or on construction paper. Your poster can show prices of things, sizes of things, large numbers, or a combination of all kinds of numbers that are found everywhere.
3. Read your number poster to your class.

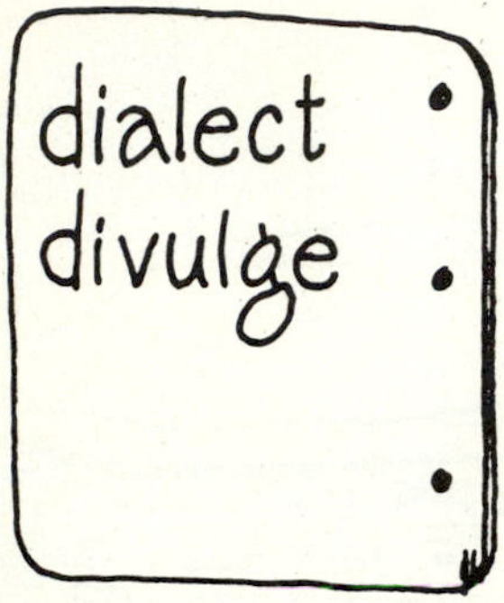

Alphabet Shopping

LANGUAGE CONCEPTS

Each letter of the alphabet has a name.
Many words begin with the same sound and symbol.

1. Choose one alphabet card for the day.*
2. Write on it words that begin with the letter or letters you choose.
3. Put the words you can already read on the front side.
4. Put the words you are not sure about on the back side.
5. Read your list with another alphabet shopper at the end of the day. Who can read the most words?

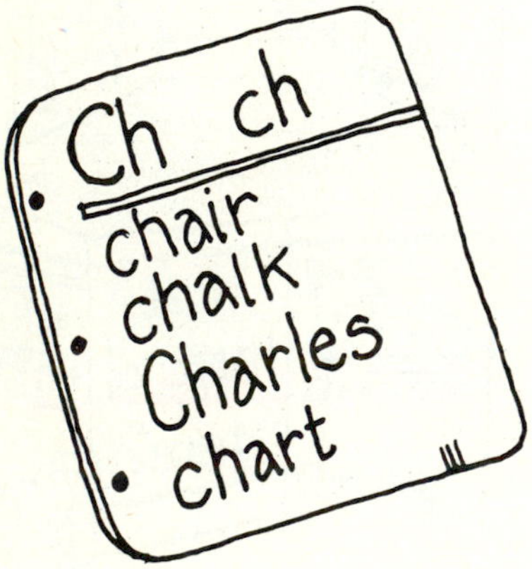

Score Five

LANGUAGE CONCEPT

Some words occur frequently in our language.

1. Take a word list from the Score Five stack. Each card has five words on it.†

---

* *To the teacher:* Keep a supply of cards with an alphabet letter or letters (usually consonants and consonant clusters) ready for the alphabet shoppers. Children can make the cards for you.

† *To the teacher:* Make and duplicate six to eight different lists of five frequently used words. Use the list in Appendix C for reference.

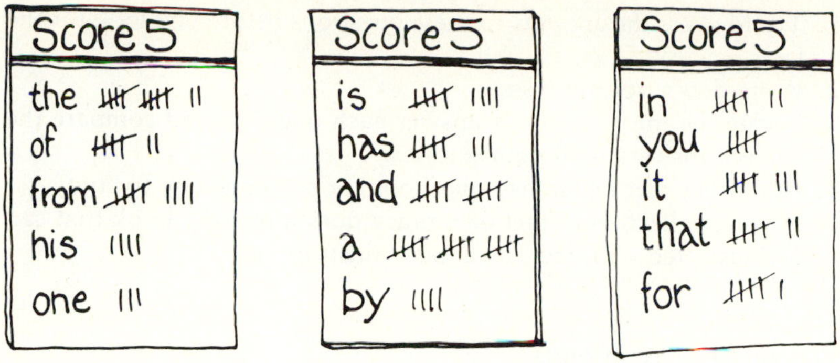

2. Read any book, magazine story, or newspaper story for ten minutes.
3. Keep a tabulation of the number of times you read each of your words.

What's in a Tree?

LANGUAGE CONCEPTS

Everything has a name.
Locating facts requires one to look in many kinds of materials.
Alphabetical arrangements help one locate information.

1. How many things can be made from a tree? a cow? a horse? a pig? a peanut?
2. Choose one subject and see how many things you can find that are made from it.
3. Look for answers in reference books, magazines, newspapers, and around the room.
4. Cut out or draw pictures to illustrate a book on your subject.

Fact or Fantasy?

LANGUAGE CONCEPTS

Locating facts requires one to look in many kinds of materials.
Alphabetical arrangements help one locate information.

Does a centipede have a hundred legs? Are bald eagles really bald? Can a porcupine throw its quills?

1. Try to guess the answers to these questions before you look for the facts.
2. Write down your guesses.
3. Locate the information to answer each question and compare the correct answers with your guesses.
4. Add other fact or fantasy questions for someone else to study.
5. Make a collection of fact or fantasy questions for a book that can be illustrated with fact or fantasy illustrations.

Where Are My Friends?

LANGUAGE CONCEPTS

Imagination promotes picturesque speech.
Stories and poems can grow out of real experiences.
Authors describe settings in ways that let readers form mental images of them.

Have you hunted for friends all around your home?

1. List places where you might find friends like Star found in "Enough Friends."

In Holes	In Trees	In Water
ants	squirrels	frogs

Under Bricks and Stones

earthworms

2. Use some of the words on your list to tell a real story into the tape recorder.
3. Put your list of friends in the Reading/Research Center for others to read.
4. Read other lists put there by your friends.

Where in the World Did That Word Come From?

LANGUAGE CONCEPTS

Locating facts requires one to look in many kinds of materials.
Alphabetical arrangements help one locate information.
Words used today come from many sources.

January comes from *Janus,* the Roman god of beginnings and endings. Janus is pictured as having two faces, one looking forward and one looking backward.

Scuba comes from the first letters in Self-Contained Underwater Breathing Apparatus.

Submarine comes from the Latin prefix *sub,* meaning "under," and *mare,* a Latin word meaning "sea."

1. Look for other words that had interesting beginnings in other parts of the world.
2. Make the words into a book.

Chapter 6

The Language Study Center

What Is a Language Study Center?

A Language Study Center is a place

for practicing skills needed for encoding and decoding language
for looking at specific ingredients of language
for understanding repeating patterns in spoken and written language
for increasing awareness of language structure through oral language activities

A Language Study Center deals with a wide range of skills and attitudes toward language. Many of the activities fit into the category of *word study*—they develop the ability to anticipate the pronunciation and meaning of words through context clues, root words with affixes, letter combinations that occur frequently, other phonetic skills, and use of dictionary-type aids.

Another major category of activities deals with *language structure.* These activities develop the ability to anticipate meanings from clues in the structure of sentences, paragraphs, chapters (introductory and summary paragraphs), and stories (sequence of events).

The Language Study Center provides continuing opportunities for acquiring a sight vocabulary of structure words, especially of frequently used words, and at the same time underlines the need to anticipate the positions of nouns, verbs, and descriptive words in sentences. This emphasis might be considered *functional grammar*, as contrasted to formal grammar studies.

Group activities in the Language Study Center relate the refinement of language understanding more to oral activities than to written ones. They offer opportunities for teachers to anchor literary-level language in the ears of students before there is any emphasis on reading and writing. The group activity selections illustrate ways of working that are useful with the great variety of materials in the reading/language arts curriculum of most school systems. They illustrate

listening to stories and poems, with students joining in by saying lines and phrases that repeat over and over
dramatizing that will reflect the variety of meanings available to students hearing the same selection
participating in unison reading as a means of releasing some students to say things in new ways
participating in choral reading as a means of refining interpretations through voice modulation, pitch, and stress
listening to the teacher read effectively while following the print

Group activity selections help students learn to control meaning through intonation. In turn, students learn how to use punctuation in writing to represent some of that control. Phoneme-grapheme relationships become visible and meaningful to them as they observe regular spelling over and over on charts and in printouts of selections the whole class uses. They learn to use a variety of dialects in speech as they do oral interpretations of characters and situations. They come into an awareness of the worth of their own language power as they see how it works for them in a variety of activities.

Language Skills Developed and Practiced

The child develops auditory discrimination through hearing contrasting language sounds and rhyming endings.

The child develops visual discrimination through identifying words that begin alike, are alike, and end alike.
The child learns to substitute beginning sounds and blends.
The child uses phonics to discover medial and ending sounds.
The child learns about silent letters.
The child identifies words that begin with the same sound and the same letter of the alphabet.
The child hears and sees common endings.
The child understands and uses simple contractions.
The child recognizes and uses compound words.
The child learns alphabetical order.
The child learns words that have the same meaning and words that have many meanings.
The child learns simple rules of punctuation and capitalization.
The child distinguishes name words from action words.
The child becomes aware of descriptive words and how they pattern in English sentences.
The child develops a sight vocabulary of frequently used words.
The child recognizes quotation marks and apostrophes.
The child recognizes common abbreviations.
The child changes meaning with voice inflections.
The child uses a variety of sentence patterns.

Group Activities

The Amorous Octopus

A is for the Amorous Octopus.
B is for the brave Amorous Octopus.
C is for the cunning Amorous Octopus.
D is for the daring Amorous Octopus.
E is for the eager Amorous Octopus.
F is for the fantastic Amorous Octopus.
G is for the graceful Amorous Octopus.
H is for the haughty Amorous Octopus.
I is for the intelligent Amorous Octopus.
J is for the jealous Amorous Octopus.
K is for the kayoed Amorous Octopus.
L is for the luxurious Amorous Octopus.
M is for the magical Amorous Octopus.
N is for the nervous Amorous Octopus.
O is for the ornery Amorous Octopus.

P is for the peculiar Amorous Octopus.
Q is for the quick Amorous Octopus.
R is for the ravenous Amorous Octopus.
S is for the speculatory Amorous Octopus.
T is for the toothy Amorous Octopus.
U is for the ultra-modern Amorous Octopus.
V is for the vaccinated Amorous Octopus.
W is for the warlike Amorous Octopus.
X is for the x-rayed Amorous Octopus.
Y is for the yearning Amorous Octopus.
Z is for the zealous Amorous Octopus.

LANGUAGE CONCEPTS

The letters of the alphabet are used over and over to write words.
Descriptive words and phrases help make meanings clear.
Alphabetical arrangements help one locate information.
Alliteration is the use of two or more words together that begin with the same sound.

1. Find out some things about the origin of our alphabet. How did the letters get their names? Who decided on twenty-six? Why isn't there a letter for every major sound? Who created the shapes?
2. Prepare a strip chart of the words describing the Amorous Octopus. Cover each word with a piece of paper that can be removed to reveal the word when it comes in the reading.
3. Read three or four lines of "The Amorous Octopus." After that, stop at the descriptive word and let children predict what it will be. After several suggestions, uncover the word on the strip chart to check out the predictions.
4. Record a list from A to Z of words that tell actions the Amorous Octopus might do.
5. Copy the list as a resource for writing.
6. Record a list of adverbs that describe the actions of the Amorous Octopus.
7. Copy the adverbs as a resource for writing.
8. Plan alphabet books on many topics.
9. Talk about and demonstrate alphabetical arrangements in dictionaries, encyclopedias, and indexes.
10. Talk about and demonstrate letters that have several sounds as first letters of words—*c*, *s*, *g*, and the vowels.

School for the Animals

Professor Frog in his deep voice announced,
"I'm starting a school on the big rock near the lake."
The first day in came one thin little frog.
He learned about number ONE.
"Tomorrow bring a friend, then we can learn something new,"
said Professor Frog.

Next morning in came the thin little frog.
Following the frog was a white shaggy dog.
They learned about the number TWO—
That one and one make TWO.
"Now tomorrow bring another friend,
then we can learn something new," said Professor Frog.

Next morning in came the thin little frog.
Following the frog was a white shaggy dog.
Following the dog was a gray fuzzy cat.
They learned about the number THREE—
That two and one make THREE.
"Now tomorrow bring another friend,
then we can learn something new," said Professor Frog.

Next morning in came the thin little frog.
Following the frog was a white shaggy dog.
Following the dog was a gray fuzzy cat.
Following the cat was a very sleek rat.
They learned that day about number FOUR—
That three and one make FOUR.
"Now tomorrow is the last day we will have school,"
said Professor Frog in his very deep voice.
"Tomorrow bring another friend,
then we can learn something new."

Next morning in came the thin little frog.
Following the frog was a white shaggy dog.
Following the dog was a gray fuzzy cat.
Following the cat was a very sleek rat.
Following the rat was a very blind bat.
They learned that day about number FIVE—
That four and one make FIVE.

That is, everyone learned it except the very blind bat.
Bat slept through the whole lesson.

LANGUAGE CONCEPTS

Numerals and numbers have word names.
Descriptive words and phrases help make meanings clear.
Readers use recognition skills to confirm or deny their predictions.
Many words rhyme with other words.

1. Read "School for the Animals" to the group. Let the students join in the repeating parts as they have confidence.
2. Let children form groups to illustrate what the animals learned at school. Let them regroup to show other combinations that the animals did not learn.
3. List the words for numerals from "School for the Animals." Let children test their ability to recognize the words for numerals that are in the story. Ask them to add other numeral words they know.
4. Talk about descriptive words. Listen to the words that describe the animals. Ask children to change the descriptions.

Examples fat ugly frog
black shiny dog

5. List the animals in the story. Ask children for the names of other animals that rhyme. They can be added to the story.
6. Duplicate "School for the Animals." Help children see that the language they have anchored in their ears is easy to read.

Words I Like

"Cool" is a word I like.
It makes me drool
For a pool
Or a drink very cool
After school.

"Light" is a word I like.
I think that I might
Need a light
In the night
When I dream of a fight
When I haven't done right.

"Rain" is a word I like.
Hear it rain
On the windowpane
And gush down the drain.
See it water the grain.
Rain! Rain! Rain!

LANGUAGE CONCEPTS

Many words end with the same sound and symbol.
Changing one letter in a word can change its pronunciation and meaning.

1. Read the rhymes with the class, then collect words that different members like.
2. Choose one of the words and show how to develop a list of rhyming words by changing the first one or two letters of the word.

Example cake: bake, take, make, rake, fake

List all the words class members can think of that rhyme with the chosen word.

3. Make up phrases that use these words. Arrange them in rhymes like "Words I Like."
4. Let each student choose a word and write a rhyme about it. Put the rhymes into a book titled "Words I Like."
5. Write other words students like on cards and put them in the Language Study Center. Students can add rhyming words and phrases.

Comparisons Using As . . . As

Fog—
as silent as feathers flying through space
as stealthy as a well-practiced burglar
as thorough as a well-trained artist
creating a scene
as lovely as an oriental painting.

Desert—
from the air looks
as broad as an ocean

as colorful as rare jewels
as lined as a pencil tablet
as surprising as a three-ring circus.

LANGUAGE CONCEPTS

The same picture suggests different words or ideas to different people
Words help form pictures in the mind.
Authors describe settings in ways that let readers form mental images of them.

1. Write the above comparisons on the chalkboard. Read them with the class. Talk about ways authors use comparisons in writing.
2. Add other comparisons about fog and the desert.
3. Choose another subject to work on. See how many as . . . as comparisons children can think of on a subject that is familiar to them.
4. Project outstanding slides of skies, water, mountains, and other topics that students can provide. Work on class or individual comparisons using them.
5. Have class members collect comparisons as they read. Copy them on cards and place them in the Language Study Center. Make them available in the Writing Center for literary-level language.

At the Circus

At the circus there were clowns—
Tall ones, short ones, fat.
Funny faces they all had—
Tall ones, short ones, fat.
With a ha-ha! here
And a ha-ha! there
Here a ha! There a ha!
Everywhere a ha-ha!
At the circus there were clowns—
Tall ones, short ones, fat.

At the circus there were horses—
Black ones, white ones, brown.
Prancing, dancing, bowing, too—
Black ones, white ones, brown.

With a pretty rider here
And a pretty rider there
Here a rider, there a rider,
Everywhere a pretty rider.
At the circus there were horses—
Black ones, white ones, brown.

At the circus there were elephants—
Little ones, big ones, smart!
Parading proudly around the rings—
Little ones, big ones, smart!
With a clump! clump! here
And a clump! clump! there
Here a clump! There a clump!
Everywhere a clump! clump!
At the circus there were elephants—
Little ones, big ones, smart!

At the circus there were tigers—
Old ones, young ones, fierce!
Jumping, rolling, standing up!
Old ones, young ones, fierce!
With a roaring here
And a roaring there
Here a roar! There a roar!
Everywhere a ROAR! ROAR!
At the circus there were tigers—
Old ones, young ones, fierce!

At the circus there were acrobats—
Fast ones, slow ones, brave!
Leaping, swinging, gliding, too—
Fast ones, slow ones, brave!
With a leap up here
And a leap down there
Here a leap! there a leap!
Everywhere a leap! leap!
At the circus there were acrobats—
Fast ones, slow ones, brave!

At the circus there were lions—
Loud ones, quiet ones, swift!
Growling, snarling, jumping too—
Loud ones, quiet ones, swift!

With growling here
And growling there
Here a growl! There a growl!
Everywhere a GROWL! GROWL!
At the circus there were lions—
Loud ones, quiet ones, swift!

At the circus there were people—
Tall ones, short ones, slim.
And laughing faces they all had—
Tall ones, short ones, slim.
With a ha-ha! here
And a ha-ha! there
Here a ha! There a ha!
Everywhere a ha-ha!
At the circus there were people—
Tall ones, short ones, slim.

LANGUAGE CONCEPTS

The letters of the alphabet are used over and over to write words.
Antonyms are words that have opposite meanings.
Descriptive words and phrases help make meanings clear.
Onomatopoeic words are those whose sounds suggest their meanings.

1. Copy "At the Circus" on the chalkboard, copy it on a chart, or make a transparency for projection. Ask students to read along with you, saying the words they can recognize or predict.
2. After enjoying the selection, look at it carefully to find

   words that are antonyms.
   words that are onomatopoeic.
   words they can read at sight.
   lines that repeat.

3. Add a stanza to the selection to illustrate the repetition of words and lines in the pattern.
4. Change the setting to a zoo and let volunteers write stanzas for animals they select.
5. Collect the stanzas about zoo animals and bind them into a book for the Reading/Research Center.

Put Togethers

Look! There's a dragon!
Look! There's a fly!
Put them together.
You have a dragonfly.

Look! There's butter!
Look! There's a cup!
Put them together.
You have a buttercup.

Look! There's a fire!
Look! There's a man!
Put them together.
You have a fireman.

Here is a tooth.
Here is a pick.
Put them together.
You have a toothpick.

Here is some chalk.
Here is a board.
Put them together.
You have a chalkboard.

Here is a button.
Here is a hole.
Put them together.
You have a buttonhole.

Here is a table.
Here is a spoon.
Put them together.
You have a tablespoon.

Have you seen a horse?
Have you seen a fly?
Put them together.
You have a horsefly.

Have you seen a foot?
Have you seen a ball?
Put them together.
You have a football.

Have you seen a pole?
Have you seen a cat?
Put them together.
You have a polecat.

DO YOU WANT THAT?

LANGUAGE CONCEPTS

Compound words are two or more words combined into one.
Some words occur frequently in our language.

1. Read a stanza or two of "Put Togethers" while students listen carefully. Continue by reading the first two lines, then letting students join in on what they think the next two lines will be.
2. Copy the selection on a chalkboard or on a chart. Use it for a hunting game. Let children discover, then underline or circle

   words they can read.
   words that are alike.
   words that are made of two other words (compound words).

3. Read "Put Togethers" in unison, letting different students lead the reading. When a student discovers that he or she can read the entire selection, give that student a copy to take home to read with parents and family.
4. Prepare some incomplete models of "put togethers" on charts or on the chalkboard. Have students complete them to make new stanzas for "Put Togethers."

Example Look! There's a __________ !
Look! There's a __________ !

Here is a __________ .
Here is a __________ .

Have you seen a __________ ?
Have you seen a __________ ?

5. Begin a list of compound words for the Writing Center. Students can write their own Put Together books.

Five Somethings

I have *one* swing
  to play on in the sun.

I have *one* truck
    that will run and run.
I have *one* toy soldier
    who holds a great big gun.
        Just *one.*
Do you have *one* something?
        What is it?

I have *two* cars
    that are very new.
I have *two* red socks
    and *two* shoes, too.
I have a picture of *two* balloons
    that I drew.
        Just *two.*
Do you have *two* somethings?
        What are they?

I have *three* baby kittens
    that were given to me.
I have *three* little squirrels
    that live in this tree.
I have *three* shiny marbles
    I want you to see.
        Just *three.*
Do you have *three* somethings?
        What are they?

I have *four* little plants
    growing close to my door.
I have *four* pretty shells.
    I'll hunt for some more.
I have *four* shiny airplanes
    that really can soar.
        Just *four.*
Do you have *four* somethings?
        What are they?

I have *five* downy ducks
    that quarrel and dive.
I have *five* tiny turtles
    that are really alive.

I have *five* buzzing bees
that live in a hive.
Just *five*.
Do you have *five* somethings
to tell me about?
What are they?

LANGUAGE CONCEPTS

Numerals and number names tell the rank order of things.
Numerals and numbers have word names.

1. Give a copy of "Five Somethings" to each child. Read each stanza and let children respond to the question. List responses under five columns.

One	Two	Three	Four	Five

2. Add to the list by letting children find words in the poem to go under each heading.
3. Add more by letting children discover things about the classroom that are found singly or in groups of two, three, four, or five.
4. Have a discovery time with the selection. Children find

   words they can read.
   words that are alike.
   number words.
   words that rhyme.
   words that end alike

5. As children discover that they can read the whole selection, let them cut the stanzas apart and make them into books to take home to read with their families. They can illustrate them with their own drawings or with pictures from magazines.

Independent Activities

Count Them

LANGUAGE CONCEPTS

Numerals are symbols of how many and how much.
Numerals and numbers have word names.

1. Cut from magazines pictures of things that can be counted.
2. Paste the pictures on cards.
3. Label the pictures with number words.
4. Put your cards on a ring for others to read.

Name Chant

LANGUAGE CONCEPTS

Language can be expressed in rhythmic patterns.
Every person has a name.
Words have a different number of syllables or beats.

1. Make first-name cards for all the persons in your class.
2. Arrange them in stacks with the same number of syllables or beats—one, two, three, or four. (You may have one with more than four beats, but not many.)

   Example

One Beat	**Two Beats**	**Three Beats**	**Four Beats**
Ann	David	Angela	Elizabeth
______	______	______	______

3. Say the names in a chant, going from one-beat words to four-beat words.
4. Ask some friends to join you in the chant.
5. Say it for the class.
6. Reverse the chant.

Color Talk

LANGUAGE CONCEPTS

Colors of things are described with words.
Many words have more than one meaning.

Go on a color walk with a friend.

1. Just look around you, or walk around your classroom, walk around the school grounds, walk in a park, or look out the window.
2. Choose one basic color at a time—like red.

3. See how many shades of the color you can find.
4. Make a list for each color.
5. Keep it to use when you write.

Two-faced Words

LANGUAGE CONCEPTS

People communicate by speaking and writing in sentences.
Words help form pictures in the mind.
Many words have more than one meaning.

I *wave* good-bye to my friends.	The *wave* crashes on the beach.
The *bark* on the tree is rough.	The dogs *bark* at the car.
I *ground* the pepper for my salad.	The *ground* is covered with stones.

1. Fold a piece of paper in half.
2. Think of a word that has two meanings.
3. Write a sentence and draw a picture to show one meaning on each half of the paper.

4. Put your paper in the Two-faced Words folder.*
5. Make the pages into a book when there is a collection.

Greetings Around the World

LANGUAGE CONCEPTS

People use common courtesies when communicating with other people.

Any sound that can be spoken can be represented with letters of the alphabet.

People greet one another everywhere and in all languages. They have special words for the greetings just as we have in English.

1. Make a list of different greetings you hear, such as

good morning	hi
good afternoon	pleased to see you
good night	good-by
hello	greetings

2. Think of words you already know from other languages that mean the same thing. Find friends who know other languages and ask them to help you.
3. Make a list of greetings from around the world—Hawaiian, Spanish, French, German, Navajo, and so forth. Some large dictionaries have words from other languages in them. Most public libraries have foreign-language dictionaries.
4. Try greeting your classmates in different languages.

Greetings Collector

LANGUAGE CONCEPT

Meanings change by voice inflection, rate of speaking, and other oral characteristics that do not show in print.

Some people have such special greetings that we can recognize them by their greeting. Collect some of these.

* *To the teacher:* Provide a folder for examples of two-faced words. Always use the same size paper so that the pages can be bound into a book.

1. Get some three-by-five cards to use while collecting the greetings.
2. On one side of the card write the name of the person you heard use the greeting. On the other side of the card write the greeting.
3. Read the cards with a friend. Try to imitate the voice of the person who uses the greeting.
4. Let the friend guess the person. Next, turn the card over and read the person's name.
5. Have fun collecting and reading greetings you hear on TV and radio, and from teachers, classmates, and friends.

Time Words

LANGUAGE CONCEPT

Time concepts have specific names.

Special words tell us the time when we don't have a clock. Do you know some of those words?

1. Write words that tell time on strips of tagboard or on other heavy paper. Remember that days of the week and months are time words.
2. Punch holes at each end of the cards for the laces to go through. String the words on shoe laces.
3. Hang your string of time word cards in the Language Study Center. Keep adding others as you think of them.

* Eat Your Own Words

LANGUAGE CONCEPTS

Each letter of the alphabet has a name.
Each letter of the alphabet has a recognizable shape.
The words we say are written with the letters of the alphabet.

1. Take a sack of cereal letters.*
2. See how many words you can build with the letters.
3. Choose four or five words to use in sentences.
4. Write the sentences with the cereal words.
5. Now, eat your words!

* Words that Begin like My Name

LANGUAGE CONCEPTS

Capital and small letters are used in writing.
Every person has a name.
Many words begin with the same sound and symbol.

---

* *To the teacher:* Put letters from cereal alphabets into small plastic sacks for children to choose. Provide slips of paper for word lists and sentences so you can check them.

1. Write your name.
2. Write other words that begin with the same sound as your name.
3. Try to make each new word longer by one letter, or find words that have increasing numbers of syllables—one, two, three, four, and five. How far can you go?

Who Am I?

LANGUAGE CONCEPTS

Capital and small letters are used in writing.
Descriptive words and phrases help make meanings clear.
We can describe things without telling their names.

1. Choose a descriptive word or two for each letter in your name. Try to choose words that really describe you.

Example M—mighty, mean
I —intelligent, industrious
C —cheerful
H —honest, healthy
A —ambitious, amiable
E —expert
L —laughable, likeable

2. If you enjoyed doing the list for your own name, describe some of your friends with words that begin with each letter in their names.
3. Use a dictionary to find the words you need.

Join Us

LANGUAGE CONCEPTS

People communicate by speaking and writing in sentences.
Most verbs have different forms to express the meaning of number.
Most nouns have different forms to express number.
The same language patterns are used over and over in writing.

1. Take the word strips from the plastic bag.*
2. Stack them on the proper square—noun or verb.

---

* *To the teacher:* After you make the word strips, put them in a plastic bag. Provide the Noun and Verb squares. Remember to include nouns and verbs that are singular and plural. Many nouns have an added *-s* or *-es* for plurals. Many verbs have an added *-s* for singular.

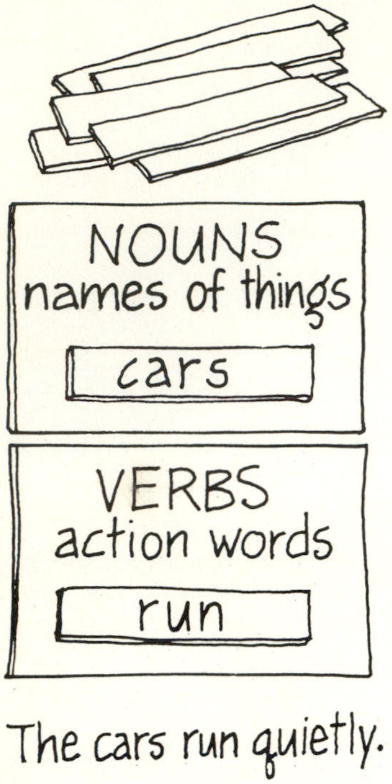

3. Choose a noun.
4. Find a verb to go with it.
5. Say or write a sentence using the two words plus some descriptive words.
6. See how many sentences you can make with the same noun and verb.

Compound Words in Dictionary

LANGUAGE CONCEPTS

Alphabetical arrangements help one locate information.
Some words occur frequently in our language.
Compound words are two or more words combined into one.

1. Look through the dictionary for compound words. Under *s* you will find *snowman*.
2. When you come to certain words, you will find many compounds.

Examples	**Butter**	**Candle**
	butterball	candleberry
	butterburr	candlefoot
	butterfat	candlelight
	butterfish	candlenut
	buttermilk	candlepower
	butterscotch	candlewick

3. Make cards for words that are in compounds as many as ten times.
4. Put the cards in the Reading/Research Center.

Kangaroo Words

LANGUAGE CONCEPT

Synonyms are words that have similar meanings.

A kangaroo word is one that contains a smaller word with almost the same meaning.

Examples mountain/mount
automobile/auto
telephone/phone

Sometimes it is necessary to hop over some letters to find the smaller word.

Examples blossom/bloom
evacuate/vacate

1. Add to this list.
2. Illustrate the words for a poster.

Sports Words

LANGUAGE CONCEPTS

People communicate by speaking and writing in sentences.
Many words have more than one meaning.

Many words acquire new meanings when they are used in sports.*

Examples	fly	love	tackle
	spare	butterfly	iron

In what sports are these words used?

1. Think of other words that have a special meaning when used in sports.
2. Write and illustrate sentences using each word with its sport meaning and with one other meaning.
3. Make the pages into a book for the Reading/Research Center.

Rhyming Names

LANGUAGE CONCEPTS

Everything has a name.
Many words rhyme with other words.

1. Think of names of animals and people. Look in the dictionary for ideas.
2. Find a word that rhymes with each word you choose.
3. Write the two words on a card.
4. Put them in the Writing Center for others to use.

* *To the teacher:* Sports sections of the newspapers will be helpful for this activity.

I'm Abbreviated

LANGUAGE CONCEPT

Abbreviations are used in places where whole words are not needed.

Whole Words	**Abbreviations**
quart	U.S.
inch	co.
cup	qt.
pound	N.Y.
United States	in.
television	lb.
New York	c.
Monday	TV
company	Mon.

1. Match the whole words with their abbreviations.
2. Cut other abbreviations from magazines and newspapers.
3. Make a book of abbreviations and their words.

A Wish Book

LANGUAGE CONCEPTS

Numerals are symbols of how many and how much.
Everything has a name.

1. Cut pictures of things you would like to have from magazines and newspapers.
2. Write the names of the things and the cost.
3. Paste your pictures on pages and make into a Wish book.

That's the Size of It!

LANGUAGE CONCEPTS

Sizes of things are described with words.
Synonyms are words that have similar meanings.

1. Make a list of words that tell the size of things, such as tiny, gigantic, huge, or itsy-bitsy.

2. Put each word on a card.
3. Arrange your size words in order, starting with the one that describes the largest thing and ending with the one that describes the smallest thing.
4. Opposite each word, write the name of something you know that is that size.

Alphabet Pyramids

LANGUAGE CONCEPTS

Descriptive words and phrases help make meanings clear.
There are words for the many movements of people, animals, and things.
Everything has a name.
Many words begin with the same sound and symbol.

Most pyramids are made of stone or dirt, but you can make some with words. Try from A to Z.

1. Choose the name of an animal or insect.
2. Write the name as the top layer of your pyramid.
3. Add a second layer with a descriptive word and the name—two words.
4. Add a third layer with a descriptive word, the name, and an action word—three words.
5. Try a fourth layer with another descriptive word describing the action word—four words in all.

Examples

ant	bear
angry ant	big bear
angry ant acting	big bear barking
angry ant acting atrociously	big bear barking beautifully

Now you are on your own. A dictionary will be helpful.

Feed the Animals

LANGUAGE CONCEPTS

Many words begin with the same sound and symbol.
A vowel can represent a variety of sounds at the beginning of a word.

These animals are always hungry for words! They will eat only words beginning with the sounds that begin their names.*

1. Feed them from the Word Box.
2. Make other word cards to feed them.
3. Make other animals that are hungry for words.

I'm a Contractor

LANGUAGE CONCEPTS

Contractions are two or more words shortened and joined with an apostrophe to show that the sounds and letters are missing.

---

* *To the teacher:* Make animal pictures with slots at the mouth for word cards to go through. Mount them on substantial cardboard and laminate them. Provide a collection of word cards. Encourage children to make other cards for the Word Box.

1. Take the contraction cards from the pocket and put them in the pocket for the words they contract.
2. Find other contractions in your reading and make cards for them.
3. Make one list of contractions you find within quotation marks and one list of those you find outside quotation marks.
4. Do you think contractions have anything to do with speaking?

I Don't Like Blanks

LANGUAGE CONCEPTS

People communicate by speaking and writing in sentences.
We perceive our own meanings from our experiences.

Contractions are two or more words shortened and joined with an apostrophe to show that the sounds and letters are missing.

1. Try writing sentences by filling in these blanks with things you don't like.

   I don't like _________ in a _________ .
   I don't like _________ on my _________ .
   I don't like _________ with lots of _________ .
   I don't like _________ and _________ .
   I don't like _________ under my _________ .

2. Get ideas by looking at pictures in books and magazines.
3. Use some of the pictures to illustrate your sentences.
4. Put your best sentences on a bulletin board for others to enjoy.

Antonym Train

LANGUAGE CONCEPTS

The letters of the alphabet are used over and over to write words. Antonyms are words that have opposite meanings.

1. Make an antonym train by drawing an engine and cars.
2. Write a word that you know has an opposite on the engine.
3. Join cars to the engine by adding words of opposite meaning.
4. A thesaurus will help you find antonyms.

The Opposite Pocket

LANGUAGE CONCEPTS

People communicate by speaking and writing in sentences.
Antonyms are words that have opposite meanings.

In a pocket there are pairs of words that are opposites.

1. Find them.
2. List them together.
3. Try to make sentences using two words of opposite meaning in the same sentence.
4. Add other words with opposite meanings to the pocket.

Discovering Sentences

LANGUAGE CONCEPTS

Descriptive words and phrases help make meanings clear.
There are words for the many movements of people, animals, and things.
Most sentences have at least one verb or a form of *be* or *have* in them.
Words that are used as nouns in sentences can be used in other ways.
Some words occur frequently in our language.

1. Cut from newspapers and magazines interesting words that name things, tell how things move, and describe.
2. Cut out other words such as *a*, *an*, *to*, *the*, *of*, and so forth.
3. Choose four colors of tagboard or cards to mount the words on.
4. Mount each word on a separate card. Put all names of things on one color, all words of movement on one color, all descriptive words on one color, and all other words on one color.
5. Find a box to hold the cards.
6. Ask a friend to play with you or play by yourself.
7. Turn all cards face down, shuffle, and then draw seven cards. Draw at least one of each color.
8. Try to combine three or more cards into a seven- or eight-syllable phrase or sentence that makes some sense.
9. Each time a player makes a phrase or sentence of seven or eight syllables, one point is scored.

10. Return the cards to the pile and repeat the procedure until one player scores five points.

New Put Togethers

LANGUAGE CONCEPTS

Imagination promotes picturesque speech.
Compound words are two or more words combined into one.
New words can be created by anyone.

1. Choose a collection of buttons, beads, beans, clay, or other material.
2. Arrange them to create a new creature, such as

   a beanboy
   a beadbird
   a zippermouth
   a pencilpot

3. Display your new put togethers with their labels.

Miniature Mountains

LANGUAGE CONCEPTS

Imagination promotes picturesque speech.
Everything has a name.

Artists sometimes collect rocks from an area to remind them of the colors of the mountains they are painting. Often the rocks are shaped like some of the mountains and have strata of different colors through them.

1. Look through the collection of rocks in the Arts and Crafts Center and find those that remind you of mountains.
2. Tape your miniature mountains to a card or mount them on clay so they will not turn over.
3. Name your mountains and tell the class about them.

A Triangle Hunt

LANGUAGE CONCEPTS

Abstract forms may suggest ideas that can be expressed in words.
Some symbols other than our alphabet communicate meaning.

Triangles are everywhere! Try to find some.

1. Look in the classroom, in the yard, at home, at a shopping center, or wherever you go.
2. Make a list of things you find that are triangles.
3. You can begin with the triangle that is in the capital letter *A*.
4. Have a contest with some friends to see who can list the most triangles in one day or in two days.
5. Ask for help with spelling if you need it. You can choose a good speller to be your secretary for the game.

Friends Finding Things

LANGUAGE CONCEPTS

We can describe things without telling their names.
Some things have several names.

1. Choose a friend to look for things with you.
2. Decide on one or more things you can find outdoors or in books, such as insects, birds, different trees, cloud formations, or natural designs like triangles and pointed things.

3. List the things you find together.
4. Use the list to write riddles for other friends to read.
5. Keep a list of all the answers to the riddles that could be correct.

Finding Contractions

LANGUAGE CONCEPT

Contractions are two or more words shortened and joined with an apostrophe to show that the sounds and letters are missing.

Do you know that you make some of your words shorter than they are? You do when you make contractions.

Everyone makes contractions when talking. Sometimes we write contractions.

1. List the contractions in "Tongue Tinglers," p. 231.
2. Add to the list other contractions you know.
3. Make word cards that show how you shorten and join the words when you make a contraction.
4. Use some of the contractions in your writing.

Number Hunt

LANGUAGE CONCEPT

Some symbols other than our alphabet communicate meaning.

Make a card game.

1. You will need twenty cards the same size for five sets of four cards each.
2. On each card in a set show a different way to write the same number.
3. Make a set for each number—one through five.
4. Play a game with each player drawing in turn to get a set of four cards of the same value.
5. The player with the most sets wins.

Who's on My Family Tree?

LANGUAGE CONCEPTS

Every person has a name.
Proper nouns begin with a capital letter.
Initials can stand for names.

1. Collect names of members of your family: father, mother, brothers, sisters, grandparents, great-grandparents, great-great-grandparents, aunts, uncles, and cousins.
2. Write the full name of each family member on a separate card.
3. Make a family tree. On the leaves write *initials only* for each name you have on the cards.
4. Play a family tree game with some of your friends. Draw names from the stack of cards and match them with the initials on the tree.

Alphabet Puzzle

LANGUAGE CONCEPTS

The English alphabet has twenty-six letters.
Capital and small letters are used in writing.

Match the capital and small letters to complete each puzzle.*

---

* *To the teacher:* On three-by-five cards write capital letters at one end and corresponding small letters at the other end. Cut each card apart so that each

Homonym Hunt

LANGUAGE CONCEPT

Homonyms are words that sound alike but have different meanings.

---

set is cut in a different way from the others. Scatter the cards on the floor, then let the children match them up.

1. Cut some green pears and some yellow pears out of paper.*
2. Write a pair of homonyms on the pears—put one word on a green pear and the other on a yellow pear.
3. Play a game by matching the pear pairs.
4. Here are some pairs of words to start with.

week/weak	maid/made
not/knot	see/sea

5. Add homonyms to the game as you find them.

You're My Opposite

LANGUAGE CONCEPTS

Many words have more than one meaning.
Antonyms are words that have opposite meanings.

1. Collect antonyms until you have at least ten pairs.
2. Write each antonym on a card—you should have a total of twenty cards.
3. Choose three playing partners.
4. Shuffle the cards and deal them so each player has five cards.
5. Take the pairs of antonyms out of your hand and then take turns calling for cards that are in the others' hands to complete your sets of antonyms. Call from any player.

---

* *To the teacher:* Keep a supply of green and yellow paper for the children to use.

6. When you get a pair, take it out. The first player to get rid of all the cards wins the game.
7. Add other antonyms to your game if your friends enjoy playing.
8. Use your master list to check for correct plays.

What Is the Word in That State?

LANGUAGE CONCEPTS

The letters of the alphabet are used over and over to write words.

1. Write the names of states and discover words in them.*
2. Write clues to the words.

Examples What questions do, in Alaska ________
A young animal, in Alabama ________
A bird's home, in Tennessee ________

3. Duplicate your list for others to use.

Discovering New Friends

LANGUAGE CONCEPTS

People communicate by speaking and writing in sentences.
We perceive our own meanings from our experiences.

1. Go for a walk in your neighborhood, a park, or around the school grounds.
2. Look for insect and animal friends.
3. List the ones you find and write something about why you like them as friends.

Examples Ladybugs keep aphids off plants.
Robins eat worms that destroy our plants.
Mockingbirds make beautiful songs that I enjoy.

4. Make your discoveries into a book for your friends to read.

---

* *To the teacher:* A dictionary should be available for this activity, as well as a list of the names of all the states.

Discovering Synonyms

LANGUAGE CONCEPTS

Understanding and following directions helps one solve problems.
Many words have more than one meaning.
Synonyms are words that have similar meanings.

Synonyms in this game come in sets of four—no more!

1. Get forty or fifty cards the same size. Cut them or use three-by-five cards.
2. Write each word for this game on both ends of a card.
3. Find at least ten words for which you have three synonyms.

Examples steep/sheer/sloping/abrupt
underneath/under/below/beneath
embroider/decorate/beautify/adorn
bump/knock/collide/hit
magnificent/gorgeous/beautiful/fine
resemble/match/copy/imitate

4. Shuffle the cards and deal eight to each player. Put the others in a pile for drawing.
5. Draw and discard around the circle. No player can have more than eight cards at one time.
6. When a player gets four cards that go together, the cards are read to the group. If they are right, they can be made into a set and taken out of the hand. The player then begins drawing again in turn up to eight cards—then discards again.
7. The player with the most sets of four wins.
8. Keep making other sets. Use a thesaurus.

Puzzle Announcements

LANGUAGE CONCEPT

Some letters are called consonants and some are called vowels.

N__ g__s t__d__y!
Tw__ d__v__s __r__l__v__ng __n th__ tr__ __ __n
fr__nt __f th__ b__rn.

1. Can you read these announcements? To give you a clue, choose a vowel (*a, e, i, o,* or *u*) to put in each blank to make words.
2. Try writing your own puzzle announcements. Write your sentence as you ordinarily would and then cross out the vowels.

Example N~~o~~ b~~u~~s t~~o~~d~~a~~y.

3. Rewrite the announcement on a strip of paper, putting a blank where each vowel should go.

Example N__ b__s t__d__y

4. Place your puzzle in the Reading/Research Center for others to use.

Just One!

LANGUAGE CONCEPT

The letters of the alphabet are used over and over to write words.

A leprechaun got into the letter cases at the print shop. It took some letters. The printer had to write without them. Here is how he wrote

__i__ __onal__ __evour a __ozen __oughnuts?
__nn __nd __d__ __re e__ting b__n__n__s.

1. Each sentence has only one letter missing. Discover the missing letters and write the sentences.
2. Now make some sentences of your own, leaving out just one letter in each.
3. Write them on strips of paper for others to guess and read.

Palindromes

LANGUAGE CONCEPT

Palindromes are words that read the same forward and backward.

These are some of the palindromes in our language.

ANNA BOB DEED MUM

1. Watch for them as you read.
2. Look in the dictionary to find some others.
3. Keep a list of palindromes.

Slurvians

LANGUAGE CONCEPT

We can use language for fun and nonsense.

1. Choose a title, a saying, or a line from a well-known poem or rhyme.
2. Write the same sounds as in the original, but use different words. Use only real words. You will have to slur your words to get a slurvian.

Examples Ladle Rat Rotten Hut
(Little Red Riding Hood)
Rocker pie bay bee honor treat hop
(Rock-a-bye baby on a tree top)

3. Write some slurvians on cards for classmates to figure out.

Chapter 7

The Arts and Crafts Center

What Is an Arts and Crafts Center?

An Arts and Crafts Center is a place

for self-expression through multiple media
for communicating in realistic and in abstract forms
for illustrating poems, stories, and books
for viewing and reviewing communication processes used by many artists

The Arts and Crafts Center is a vital ingredient in the language learning environment. It serves as a launching pad for oral language expression. From oral expression come writing and reading in natural, personal forms. Ideas never expressed before germinate as children apply paint to paper, model with clay, cut and tear paper, and arrange a variety of materials into a collage. Ideas that are difficult, if not impossible, for many children to grasp from reading are available in the paintings, sculpture, and crafts of artists. These ideas, once spoken, are basic to the further development of writing and reading.

Arts and Crafts Center activities are often recreational and should be done for the sheer pleasure of the "doing." They do not have any planned language follow-up activities.

The Arts and Crafts Center is a treasure house of creative materials available for teacher and children. Some essentials are provided by the school, such as

newsprint
paints
brushes
crayons
paste
different types of art paper

Much material is provided by the children and parents, such as

scraps of fabric
scraps of wood
wood shavings
wallpaper
newspapers
magazines
color chips on cards from paint stores
bottles and bottle caps
buttons
scraps of yarn
string
nuts and bolts
pliable wire
plastic egg cartons
paper plates
pieces of cardboard
cellophane
used greeting cards
foil
crepe paper
sandpaper
glitter
macaroni

Art exists in all other learning centers and in all aspects of life. It provides material for illustrating books for the Writing and Publishing Centers, for making puppets, costumes, and props for the Dramatization Center, and for developing visually attractive materials for any other center.

Language Skills Developed and Practiced

The child increases vocabulary of descriptive words found frequently in reading materials—words of color, size, shape, texture, contrast, and comparison.

The child increases vocabulary of names of things frequently found in reading—names of animals, plants, weather, people, and nonsense and fun names.

The child increases vocabulary of motion words found frequently in reading—words describing the movement of people, machines, and the elements.

The child learns ways of expressing ideas without reading and writing them.

The child develops skills in summarizing ideas for dictation or writing.

The child increases awareness of the multiple materials available for expressing ideas and feelings.

The child expresses ideas in abstract as well as in realistic forms.

The child builds a base for creative language production with ideas that form during the process of exploring with materials.

The child uses ideas and skills of many artists to influence personal production.

Group Activities

I Move

I MOVE can mean a lot of things.
It may mean I just WALK,
Or just SHOW feelings with my hands
When I want to TALK and TALK.

It can mean RUNNING very fast
Or CLIMBING up a tree,
Or SHOWING you a great big grin
When I'm happy as can be.

It can be SWINGING in the swing
That my big brother MADE,
Or PLAYING in the sand
With my shovel and my spade.

It can be MAKING UP a dance
To a tune I like to hear,
Or BEATING on my big red drum,
Or SHAKING hard with fear.

I MOVE can mean just GIGGLING,
Or WINKING with my eyes.
It can mean just LOOKING
For cloud poodles in the skies.

I MOVE and you MOVE
Many, many times a day.
Tell me. How do you MOVE
While you WORK and PLAY?

LANGUAGE CONCEPTS

There are words for the many movements of people, animals, and things.

Movements of people, animals, and things can be acted out.

1. Read "I Move" and ask students to answer the question in the last stanza. List words of movement that are suggested, then try to compose some additional stanzas. Or copy the selection with room at the end for students to add statements about movement, such as

   Alberto KICKS when he plays soccer.
   Jenny WRITES when she has an idea.
   Sara WIGGLES when she doesn't know an answer.

   Make the expanded I Move book into a class book. Ask volunteers to illustrate it with stick figures.
2. Paint pictures of favorite activities. Try to show some sense of movement in the paintings—position of arms, legs, hands; facial expressions; lines to indicate direction of movement; and other devices that students might suggest.
3. Go on a walk to watch things move: vehicles, plants, insects, birds, clouds, and water. Keep individual or group lists of words describing movement observed. Use the list back in the classroom to see who can illustrate at least one of the words to show movement.

4. Arrange pictures for a "picture walk" around the classroom. As you move from picture to picture, let students talk about things in the pictures that can move.
5. Read "I Move" and ask students to listen to the words of movement and make the motions when appropriate. Choose one or more of the movements to paint.
6. Make sculptures if materials are available. Try to show differences in walking, running, skipping, jumping, and other well-known movements.
7. Make a Mural of Movement. Choose pictures from magazines that are good illustrations of the movement of animals, vehicles, people, and plants. Look for pictures of moving clouds, of wind in the trees, and of water running. Arrange the pictures in a pleasing design and glue them down. Display the mural so students can have access to the pictures as they develop abilities to portray movement in paintings and sculpture.

I Like

I like ice cream in a dish.
I like lemon on my fish.
I like jelly on my bread.
I like apples very red.

I like houses with lots of noise.
I like to play with girls and boys.
I like rocks and balls and bats.
I like lots of funny hats.

I like birds and cats and dogs.
I like walking on fallen logs.
I like riding on my bike.
I like taking a long hike.

Say! I'm doing all the talking.
What do *you* like?

LANGUAGE CONCEPTS

People communicate in many ways through many media.
Descriptive words and phrases help make meanings clear.
Everything has a name.

1. Read the selection. After a discussion of the question at the end, ask students to paint pictures of two things they really like: food, places to go, games to play, clothes to wear, and so on.

   Try to put the two things into a couplet. For those that are successful, attach the couplet to the painting and display it.

   If a couplet doesn't come, attach the statements

   I like ________
   I like ________

   to the painting and display it.
2. Paint pictures in your mind. Read "I Like," taking turns reading one line each. When you come to the name of a thing, add one word that describes that thing.

Example I like *chocolate* ice cream in a *big* dish.

Read until one student misses. Drop that student from the game and go on.

The next time through, add two words that describe.

Example I like *very sour* lemon on my *freshly caught* fish.

If anyone is left, try three!

Example I like *sweet, gooey grape* jelly on my *brown toasted wheat* bread.

3. Make a rhebus poem of "I Like" or "I Don't Like." Make simple drawings in the blank spaces.

   I don't like ________ in a dish.
   I don't like ________ on my fish.
   I don't like ________ on my bread.
   I don't like ________ very red.

   Pass the "I Don't Like" versions around to see if classmates can read the poem. If they read the simple rhebus, try a harder version.

   I don't like ________ in a ________ .
   I don't like ________ on my ________ .
   I don't like ________ and ________ .
   I don't like ________ under my ________ .

   Try to rhyme the rhebus.

   If the "don't" version is successful, use the "like" version to continue to enjoy the selection.

4. Use modeling clay to sculpt one thing that is liked and one thing that is not liked. Provide a "Yes" and a "No" section on a table for display.

Mongon Wears Shoes

Mongon was Melissa's very special friend. He was part monster and part dragon. That's how he got his name. Mongon was slightly dumb, especially about human ways.

One day he got up very early to take his morning walk. It wasn't long until he met Mr. Lizard dashing across the road.

"Good morning, Mr. Lizard," greeted Mongon. "Did you know that Melissa is starting to school tomorrow?"

"Oh, my!" replied Mr. Lizard. "You'll surely miss playing with her, Mongon. What are you going to do?"

"I'm going with her!" came back the answer quickly.

"You are?" asked Mr. Lizard in surprise. "But I guess you can since you are never seen by adults. The teachers won't know you are there. What are you going to wear? Wearing the right things to school is important."

"I'll wear my blue bathrobe and an orange box for a hat."

By this time Frisky Squirrel and Becky Roadrunner were awake and listening. This announcement brought both of them from their homes.

"No! Not a robe for school!" said Frisky. "You wear a sweater if it is a cool day."

"And a cap on your head," said Becky.

"You really don't need a cap or hat most days," said Mr. Lizard.

"But I like a cap," said Mongon. "I'll wear a sweater, I'll wear a cap, and I'll wear a gown for my nap."

"No! No! No! Mongon," shouted the friends. "Wear your sweater. Wear your cap. Your shirt and jeans are for your nap."

"O.K.," said Mongon. "I'll wear my sweater. I'll wear my cap. I'll wear my shirt and jeans and carry my lunch in my old jack-o-lantern."

"Oh, no, Mongon! Wear your sweater. Wear your cap. Wear your shirt and jeans and carry your lunch in a lunch box," said Mr. Lizard.

"Remember, I gave you a lunch box for your birthday," said Becky. "I think your paint brushes are in it now, but you can put them in a glass."

"So that's what that box is for," said Mongon. "O.K. I'll wear my sweater. I'll wear my cap. I'll wear my shirt and jeans. I'll carry my lunch in my lunch box, and I'll put my red scarf on one foot and my green scarf on the other foot. Won't I be dressed up?"

"No! No! No! Mongon," shouted his friends.

Frisky stepped forward. "We want you to look just right for school so Melissa will be proud of you. Too, we don't want the kids to make fun of you."

"Shoes are for your feet, Mongon. You must wear your shoes to school," said Becky.

"But I hate shoes!" wailed Mongon.

"No shoes, no school," said Mr. Lizard.

"Well, I guess I'll have to wear them. I'll wear my sweater. I'll wear my cap. I'll wear my shirt and jeans. I'll carry my lunch in my lunch box, and I'll wear my shoes on my feet."

"Now you'll be dressed just right for school!" said Becky.

"Bye! See you later," called Frisky as he dashed home.

"Thanks for all the help," called Mongon as he continued on his walk.

"Bye," called Mr. Lizard and Becky Roadrunner as they raced to their favorite early morning eating place.

LANGUAGE CONCEPTS

Imaginary creatures can have names.
Oral reading can bring an audience pleasure and information.

1. Read the story "Mongon Wears Shoes." Let the students join in on the parts that are repeated. After one or two readings, duplicate the story so the students can follow along and read when the dependable lines occur.
2. Talk about clothing suitable for school in your community.

   what to wear during hot weather
   what to wear during cold weather
   what colors of clothing go together better than others

3. Reread the first paragraph of the story. Let each student draw or paint a personal interpretation of Mongon. Before the drawing and painting, you might talk about questions such as

   Is he large or small?
   What kind of eyes does he have?
   What kind of nose does he have?
   What kind of mouth does he have?
   What kind of feet does he have?

   Expect a wide range of interpretations.

4. Make a copy of the story. Cut the main ideas apart and paste each one on a separate sheet of paper. Let each student choose a passage to illustrate. Make these into a book for the classroom library.

The Zingitty Zangetty Zoo

The Maple Street friends were gathered in Jim's carport, deep in thought. School had been out almost a month and they had run out of things to do. Suddenly Jerry suggested, "Let's make a zingitty zangetty zoo!"

"What's that?" asked Maria.

"A zingitty zangetty zoo is one that has only imaginary animals—like this. Get some paper and boxes and make animals called poxes," answered Jerry.

"Oh, I get it," called Jim. "I put glue and toothpicks together and make gluethpicks."

"Or a shoe and a magazine makes a shoegazine," said Susan laughingly.

"How about some lids and a mayonnaise jar—maybe a layonnaise?" suggested Maria.

"You've got the idea! Let's head for home and see what we can find and bring it back soon!" exclaimed Jerry.

"How about some boxes for cages? Mom has a stack in our garage that I know she would be glad to get rid of," said Maria.

"Hey! that's a great idea! We could decorate them, fix bars on them, and have a great show. Let's get started! See you later!" yelled Susan as she dashed for home.

Before long Maria, Jerry, Jim, and Susan came back loaded down with bottles and wood blocks, cans and candles, fans and food, and lots more.

"Look, kids! I found this old clock for a face for my animal. I'll glue these spools on for arms, body, and legs!" said Jerry excitedly.

"Then you'll have a round-faced splock, a very endangered species," suggested Maria.

"Or a clock-faced ool," said Susan.

"Mother said I could use this old fan. It would make a pretty tail for a bird. I'll use this small can for a body. The corks are for the head and feet. I can make legs with these pipe cleaners," said Maria.

"You'll have a terrific fan-tailed cacorpipe," said Jim. "What do you have, Susan?"

"Mother gave me a potato, some big tacks to use for eyes, and some wire. I think I'll have a tack-eyed wotato," replied Susan.

"My! That sounds fierce! You had better be careful, for I bet that one would bite," teased Jerry. "What are you going to do, Jim?"

"I have some old candles and small bottles. If Susan will let me have a little of her wire, I think I could make a wire-tailed cottle," answered Jim.

"Sure, I have plenty of wire for both of us," said Susan. "Help yourself."

"To work we all go.
Hippity ho!" sang Jerry.
Quickly Maria added,
"Soon we'll be through
With our zingitty zangetty zoo!"

LANGUAGE CONCEPTS

Imagination promotes picturesque speech.
New words can be created by anyone.
We can use language for fun and nonsense.
Words can be used for pleasure only.

1. Read the selection to the class. Put lots of expression and enthusiasm into the reading. Try to generate ideas in the minds of listeners.
2. Talk about objects that could be combined into zingitty zangetty zoo creatures. Choose names for the finished animals.
3. Draw or paint pictures of animals for a zingitty zangetty zoo. Make them into a Zingitty Zangetty Zoo book with labels.
4. Make collages from magazine pictures. Combine two or more things to make imaginary animals. Add facial features, arms, and legs with pens when appropriate.
5. Make a zingitty zangetty zoo as a class project. Prepare information for visitors—natural habitat, feeding requirements, and care of the new creatures.

Beauty Is Blue Sky

Beauty is a song with just the right rhythm for me.
Beauty is a male cardinal at my bird feeder.
Beauty is my choice rock that looks like a miniature
mountain.

Beauty is the look of love in my mother's eyes when I please her.
Beauty is the wind whispering in the trees.
Beauty is blooming wild flowers on a hillside.
Beauty is the gracefully moving hand of my favorite guitarist.
Beauty is blue sky, free of smog.

LANGUAGE CONCEPTS

Many words have more than one meaning.
We perceive our own meanings from our experiences.

1. Write the word *Beauty* on the chalkboard. Ask students to think about what the word means to them. This can be a quiet time and then one of sharing ideas.
2. Following some sharing, read "Beauty Is Blue Sky." Pass out duplicated copies of the selection and ask students to add lines from ideas they got from the discussion.
3. Make blottoe paintings using multiple colors of tempera. Let students see in the abstract paintings an extension of the idea "Beauty is . . . ." Label the paintings and display them in the classroom.
4. Make a Beauty Mural. Find magazine pictures that are beautiful to at least one student. Arrange them in a satisfying design and glue them onto the mural. Display it for students to enjoy and contemplate.
5. Make a Contrast Book. Each student can make a page of "Beauty is . . . ." On the facing page do "Ugly is . . . ." The ideas can be illustrated and the book placed in the classroom library.

Independent Activities

Leaf Rubbings

LANGUAGE CONCEPTS

Descriptive words and phrases help make meanings clear.
Rhyming is the use of two or more words that end with the same sound.

You may have rubbed an ache, but did you ever rub a leaf?

1. Collect leaves of different shapes and sizes.
2. Put a smooth piece of paper over a leaf.
3. Use the blunt end or side of a crayon to rub over the paper while it is on top of the leaf. Use more than one color on the same leaf.
4. Rub until the design of the leaf comes through the paper.
5. Mount your leaf rubbing on colored paper.
6. Write a sentence or rhyme to describe your leaf rubbing.
7. Make some leaf rubbings to take home.

Portraits by Friends

LANGUAGE CONCEPT

We can describe things without telling their names.

Did you ever have a portrait taken with a camera? Was your portrait ever painted by an artist? Find a friend who will paint your portrait.

1. Stand or sit in a place where the artist can see you easily. Keep the same position while the picture is being painted.
2. Watch to see that colors are matched.

hair	skin
eyes	clothes

3. Watch to see that shapes are matched.

head	mouth
eyes	nose
ears	hair style

4. Change places, and you paint the portrait of your friend.
5. Display your portraits and let others guess whose they are.

Transparent Illustrations

LANGUAGE CONCEPTS

We perceive our own meanings from our experiences.
People express feelings and emotions through creative activities.
Stories and poems can be written with words and pictures or with words only.

Make see-through illustrations for your Oriental poetry books.

1. Collect leaves, twigs, feathers, pressed flowers, scraps of tissue, cellophane, and other flat objects to illustrate your ideas.
2. Place an arrangement on a piece of wax paper that is larger than the book page.
3. Put another piece of wax paper on top.
4. Cover the wax paper arrangement with a piece of paper (not wax) or a piece of fabric.
5. Press with a warm iron, being sure to seal the edges.
6. Now cut your arrangement to the same size as the book page with pinking shears.
7. Use the illustration in a book. The objects will show from both sides of the page.

Doodle-dee-doo!

LANGUAGE CONCEPTS

Feelings of people and animals are described with words.
Imagination promotes picturesque speech.

1. Doodle for a while.
2. Find a face in your doodle.
3. Outline it with heavy lines.
4. Label it with a feeling word. You might find the face sad, angry, happy, glad, ho-hum, bored, gleeful, or overjoyed.
5. Add your doodle-dee-doo to the collection of them in the classroom.

Mr. String-a-long

LANGUAGE CONCEPTS

Shapes of things are described with words.
Imagination promotes picturesque speech.

Here is Mr. String-a-long. He can make shapes with string: a triangle, a circle, or even something unique.

1. Take a piece of string.
2. Dip it into liquid starch.
3. Place it on a piece of colored paper to make a design or a shape.
4. Give your design or shape a name.
5. Take it home to show your family.

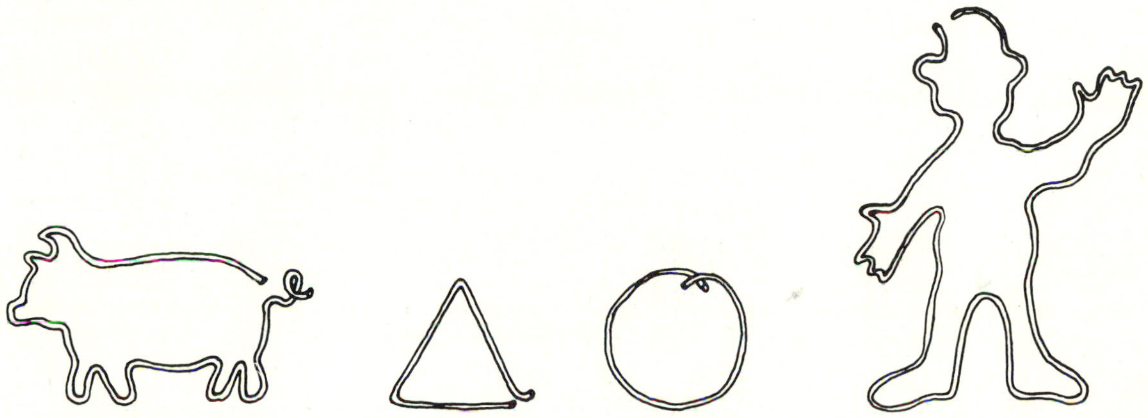

Moving Pictures

LANGUAGE CONCEPTS

There are words for the many movements of people, animals, and things.
Titles are used to tell the main idea of a production.

1. Make fingerpaint pictures with lots of movement in them.
2. When the whirls and swirls are right for you, let the painting dry.
3. Mount the paintings you like for a Moving Pictures bulletin board.
4. Label the paintings with words of movement: swirling, zigzagging, twirling, or waving.

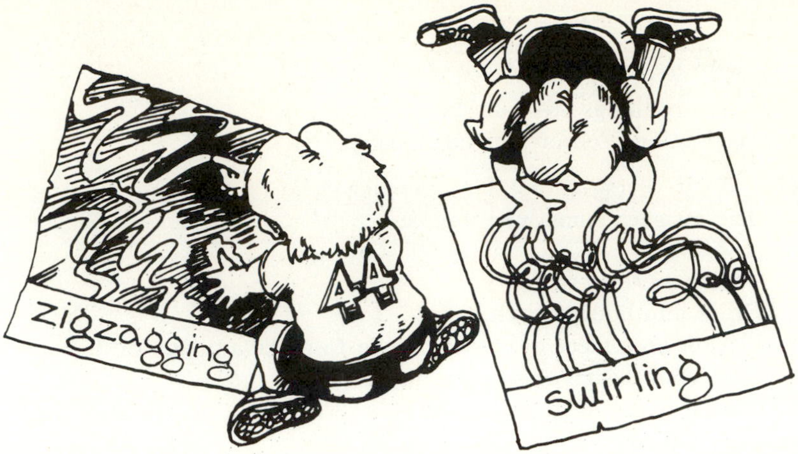

Stick Puppets

LANGUAGE CONCEPTS

People communicate in many ways through many media.
Meanings change by voice inflection, rate of speaking, and other oral characteristics that do not show in print.

Make stick puppets to use as actors in stories you like to tell. Here's how to do it.

1. Choose sticks about 12 in. long.
2. Make heads for your characters out of cardboard.
3. Decorate the faces with paint, yarn, paper, and other things.
4. Glue or tie the faces to the sticks.
5. Use a table or desk for a stage. Tell your story as you show the action with the puppets. You may need some help if there are too many puppets for two hands.

Want Ad Art

LANGUAGE CONCEPTS

Abstract forms may suggest ideas that can be expressed in words.
We perceive our own meanings from our experiences.

1. Take a page from the Want Ad section of a newspaper.
2. Look at the lines and spaces until you see something like a city

skyline, a skyscraper, a house plan, an abstract scene, a map, or a machine. Turn the paper around as you look so you can see it from different angles.

3. Outline what you see with heavy crayon or paint strokes.
4. Fill in the outlined space with a wash that lets the print show through.
5. Add people, buildings, and other objects by cutting them from the newspaper and pasting them onto your picture.
6. Make a title for your painting and display it for others to enjoy.

Masks for Me

LANGUAGE CONCEPTS

People communicate in many ways through many media.
Meanings change by voice inflection, rate of speaking, and other oral characteristics that do not show in print.
We perceive our own meanings from our experiences.

Make a mask.*

1. Use a paper sack, scissors, paste, crayons, colored paper, and yarn.
2. Cut holes for the eyes, the nose, and the mouth.

* *To the teacher:* Replenish the junk box with scraps of colored paper, bits of yarn, sequins, fur, feathers, and other decorative materials.

3. Decorate the mask.
4. Wear the mask to tell an original story, to tell a story you have heard, to act out a part for a play, or just for fun!
5. Change your voice to fit the character you play.

Special Occasion Mobiles

LANGUAGE CONCEPTS

Greeting cards and letters are special ways of saying things.
Feelings of people and animals are described with words.

Make mobile greeting cards for special occasions, like a birthday, a holiday, or when a friend is sick.

1. Write on a circular, triangular, or square piece of construction paper.
2. Make the writing of the message bold.
3. Cut along lines, as in the illustration, so the mobile will hang from a string.
4. Give or send your special occasion mobile to someone.

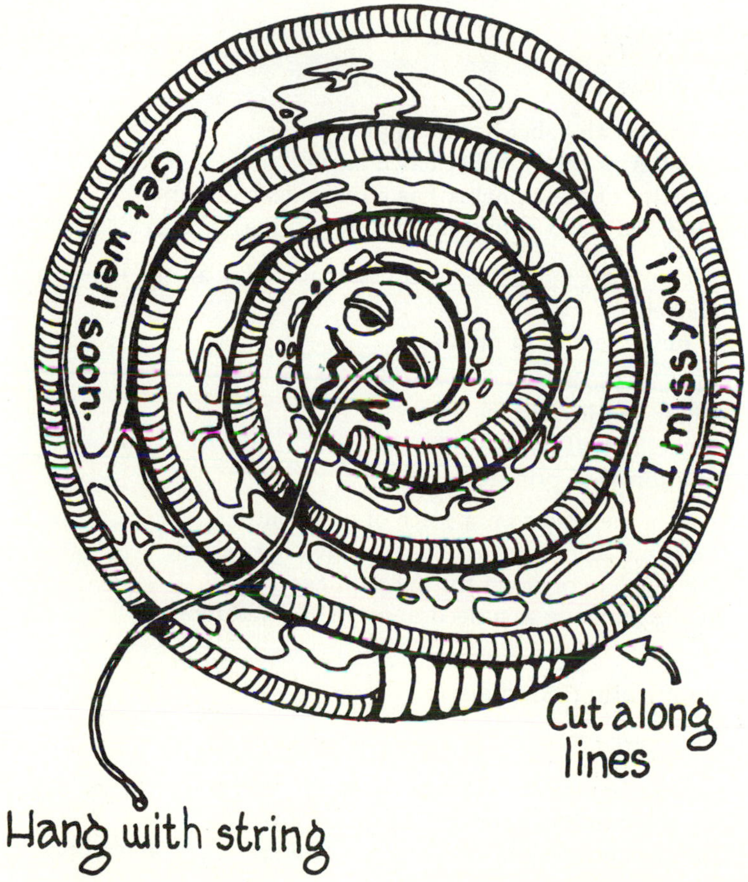
Get well soon.
I miss you!
Cut along lines
Hang with string

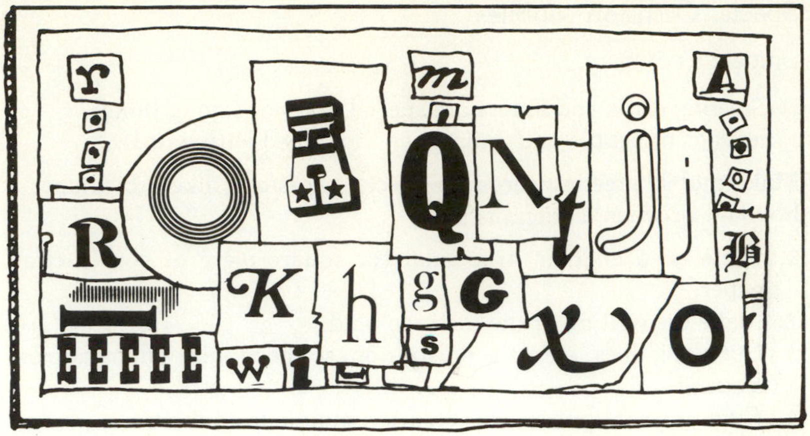

ABC Montage

LANGUAGE CONCEPTS

The English alphabet has twenty-six letters.
Each letter of the alphabet has a name.
Each letter of the alphabet has a recognizable shape.
Capital and small letters are used in writing.

1. Look through magazines and newspapers for all the letters of the alphabet.
2. Cut out letters for a montage.

   large and small
   capitals and lower-case letters
   many colors of letters
   many forms of printing

3. Arrange the letters on a piece of cardboard.
4. Rearrange them until you have a pleasing design.
5. Paste the letters down for the montage.
6. Use the montage as a decoration in the classroom.

Communicating Animals

LANGUAGE CONCEPTS

People communicate in many ways through many media.
Sounds are imitated and described with words.
Movements of people, animals, and things can be acted out.

1. Take a paper sack.
2. Get some scraps of construction paper, a pair of scissors, and some paste.
3. Cut out a face, a body, and a tongue.
4. Paste your animal on the paper sack.
5. Make the sounds of your animal puppet.
6. Make up a puppet show with your animal as the main character.

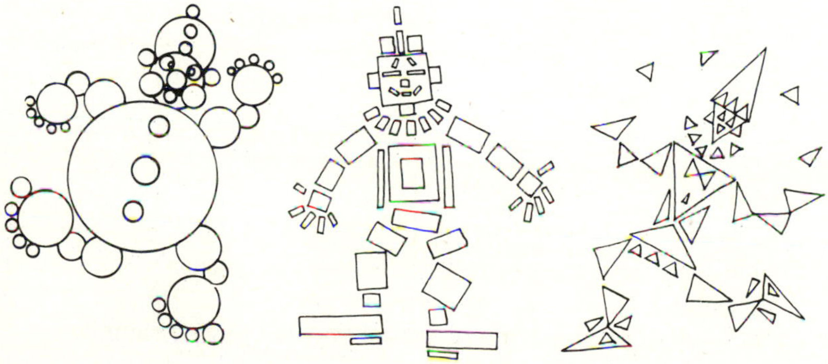

Clowns

LANGUAGE CONCEPTS

Abstract forms may suggest ideas that can be expressed in words. Imagination promotes picturesque speech.

1. Draw pictures of clowns using only circles, or draw some with only triangles or rectangles.

2. Choose your best drawings.
3. Mount them on construction paper.
4. Put them on a display board.
5. Tell your friends about your clowns—their names, where they might work, what they say, and how they feel.

Popcorn Clowns

LANGUAGE CONCEPTS

People express feelings and emotions through creative activities.
New words can be created by anyone.

1. Pop popcorn for popcorn clowns. Make enough for everyone to have some to eat too.
2. Put different colors of dry tempera paint in paper bags. Add some popcorn to each and shake to make colored popcorn for your popcorn clowns.
3. Draw an outline of a clown on a piece of heavy paper or cardboard.
4. Paste the colored popcorn in the outline to make clothes for the clown.
5. Fill in by drawing the face, hands, feet, and ears.
6. Display your popcorn clown.

Greeting Cards

LANGUAGE CONCEPTS

People use common courtesies when communicating with other people.
Greeting cards and letters are special ways of saying things.

If you like to receive greeting cards, maybe you would like to make them too.

1. Make greeting cards that you can give on special occasions, such as birthdays, Valentine's Day, Christmas, or when a friend is sick.
2. Collect old greetings for the pictures and the beautiful paper. Find scraps of paper from wrappings, advertisements, and any other place you see them.
3. Design your own cards and decorate them with cut-outs, original

drawings, pressed flowers, pressed leaves, glitter, sequins, and other decorative material.
4. Visit greeting card displays in stores for ideas.
5. Write your messages on the cards and send them to friends and family.

Nature Greetings

LANGUAGE CONCEPTS

People communicate in many ways through many media.
Greeting cards and letters are special ways of saying things.

Design and make your own greeting cards with scraps from nature.

1. Collect leaves, twigs, dried flowers, feathers, and other objects found in nature that can be flattened.
2. Arrange the objects between wax paper and press them as described in "Transparent Illustrations," but put them on only half the paper you plan to use.
3. Cut and fold the arrangements as covers for greeting cards. No two arrangements will be exactly alike.
4. Use plain paper just a little smaller than the wax paper for the inside part.
5. Write get well, birthday, and other greetings on the plain paper.

Paper Sack Pets

LANGUAGE CONCEPTS

Understanding and following directions helps one solve problems.
Words help form pictures in the mind.
Stories and poems can grow out of real experiences.
Stories and poems can grow out of imagination.

You can have any pet you want.

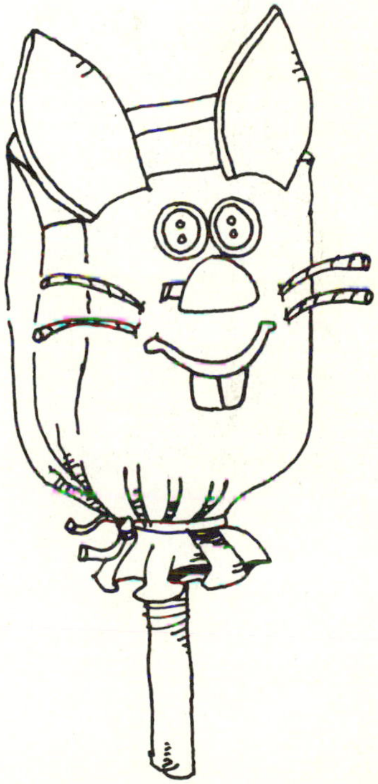

1. Fill a paper sack with torn-up newspaper.
2. Put a stick in the bag with some of it left out for a handle.
3. Tie a string around the neck of the sack. Make it tight.
4. Add a face with cut paper, string, buttons, cloth, or anything else you have to decorate a puppet.

5. Play with your paper sack pet. As you play, talk with your pet. You may make up a good story.
6. Tell your story on tape. Listen to the tape and let the puppet act out its part.

Trifold Treasures

LANGUAGE CONCEPTS

Understanding and following directions helps one solve problems.
A reader can enjoy the way an author says things as much as what the author says.

1. Cut construction paper or tagboard into strips 5 in. by 12 in.
2. Fold this strip into three parts to make a trifold.
3. Draw or paint attractive covers and borders for the trifolds.
4. Mount original poems in each space.
5. Place the trifolds in the classroom for decoration and for reading enjoyment.

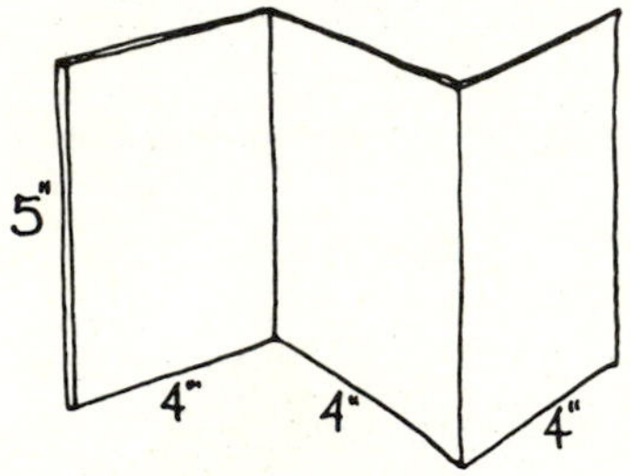

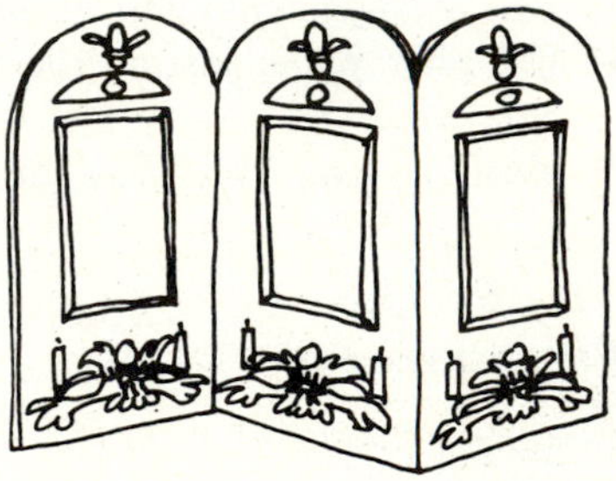

Newspaper Costumes

LANGUAGE CONCEPTS

We can use language for fun and nonsense.
Movements of people, animals, and things can be acted out.
A reader can enjoy the way an author says things as much as what the author says.

Costumes for storytelling, role playing, and dramatizing can be made out of newspapers.

1. Cut, fold, staple, and tape newspapers to make hats, shirts, capes, dashikis, skirts, and other costumes for

   a character in a fun and nonsense story
   a character in a story that you are acting out with others
   a character in one of your own stories
   a parade costume
   a Halloween costume

2. Use comic pages for color.
3. Decorate with tempera, crayons, or ribbons, yarn, and other scrap materials.

Groovy Initials

LANGUAGE CONCEPT

Initials can stand for names.

1. Write your initials in large letters on a piece of paper 8½ in. by 11 in. Make them bold.
2. Select a combination of three or four colored crayons.
3. Begin outlining your initials with heavy strokes of the crayons. Alternate the colors.
4. Continue doing this until the whole page is covered.
5. Mount your groovy initials on a large piece of paper and display it on a bulletin board.

Cook Some Clay

LANGUAGE CONCEPTS

People communicate in many ways through many media.
Abstract forms may suggest ideas that can be expressed in words.
There are words for the many movements of people, animals, and things.
Initials can stand for names.

You can make your own clay for animals and other forms.* You will need:

* *To the teacher:* To get prints from objects, roll a slab of clay. Put the objects on top, cover with wax paper, then roll with a rolling pin. Remove the

1 cup salt
1 cup flour
1 cup water

1. Mix together the salt, flour, and water. Cook over low heat until the mixture thickens.
2. Stir the mixture while cooking.
3. Let the clay cool.
4. Pinch off a piece of clay the size of a golf ball. Roll it. Pat it. Pinch it. Squeeze it. Flatten it. Form something out of it. You can make an animal, a bowl, a reptile, a pendant, beads, a plaque, or an interesting statue.
5. Decorate what you make.

   Press sharp objects into it to make designs.
   Press leaves or other objects into the clay, then take them out to leave just their print.
   Press your initials into it.

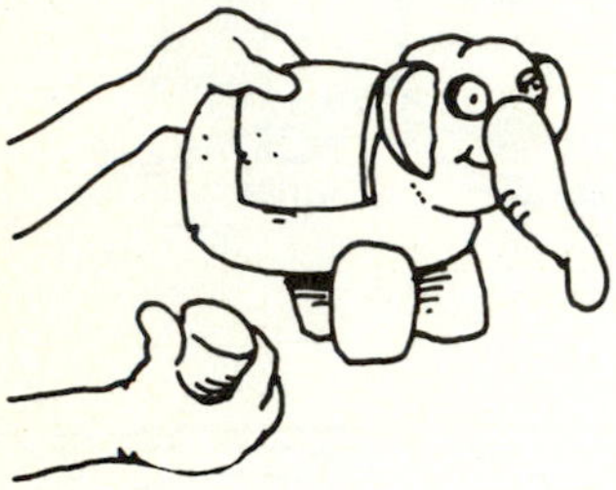
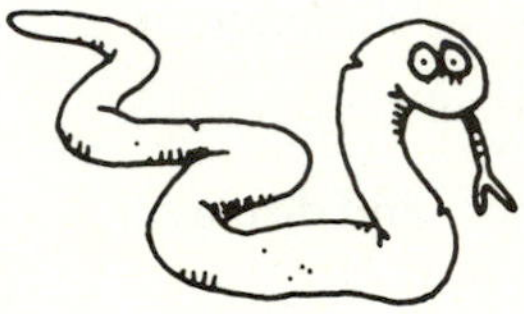
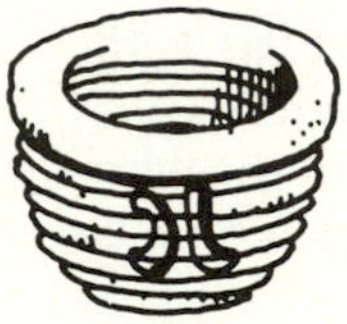

My Own Thing

LANGUAGE CONCEPTS

Imaginary creatures can have names.
Stories and poems can grow out of imagination.
Authors describe characters in ways that let readers form mental images of them.

---

paper and objects. Cut the clay from around the design for a plaque or a pendant. A large knitting needle is useful for punching holes when they are needed. Remember to punch the holes larger than you need to allow for shrinkage as the clay dries.

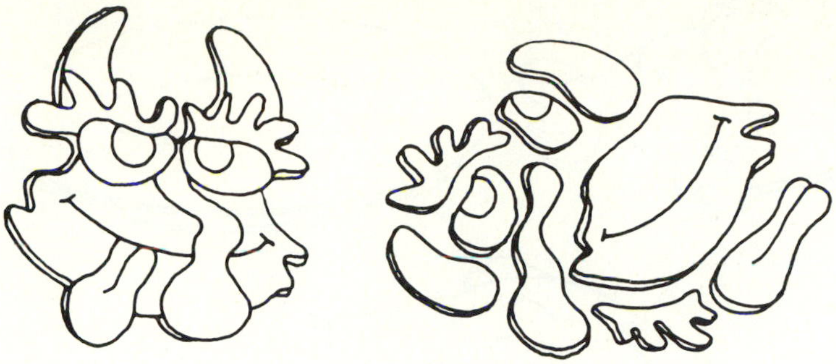

1. Cut several odd shapes out of construction paper.
2. Arrange them on a piece of paper to make a thing. You may need to add eyes or ears or a mouth.
3. Name your thing and display it on a bulletin board.
4. Write a story with your thing as the main character.

Rhyming Pictures

LANGUAGE CONCEPTS

Many words rhyme with others.
Rhyming is the use of two or more words that end with the same sound.

1. Make pictures of two things that have rhyming names: draw them, cut out pictures and paste them on cardboard, or mold them from clay.
2. Put the two things together in a picture or sculpture.
3. Make a rhyme to go with them.

What's Hiding There?

LANGUAGE CONCEPTS

Abstract forms may suggest ideas that can be expressed in words.
New words can be created by anyone.

1. Study the illustration. There is more to the lines or shapes than you can see on the paper. Could something be hiding?*
2. Take a marker and begin adding your own ideas about what might be hiding.
3. Add a title to each drawing.
4. If you can't think of real words, create new ones to go with your design.

Scissorettes

LANGUAGE CONCEPTS

Abstract forms may suggest ideas that can be expressed in words. Everything has a name.

---

* *To the teacher:* Prepare a stack of newsprint for use in this activity by simply making a creative line or shape on each sheet.

1. Cut odd shapes from colored pictures in magazines or from scraps of cloth.*
2. Make a picture by moving the shapes around on a piece of construction paper.
3. When you find a picture you like, stop, and paste it down.
4. Name your picture.

* *To the teacher:* Keep a scrap box available for bits of paper and cloth.

Chapter 8

The Cooking Center

What Is a Cooking Center?

A Cooking Center is a place

for increasing the language of the senses
for following directions
for comparing and contrasting foods before and after cooking
for creating interest in pictures of food that can be made into books and labeled
for stimulating discussions on the sources of food—people and places involved in producing ingredients

More than any other language development center, the Cooking Center assures use of words in all the major classifications—names of things, words of movement, and descriptive categories of color, size, shape, sound, smell, taste, touch, emotions, and contrast and comparison (nouns, verbs, adjectives, and adverbs). The variety of words, linked with the structure words of English, guarantees a full language learning environment.

High motivation is built into cooking activities. Most children are anxious to participate in follow-up language experiences as well as in the tasting and eating activities. They will read recipes for exact meanings and will follow the sequence of ideas presented because they learn that not to do so will produce poor results.

Cooking is an activity in which parents can be involved in a meaningful way. They can supervise activities and check on pupil participation. Also, they can demonstrate the preparation of foods indigenous to their ethnic group.

The Cooking Center necessitates eating with others and provides real opportunities for developing the language of courtesy and manners. Children can invite parents, school personnel, or other class groups to share the foods they prepare. In doing so they learn to entertain others in conversational settings.

An electric skillet or a hot plate provides enough heat for most simple cooking. Ovens can be used in the cafeteria, or children can be invited to a nearby home to observe the baking process.

Utensils can be gathered through donations. Nothing elaborate is needed. Some teachers ask for trading stamps and get enough for basic equipment.

Recipes that require no heat are useful when using cooking for language development.

Language Skills Developed and Practiced

The child increases vocabulary of names—of foods, ingredients, utensils.

The child increases vocabulary of motion—words used for preparing, cooking, serving.

The child increases vocabulary of description—words of smell, taste, color, size, shape, texture, sound, and emotions.

The child increases ability to use the language of contrast and comparison—softer/harder, smoother/lumpier, larger/smaller, wet/dry, sweet/sour.

The child follows directions in recipes.

The child makes decisions from observation and communicates those decisions.

The child records experiences in word lists and in books.

The child develops interest in reading recipe books and recipes in newspapers and magazines.

The child increases ability to read for specific information.

The child uses the vocabulary of courtesy and manners in a functional setting.

The child develops interest in sources of food.

Cooking Words Wall

As a part of the Cooking Center, display words that grow out of the experiences. Suggest categories of words with labels, but keep the lists open ended so that children can add new ones. Use the lists for spelling references and for reading games that review vocabularies inherent in cooking and eating. Talk about words that have more than one meaning, such as *orange*.

Taste Words	Smell Words	Texture Words
delicious	minty	sticky
yummy	lemony	gooey
spicy	strong	hard
bitter	pungent	soft

Shape Words	Size Words
round	small
mounds	pinch
squares	cup
heart	tiny

Name Words	Motion Words	Color Words
sugar	stir	orange
salt	blend	avocado
cookies	mix	brown
butter	pour	burned

Group and Independent Activities

We Are Making Soup at School

Sing to the tune of "She'll Be Coming 'Round the Mountain"

We are making soup at school, yum, yum, yum.
We are making soup at school, yum, yum, yum.
We are making soup at school.
We are making soup at school.
We are making soup at school, yum, yum, yum.

First we put the carrots in, yum, yum, yum.
First we put the carrots in, yum, yum, yum.
First we put the carrots in.
First we put the carrots in.
First we put the carrots in, yum, yum, yum.

Then we add the white potatoes, yum, yum, yum.
Then we add the white potatoes, yum, yum, yum.
Then we add the white potatoes.
Then we add the white potatoes.
Then we add the white potatoes, yum, yum, yum.

Next we stir some yellow corn in, yum, yum, yum.
Next we stir some yellow corn in, yum, yum, yum.
Next we stir some yellow corn in.
Next we stir some yellow corn in.
Next we stir some yellow corn in, yum, yum, yum.

Then we add some salt and pepper, yum, yum, yum.
Then we add some salt and pepper, yum, yum, yum.
Then we add some salt and pepper.
Then we add some salt and pepper.
Then we add some salt and pepper, yum, yum, yum.

Now take turns and stir the soup, yum, yum, yum.
Now take turns and stir the soup, yum, yum, yum.
Now take turns and stir the soup.
Now take turns and stir the soup.
Now take turns and stir the soup, yum, yum, yum.

It is tasty and smells good, yum, yum, yum.
It is tasty and smells good, yum, yum, yum.
It is tasty and smells good.
It is tasty and smells good.
It is tasty and smells good, yum, yum, yum.

Don't forget to wash the dishes, scrub, scrub, scrub.
Don't forget to wash the dishes, scrub, scrub, scrub.
Don't forget to wash the dishes.
Don't forget to wash the dishes.
Don't forget to wash the dishes, scrub, scrub, scrub.

from East Baton Rouge Parish Schools

LANGUAGE CONCEPTS

The same language patterns are used over and over in writing.
Language can be expressed in rhythmic patterns.

1. Make soup at school. Ask students to help furnish ingredients—one carrot, one potato, one onion, and other items that they

might bring from home for vegetable soup. Use an electric cooker to cook the soup in the classroom.

2. Sing "We Are Making Soup at School" to the tune of "She'll Be Coming 'Round the Moutain." Students can join in as they pick up the pattern.
3. As your soup recipe is developed, sing stanzas and keep a record. The soup does not have to be just like that in the song.
4. After the eating and clean-up, edit your soup song to make sure the text fits the tune.
5. Duplicate copies of the new soup song for students to illustrate and bind. They can make individual books to take home for singing and reading.

Popcorn Pops

Popcorn pops when it is hot,
Dancing around in a great big pot.
Around and around,
Up and down,
Around and around,
Up and down,
Dancing around in a great big pot.
It pops when it is hot.

Popcorn's a sight for me to see,
A beautiful sight for you and me.
Fluffy and white,
It flies like a kite.
Fluffy and white,
It flies like a kite.
A beautiful sight for you and me,
It is a sight for me to see.

Popcorn's a thrill for me to smell.
I know the scent very well.
Inviting and buttery,
Enticing and salty,
Inviting and buttery,
Enticing and salty,
I know the scent very well.
It is a thrill for me to smell.

Popcorn is lots of fun to hear,
Popping in a pot so very near.
    Crackle and pop,
    When will it stop?
    Crackle and pop,
    When will it stop?
Popping in a pot so very near,
It is lots of fun to hear.

Popcorn feels good to my touch.
I like to feel it very much.
    Puffy and rough,
    Soft and warm,
    Puffy and rough,
    Soft and warm,
I like to feel it very much.
It feels good to my touch.

Popcorn is good for me to taste.
Don't let any of it go to waste!
    Marvelous and crunchy,
    Delicious and yummy,
    Marvelous and crunchy,
    Delicious and yummy,
Don't let any of it go to waste!
It is good for me to taste.

Popcorn popping in the pot,
I like to eat it when it's hot.
    A little to start,
    Then more and more,
    A little to start,
    Then more and more,
I like to eat it when it's hot,
Popcorn popping in the pot.

Popcorn popping in the pot,

    Around and around,
    Up and down.

    Fluffy and white,
    It flies like a kite.

    Inviting and buttery,
    Enticing and salty.

Crackle and pop,
When will it stop?

Puffy and rough,
Soft and warm.

Marvelous and crunchy,
Delicious and yummy.

A little to start,
Then more and more,
and more,
and more,
and more.

I CAN'T STOP!

LANGUAGE CONCEPTS

Colors, shapes, smells, tastes, feel, and sounds of things are described with words.

Onomatopoeic words are those whose sounds suggest their meanings.

The same language patterns are used over and over in writing.

1. Pop corn as a class project. Before you start, pass out grains of corn. Talk about and experience the color, size, shape, texture, smell, taste, and feel, and record some of the descriptive vocabulary.
2. Make a transparency or reading chart of Popcorn Pops. Begin reading and invite students to join in when they discover the pattern. Look at the pattern that repeats in most of the stanzas. Talk about this type of patterning as a literary characteristic of some poetry.
3. Say or write the same information in prose that is in the poem. Which is more interesting? Which is easier to remember?
4. Say the word *POP* in unison. Does it sound like its own meaning? If it does, it is onomatopoeic. Think of other words that are onomatopoeic, such as

   BANG! SWISH! CRUNCH! DRIP!

   Say the words in chorus as they are suggested. Make a list as a resource for the Writing Center.
5. Make "Popcorn Pops" into an accordian book. See the Publishing

Center for instructions. Fill leftover pages with illustrations or with popcorn poems written by members of the class.

Tongue Tinglers

What taste gives your mouth a tingly feeling?
Peppermint candy is very appealing.

Have you tried the hot peppery taste of tacos or chili?
They're usually hotter that most piccalilli.

Do you know foods that have a sparkling red taste?
Strawberries and cranberry sauce—hand me with haste!

What foods you know have the cool taste of green?
Limeade, lettuce, celery are ones I have seen.

Do you like the purple taste of a ripened plum?
Some grapes and juice have that taste. I'd like some.

Do you like the taste of an orange full of tang?
Tangerines and orange juice are for my gang.

Have you tasted foods that are soft and fluffy?
Angel cake's like that when it looks real puffy.

Do you like foods well sprinkled with salt?
Potato chips and salty nuts are good with a malt.

Do you like foods that taste kinda lumpy and bumpy?
I do if raisins and nuts are what's making them humpy.

Have you tasted things that are rubbery like gum?
Licorice and jerky are. Can you give me some?

Have you tried to swallow something slippery and slick?
The doctor gives medicine like that if I'm very sick.

How many foods can you name that are sweet?
Watermelon's my favorite for a special treat.

Have you tried foods that are crispy and crunchy?
Celery or carrots—try eating a bunchy.

Do you like mellow yellow foods like scrambled eggs?
Baked pudding and bananas I could eat by the keg.

Do you like the crunchy crisp taste of some things brown?
Cinnamon toast and crispy cereal are foods I'd crown.

Have you tried drinks that are very fizzy?
Ginger ale's bubbles stay very busy.

Each day my tongue tingles with many kinds of tastes—

crunchy
lemony
soft
salty
hard sour
sweet cold hot
stringy bitter tart
peppery sticky icy
buttery puckery GOOEY!
spicy

LANGUAGE CONCEPT

Tastes of things are described with words.

1. Read "Tongue Tinglers" and ask children to make facial expressions to represent their feelings about each taste idea.
2. Record the words of taste at the end of the selection. Use the chalkboard or a chart.
3. Plan a tasting experience of several different foods. All children do not have to taste everything. Choose words from the list to describe the tastes. Add others as students have new tasting experiences.
4. Hold up pictures of food and let children suggest words of taste for them. Have the list available in the Writing Center for use in stories and poems.
5. Generate a list of similes and metaphors for taste ideas. Make the list available in the Writing Center.
6. Discuss foods liked and not liked. Is taste the only criterion? What else causes one to like or not like a food?
7. Plan a Food Fair. Invite parents to bring small amounts of ethnic foods for students to taste—Mexican, Italian, Chinese, Greek, and any other that might be represented in the class. This activity can be done on one day or it can be extended over several days.

Ridiculous Recipes

TOAD STEW

Skin enough toads to melt a pint of toad fat. Cut toads in pieces. Dice 5 poison mushrooms. Add ingredients to broth from fat. Season to taste with dragon claw powder. Cook until bubbling rapidly. Serve to ghosts and goblins on Halloween.

TARANTULA COOKIES

Grind 5 tarantulas and season to taste with spider webs. Add ½ handful of lizard tails ground very coarse. Mix in ½ cup of gasoline. Drop onto cookie sheet and watch them flame while they cook for 10 minutes. Makes 1 dozen cookies. Eat to cure warts on your nose.

CREAM OF TERMITE SOUP

20,000 termites in various stages of development
10 dried skeleton weeds
40 flowers of golden poppy
2 gallons of brittlebrush wine
1 quart of unicorn milk

Place termites, skeleton weeds, poppies, and wine in an iron kettle. Cook for 30 minutes. Add 1 quart of unicorn milk. Let cool and then eat. Especially useful for making one invisible. Small amounts are recommended.

SCORPION SCORCHER

13 dried scorpions
13 splinters from an old ladder
13 hairs from a black cat
1 quart rubbing alcohol

Grind scorpions, splinters, and hairs together. Add to alcohol. Allow to age for one year before using. Use to cure about anything.

HALLOWEEN BREW

1 quart whale fat
1 toe of bobcat
1 centipede
1 bat's wing
1 dozen fresh grasshoppers
4 gallons water

Melt fat. Fry toe of bobcat, centipede, bat's wing, and grasshoppers in the fat for 10 minutes. Pour contents into 4 gallons of boiling water. Boil one hour. Strain. Pour into leather pouches and age for 5 years. Drink to ward off evil spirits.

RATTLESNAKE TEA

1 dead rattlesnake
2 cups of flowers of sow thistle
3 gallons rain water

Bring rain water to a boil. Add rattlesnake and boil for 1 hour. Add sow thistle flowers and continue to boil 15 minutes longer. Strain liquid and pour into brown bottles. Take 3 tablespoonsful to cast a spell in October.

LANGUAGE CONCEPT

We can use language for fun and nonsense.

1. Plan a Ridiculous Recipe Picnic.
2. Each student brings a paper plate with a picture of some ridiculous food or drink pasted on it. On the bottom is the recipe.
3. At meal time students tell about the "favorite ridiculous food" that was prepared for the picnic. They can tell how they found the ingredients, how they prepared the concoction, and why they like it.
4. Have a time to exchange recipes. Students can copy recipes from the bottoms of plates and make personal recipe books of Ridiculous Recipes.
5. During the picnic time, ask students to think up ridiculous games to play.

Color Books

LANGUAGE CONCEPT

Colors of things are described with words.

1. Make a collection of pictures of foods of the same color—green foods, orange foods, brown foods, red foods, or others.
2. Make a book of foods for each color. Bind the book in consruction paper of the same color as the foods inside.

Making Butter

LANGUAGE CONCEPT

There are words for the many movements of people, animals, and things.

You will need

1 pint whipping cream at room temperature
salt
a 1-quart jar or larger, with a lid

1. Pour the cream into the jar.
2. Put the lid on tightly.
3. Take turns with a friend shaking the jar until butter forms.
4. Pour off the liquid.
5. Add 1/8 teaspoon salt to the butter.
6. Serve with crackers or bread.
7. Make a list of words telling the motions you used while making the butter.

Recipe Exchange

LANGUAGE CONCEPTS

People communicate some information in sequence.
Numerals are symbols of how many and how much.
Understanding and following directions helps one solve problems.
Abbreviations are used in places where whole words are not needed.

1. Choose a favorite recipe.
2. Copy it for duplication.
3. Make enough copies for class members.
4. Put copies in the Favorite Recipes box for others to take.
5. Make a recipe book as you collect ones you like from your friends.

Foods Change

LANGUAGE CONCEPT

Antonyms are words that have opposite meanings.

1. Read some recipes.
2. List foods from them that change when they are heated or cooled.

From Soft to Hard	**From Hard to Soft**	
eggs	apples	popcorn
bacon	chocolate	
toast	beans	

From Liquid to Solid	**From Solid to Liquid**	
pancakes	sugar	coffee

3. Plan a demonstration to show what happens to some foods when they are heated or cooled.

Family Food Budget

LANGUAGE CONCEPTS

Some symbols other than our alphabet communicate meaning.
Numerals are symbols of how many and how much.
Everything has a name.

1. Read the grocery ads in a newspaper.
2. Pretend to buy groceries for a family of four for one week. You have $80 to spend.
3. Make your grocery list. Include prices.
4. Plan menus for at least three meals using foods from your list.

Where in the World?

LANGUAGE CONCEPTS

Locating facts requires one to look in many kinds of materials.
Alphabetical arrangements help one locate information.
Words used today come from many sources.

1. Choose a picture of a meal from a magazine.*
2. List the foods you know. Include seasonings.
3. List next to the name of each food at least one place where that food is grown.
4. Find a map of the United States or the world.
5. Mark all the places the one meal might have come from.

Tasting Fruit

LANGUAGE CONCEPTS

Smells of things are described with words.
Tastes of things are described with words.

* *To the teacher:* Pictures of meals and blank maps can be supplied. Most students will need an encyclopedia, but it can be used at home or in the school library.

This is a group activity. The teacher should follow these steps.

1. Bring to class an assortment of fruits.
2. Let the children identify the fruits.
3. Let the children describe them.
4. Cut the fruits into small pieces for a tasting experience.
5. As the children taste and smell, record their sayings.
6. Play Fruit Basket Turn Over (if the children know this game).

Popcorn

LANGUAGE CONCEPTS

Smells of things are described with words.
Tastes of things are described with words.
Antonyms are words that have opposite meanings.
Onomatopoeic words are those whose sounds suggest their meanings.

This is a group activity. The teacher should follow these steps.

1. Let the children examine the popcorn before popping—its size, shape, color, texture, smell, and taste. Keep a record of words used.
2. Let the children examine the popcorn after popping. Use the same categories of words.
3. Discuss what the popping did.
4. Sing a popcorn song to the tune of "Do You Know the Muffin Man." You can sing, "Oh, do you know the popcorn man, the popcorn man, the popcorn man."

Tortillas

LANGUAGE CONCEPTS

There are words for the many movements of people, animals, and things.
Movements of people, animals, and things can be acted out.
Most verbs have different forms to express the meaning of time.

This is a group activity. The teacher should follow these steps.

1. Use words of movement while making the tortillas. Make certain the children know the meanings of the words. Keep a list of those you use and those you hear the children use. You will need

   4 cups flour
   ¾ cup lard
   ½ cup lard for greasing
   1 teaspoon salt
   1½ cups water

2. Mix together the flour, lard, and salt.
3. Add water.
4. Knead until smooth.
5. Pull off pieces of dough the size of small eggs.
6. Cover each piece with lard, then let it set for a few minutes.
7. Roll each piece until thin. Stretch and pull it to get the dough thinner and to the desired shape.
8. Cook each piece on a very hot grill until it blisters.
9. Serve the tortillas with butter or refried beans.
10. Sing "Tortilla Song" to the tune of "Here We Go 'Round the Mulberry Bush."

    This is the way we make tortillas.
    " " " " " roll "
    " " " " " knead "
    " " " " " pinch "
    " " " " " fry "
    " " " " " eat "

    Let children supply the words and decide on appropriate actions.
11. On the following day ask the children to tell what they did to make tortillas. Write the words on the chalkboard. Call attention to the endings of the verbs when they are used to tell that something has happened in the past.

Pancakes

LANGAUGE CONCEPTS

Shapes of things are described with words.
Smells of things are described with words.
Tastes of things are described with words.
Understanding and following directions helps one solve problems.

This is a group activity. The teacher should follow these steps.

1. Let the children use the recipe on a box of pancake mix to make the batter.
2. Talk about the pancake batter before you cook it—let the children feel it, smell it, taste a bit of it.
3. Put spoonfuls of batter in a lightly greased skillet.
4. Turn the pancakes once when the tops are covered with bubbles.
5. Eat the pancakes with syrup and margarine or butter.
6. Compare and contrast the uncooked batter and the pancakes.
7. Work with the children in making a pancake-shaped book, listing words and recording stories about how pancakes smell and taste.

Applesauce

LANGUAGE CONCEPTS

Tastes of things are described with words.
Many descriptive words that compare two or more things end in *-er* and *-est.*
Understanding and following directions helps one solve problems.

This is a group activity. The teacher should follow these steps.

1. Prepare apples for applesauce. (Do not have a recipe in sight.)
2. Let children taste the apples before cooking.
3. Cook the apples and season with sugar, lemon, and cinnamon.
4. Serve with crackers or toast.
5. Lead the children to compare the taste, smell, texture, and color of the apples before and after cooking. Call attention to the use of words ending in *-er* and *-est* when comparisons are made.
6. Let the children dictate a recipe for making applesauce from their observation of the process.
7. Compare their recipe to the one you used.
8. Read *Rain Makes Applesauce* by Julian Scheer and Marvin Bileck if it is available.

Quickie Doughnuts

LANGUAGE CONCEPTS

Tastes of things are described with words.
The feel of things is described with words.
People use similes and metaphors to compare and contrast things and ideas.

This is a group activity. The teacher should follow these steps.

1. Use canned biscuits.
2. Divide each of the biscuits into two thin ones.
3. Let children punch holes with fingers or use cutters to make a hole in each biscuit.
4. Drop the biscuits into deep fat and fry until brown.
5. Remove and shake in a paper sack with confectioner's sugar or a mixture of sugar and cinnamon.
6. Talk about the feel of the dough before it is cooked, and compare it with the feel of the dough after it is cooked.
7. Collect similes that are used for the comparisons.
8. Talk about the taste as the doughnuts are eaten.

A Feast for Birds

LANGUAGE CONCEPTS

People express feelings and emotions through creative activities.
Tastes of things are described with words.

1. Cut some fruit into small pieces.
2. Tear some bread into small bits.
3. Pop some corn for the birds.
4. String the fruit, bread, and popcorn on loops of thread that can be hung on tree branches.
5. Put the strings of food on tree branches where you can watch the birds have a feast.
6. List words that describe how you think the food will taste to the birds.

Chapter 9

The Dramatization Center

What Is a Dramatization Center?

A Dramatization Center is a place

for using words not characteristic of normal everyday speech
for acting out roles, real and imaginary, that are impossible in real life
for stimulating the imagination
for projecting ideas and language through puppets

The Dramatization Center gives children repeated opportunities to try out new ways of thinking about themselves and others. The children pretend they are characters they have heard or read about and assume the language of those characters. This requires the use of language that can never be characteristic of normal conversation and discussion but that will be encountered over and over in reading.

The Dramatization Center should have some storage space—either on shelves or in boxes. Hats, shoes, masks, tools, puppets, and other items permit children to change characters in a flash. Children are encouraged to play school, fly an airplane, or fly into space, or to be a barber, a nurse, a medical doctor, a beauty parlor operator, an auto mechanic, or any other character that gives them an opportunity to use informal oral language in a new setting. Puppets are available to encourage children to try out sounds and expressions not typical of their normal conversation.

Producing puppet shows in a puppet theater brings children together in planning sessions and rehearsals and helps them form friendships through cooperation. The puppet theater also provides a functional setting for extending the work of a group of children to others—parents, school personnel, and other class groups. The recognition children gain from this type of activity strengthens their self-image and permits their language skills to grow in multiple ways.

Color slides made of dramatic productions can be accompanied by a tape of the sound. The presentation can be placed in the library for others' entertainment and information. This type of extension of children's efforts and abilities builds positive attitudes toward reading and language growth.

Fairies, goblins, witches, magicians, elves, nonsense creatures, and talking animals are found in literary classics. These roles can be acted out, with the teacher telling the story first and then releasing it to the innovative ideas of children. *The Three Little Pigs, The Three Billy Goats Gruff, Hansel and Gretel, The Shoemaker and the Elves,* and *The Bremen Town Musicians* are examples of stories that are readily available. The acting out gives students opportunities to "try on" and "try out" language that is new to them. The experience helps them build a "sense of story," which is required for success in reading and writing. They practice doing things in sequence, and they learn to set the mood of characters that they will meet later in reading.

Stories from the reading curriculum can be told before they are read. The teacher can select suitable ones and announce the need for characters to act out the story as they hear it. As the teacher tells the story, the characters pantomime their parts. They have to listen carefully and think fast of ways to show actions and feelings. The audience gets emotionally involved in observing the characters in action. When the time comes to read the story, the students are ready to confirm and/or deny their predictions of the language and ideas of the author.

A theater-in-the-round can be scheduled about once a week for intermediate-age students. One student has permission to prepare the play. The story to be acted out is kept a secret. The student director reads it as many times as necessary to learn to tell it with ease and clarity. Props are prepared ahead of time. Characters are usually volunteers. They move to the center of the room, and the audience sits around the edge. The storyteller begins and the action starts. Most of the time the characters have never heard the story before. Their actions are spontaneous. Sometimes the story is acted several times with different sets of actors. This dramatization experience keeps children reading for specific purposes and forces them to gain an awareness of stories that have setting, characters, action, and plot that appeal to others. Oral interpretation of stories is improved significantly, and listening skills are sharpened.

A collection of stories with beginnings that are sharp and clear can be useful in dramatization. Teachers print out the beginnings and let volunteers develop the plot with characters and actions. After several presentations of student versions of the story, copies can be placed in the Reading Center. No comments are necessary to interest students in reading them.

Teacher resources are available for the expansion and enrichment of the Dramatization Center. Some useful ones are

Carlson, Ruth Kearney. *Sparkling Words.* Geneva, Ill.: Paladin House Publishers, 1979.

Carlton, Lessie, and Robert H. Moore. *Reading, Self-Directive Dramatization and Self-Concept.* Columbus, Ohio: Charles E. Merrill, 1971.

Croft, Doreen J., and Robert D. Hess. *An Activities Handbook for Teachers of Young Children.* Boston: Houghton Mifflin Company, 1980.

Norton, Donna E. *Language Arts Activities for Children.* Columbus, Ohio: Charles E. Merrill, 1980.

Siks, Geraldine B. *Children's Literature for Dramatization.* New York: Harper, 1964.

———. *Creative Dramatics: An Art for Children.* New York: Harper, 1958.

Woods, Margaret S., and Beryl Trihart. *Guidelines for Creative Dramatics.* Buffalo, N.Y.: D. O. K. Publishers, 1970.

Language Skills Developed and Practiced

The child gains confidence in oral production.

The child learns to use voice modulation to represent a variety of characters.

The child learns to use voice modulation to portray feelings and moods.

The child conveys ideas and feelings through facial expression, gesture, posture, and tone of voice.
The child develops an ability to convey meaning through pantomime.
The child learns to organize thoughts into sequence.
The child practices using language in ways that other people use it in reading materials.
The child memorizes repeating phrases and songs from classic stories.
The child develops sensitivity to the ideas and language of other people.
The child improves in the oral reading of stories that have been acted out.
The child increases comprehension of stories that are read.
The child uses home-rooted language in new situations.
The child uses multiple media for communication.
The child plans cooperatively for production of shows.
The child uses more than one language in the same story (in classrooms in which there are children whose home language is not English).

Group Activities

With a Friend

With a friend
I can slide.

With a friend
I can ride.

With a friend
I can walk.

With a friend
I can talk.

With a friend
I can run.

With a friend
I can sun.

With a friend
I can hunt.

With a friend
I can punt.

With a friend
I can look.

With a friend
I can cook.

With a friend
I can hop.

With a friend
I can shop.

With a friend
I can draw.

With a friend
I can saw.

To a friend
I can phone.

I can't do
that alone!

LANGUAGE CONCEPTS

There are words for the many movements of people, animals, and things.
Every person has a name.
Language can be expressed in rhythmic patterns.

1. Read the first two or three verses of "With a Friend" and pause to let children predict what comes next.
2. Invite them to say "with a friend" each time in unison, then read the second line of the verse to them. Pause occasionally for prediction of rhyming words.
3. Children choose a friend and decide what they can do together. They act out what they decide. The teacher helps them do a couplet if possible, but this is not necessary.
4. Record what the "friends" produce. Put each contribution on a separate page. These pages can be illustrated and bound into a class book.
5. If there is interest in reading the class-produced book, duplicate copies for students to take home.
6. Substitute names of class members for the word "friend" in the text. Ask the person whose name is called to act out the stanza. Some stanzas can be omitted.

Over and Over

Today I started walking to school.
A big dog stopped me and knocked me over.
My pencil went one way.
My lunch went another.
I thought of plenty to say,
BUT
I picked up my pencil,
I picked up my lunch,
and
started to school once more.

A carpenter bumped my arm with a door.
My pencil went one way.
My lunch went another.
I thought of plenty I wanted to say,
BUT

I picked up my pencil,
I picked up my lunch,
and
started to school once more.

I heard the school bell, so I started to skip.
I stumbled and fell.
My pencil went one way.
My lunch went another.
I thought of plenty I wanted to say,
BUT
I picked up my pencil,
I picked up my lunch,
and
started to school once more.

The bell rang again.
I started to run.
I stumbled and fell.
My pencil went one way.
My lunch went another.
I thought of plenty I wanted to say,
BUT
I picked up my pencil,
I picked up my lunch,
and
GOT TO SCHOOL ON TIME!

LANGUAGE CONCEPTS

People express feelings and emotions through creative activities.
Movements of people, animals, and things can be acted out.
There are words for the many movements of people, animals, and things.

1. Read "Over and Over," letting children join in on repeating lines.
2. Read it again, letting some children act out the lines.

Talk about facial expressions and hand expressions that can be used instead of words to express

disgust
pain
fear
anxiety

3. Read again, and let other children apply the suggestions that have been discussed. Encourage children to BE DRAMATIC!

Mongon Helps

Mother lets me set the table.
I put the plates all on,
Then put knives, forks, and spoons
Just where they belong.
  Of course, mother never sees
  That Mongon helps me, too.
  No one else sees Mongon.
  They don't know what he can do.

Mother lets me clean the living room.
My! You should see me dust!
I vacuum very carefully
Because I know I must.
  Of course, mother never sees
  That Mongon helps me, too.
  No one else sees Mongon.
  They don't know what he can do.

Mother lets me make my bed.
I work hard on my big spread.
I tug and smooth the covers,
Then put the pillow at the head.
  Of course, mother never sees
  That Mongon helps me, too.
  No one else sees Mongon.
  They don't know what he can do.

On wash day I can match the socks
When they are nice and clean—
Red with red and blue with blue,
Then find two white and green.
  Of course, mother never sees
  That Mongon helps me, too.
  No one else sees Mongon.
  They don't know what he can do.

Mother lets me water plants
The days they need a drink.
I get my little watering can
And fill it at the sink.
    Of course, mother never sees
    That Mongon helps me, too.
    No one else sees Mongon.
    They don't know what he can do.

Mother lets me put the trash
All in a great big sack.
I empty all wastebaskets,
Than take them all right back.
    Of course, mother never sees
    That Mongon helps me, too.
    No one else sees Mongon.
    They don't know what he can do.

Mother sometimes lets me cook.
That job I do like best.
But she shoos me from the kitchen
If we have a special guest.
    Of course, mother never sees
    That Mongon helps me, too.
    No one else sees Mongon.
    They don't know what he can do.

I like to measure with a cup
And shining measuring spoon.
I like to stir and stir and stir
While I hum a little tune.
    Of course, mother never sees
    That Mongon helps me, too.
    No one else sees Mongon.
    They don't know what he can do.

Some day I'll bake a cake
When I can read some more.
I'll measure and I'll stir it,
Then into the pan I'll pour.
    Of course, Mongon will help me.
    Expect we'll make it with a mix.
    He'll help me read directions.
    We'll be ready half-past-six.

LANGUAGE CONCEPTS

Imaginary creatures can have names.
Movements of people, animals, and things can be acted out.

1. Talk about helping at home.

   What are regular jobs?
   What are special ways to help?
   What jobs can be done without adult help?
   Does anyone have an imaginary playmate who helps?
   Did anyone ever have one? Tell about it.

2. Read "Mongon Helps." Explain that Mongon is an invisible playmate who is half monster and half dragon. He is never seen by adults, but he can be seen by children.
3. Copy the chorus of "Mongon Helps" on the chalkboard or on a chart. Practice reading it in chorus.

   Two students at a time can pantomime a stanza of "Mongon Helps." One can be *self* and one can be Mongon. Teacher reads the stanza and students act. The chorus joins in for the refrain.

   Two more students pantomime the next stanza. Continue through to the end of the selection.

   Some kind of costume designation for Mongon would be appropriate. It could be a big *M* to pin on.
4. Pantomime other experiences of home, such as

   getting out of bed
   putting on clothes
   tying shoes
   washing face
   combing hair
   brushing teeth
   eating breakfast

5. Ask for volunteers to pantomime other activities without telling what they are doing. Classmates can guess.

Example Eating an ice cream cone

get the ice cream from the freezer
get the cone from the cabinet
scoop the ice cream and put it on the cone
lick the ice cream
control the drips

drop some on the floor
clean up the mess

and so on, until guessed.

Just Playin'

Tom played he was a nurse
At the hospital close to us.
He gave the shots and served the meals,
Then ran to catch the bus.

Lena played she was president
Of our great U.S.A.
She broadcast loud on television
To cut taxes and increase pay.

Rico played that he sold real estate
And had houses and lots of land.
He made a number of sales today
With the help of his four-piece band.

Teresa played she was a dancer
In a glittering new ballroom.
The lights were low and the spotlight shone
On her sequins and ostrich plume.

LANGUAGE CONCEPTS

People communicate in many ways through many media.
Meanings change by voice inflection, rate of speaking, and other oral characteristics that do not show in print.

1. Play a game letting one person at a time act out a person at work. Let class members guess what is being done.
2. Read "Just Playin' " to the class. Discuss the work of parents and others. Write some additional stanzas for "Just Playin' " using the work of persons known to class members.
3. Copy each stanza on a card. On each card put the number of characters needed to act it out.

   Shuffle the cards well. Let some class members draw cards. They in turn choose characters and meet briefly to decide parts and what to do. Then they present the stanza to the class. Multiple copies of stanzas may be needed if additional ones were not developed before the game.

4. Make simple puppets for the characters. Let children take turns acting out their parts. Encourage them to use their own ideas and their own language as they let the puppets be

   a male nurse
   the president of the U.S.A.
   a real-estate salesman
   a dancer

   From this beginning some children might want to make other puppets and add stanzas to "Just Playin'."

City Workers

One city worker is putting up signs.
Two city workers are drawing street lines.
Three city workers are working on lights.
Four city workers are guarding historic sights.
Five city workers are collecting trash.
Six city workers are at an auto crash.
Seven city workers are putting out fires.
Eight city workers are replacing tires.
Nine city workers are cleaning the car fleet.
Ten city workers are policing the street.

LANGUAGE CONCEPTS

Everything has a name.
Movements of people, animals, and things can be acted out.
Meanings change by voice inflection, rate of speaking, and other oral characteristics that do not show in print.

1. Display "City Workers" on a chart or on the chalkboard. Read it with students. Notice the number progression and the rhyming couplets.

   Talk about work of city employees that may or may not be in the selection.
2. Ask for volunteers to act out some of the lines. Each group will have to have the number of people designated in the line selected.

   Give the groups time to plan

what they are going to say
who will say what
what props they will need
what actions they will use to best convey their work
whether they will use loud or soft voices
whether they will need one person for a boss

Groups act out their choices for others, who will be the audience.

3. Evaluate through class discussion the extent to which the actors used voice inflections, pitch, levels of sound, body movements, and facial expressions to be convincing about their work.

Ish Time

Fall came—
Ish time of the year.

I walked among the gold*ish* trees—
    the yellow golds,
    the brown*ish* golds,
    the green*ish* and
    even redd*ish* golds!

I skipped among the redd*ish* trees—
    the brown*ish* reds,
    the purpl*ish* reds,
  and sparkling, sparkling,
    bright, bold reds!

I hopped among the orangey trees and saw—
    pale yellow orange,
    brown*ish* orange,
    green*ish* orange,
  and bright, bright, redd*ish* orange!

I ran among the yellow trees and saw—
    the green*ish* yellows,
    the gold*ish* yellows,
  and sun-splashed, sparkling,
    bright bold yellows!

I strolled among the brown*ish* trees and saw—
the gold*ish* browns,
the green*ish* browns,
the black*ish* browns,
and redd*ish* browns!

I danced among the purpl*ish* trees and saw—
redd*ish* purples,
brown*ish* purples,
and dark, dark black*ish* purples!

I jumped among the green*ish* trees and saw—
pale yellow greens,
the brown*ish* greens,
the gold*ish* greens,
and darker, darker evergreens!

Fall came!
Ish time came!
The leaves came tumbling down!

I picked up leaves of many colors—
orangey speckled red and green,
redd*ish* speckled brown and gold,
yellow*ish* speckled brown and orange.

I tossed up—
green leaves with brown*ish* edges,
brown leaves with green*ish* edges,
yellow leaves with orangey edges,
and green*ish* leaves with yellow edges.

I looked at—
redd*ish* leaves with lines of brown,
gold*ish* leaves with lines of green,
and yellow leaves with lines of red.

I found a yellow*ish* leaf
trimmed with gold and red!
I kept a silver*ish* leaf
trimmed with red and purple.

Fall came!
Ish time came—
the yellow*ish*,
the redd*ish*,

the green*ish*,
the purpl*ish*,
the brown*ish*,
the silver*ish*,
the gold*ish!*

LANGUAGE CONCEPTS

Colors of things are described with words.
Movements of people, animals, and things can be acted out.
We perceive our own meanings from our experiences.

1. Show pictures, paintings, or colored slides of fall coloring in leaves. Talk about the feelings of fall and experiences that students have had relating to fall coloring.
2. Read "Ish Time" so students can get acquainted with the mood and the language.
3. Move to an area outside or inside so students will have space to move. Talk about the feel of being in a place with trees and fallen leaves. Imagine that you can feel the leaves on the ground. Imagine that you can look overhead at the array of color. Feel the abandon of playing in fallen leaves.
4. Change "I" to the names of students in the class. As you call the name, that student responds to the verb in the stanza.

   Ricardo walked . . . .
   Helen skipped . . . .
   Tom hopped . . . .

4. If space permits, let the whole class act out the verbs in a "fall dance" as the teacher or someone else reads "Ish Time."
5. Make a color slide record of the students acting out "Ish Time." They can take turns reading the stanzas onto a cassette tape to be played while the slides are shown. The show can be shared with other classes and then put in the school library for future use.

Independent Activities

Ish Dance

LANGUAGE CONCEPTS

People communicate in many ways through many media.
Language can be expressed in rhythmic patterns.

There are words for the many movements of people, animals, and things.
Movements of people, animals, and things can be acted out.

1. Choose a partner. One of you can read "Ish Time." The other can act it out.
2. Read "Ish Time" over and over to get the rhythmic pattern in it.
3. Make the rhythmic pattern into a dance.
4. Decide on movements for each stanza.
5. Use colored scarves or paper streamers with your dance.
6. Choose music to go with the dance.
7. Dance "Ish Time" for the class.

Show Me

LANGUAGE CONCEPTS

Meanings change by voice inflection, rate of speaking, and other oral characteristics that do not show in print.
Feelings of people and animals are described with words.
There are words for the many movements of people, animals, and things.

1. Make a list of statements of people's feelings and problems, such as I don't know.

Get out of my way!
That's terrible!
Don't hit me!
Could that be me?
I'm so ashamed.
I couldn't be happier!

2. Ask one or two classmates to pantomime the statements as you read them. Use your voice to help them with the meanings.
3. Take turns reading statements and acting them out.
4. With your friends, decide on the movement word that best describes each statement. It might be

shrug	jerk	shove
twist	cringe	hug

Mirror Acting

LANGUAGE CONCEPTS

People express their feelings and emotions through creative activities.
Movements of people, animals, and things can be acted out.

1. Select a partner.
2. Make facial movements, hand movements, and other movements as you face each other. Your partner mirrors the movements as you make them.
3. Change places and mirror your partner's movements as if you were looking at yourself in a mirror.

Paper Sack Plays

LANGUAGE CONCEPTS

Imagination promotes picturesque speech.
Words can be used for pleasure only.
People express their feelings and emotions through creative activities.

1. Fill a paper sack with several things that suggest a person doing something.

book	spoon	pills
pencil	money	dishrag
glove	nail	razor
envelope	needle	perfume

2. Choose three or four classmates to work with you.
3. Begin a story.
4. As you tell it, draw one thing from the sack.
5. Use this item to help portray a character in your story.
6. Pass the sack to the next classmate.
7. He or she draws an item from the sack and uses it to help portray a character in the story as he or she continues it.
8. Continue passing the sack until all articles are woven into your paper sack story.

A Clown Act

LANGUAGE CONCEPTS

We can use language for fun and nonsense.
People express feelings and emotions through creative activities.
Sounds are imitated and described with words.

Plan a puppet clown act.

1. Make miniature stick puppets of clowns.
2. Use a box for a car. Paste a picture of a car on the outside.
3. Invite an audience to watch your clown act.
4. As each clown comes out of the car

   make sound effects
   say something funny or sad for each clown
   let each clown tell what it does in the circus

Let's Make an Octopus

LANGUAGE CONCEPTS

People communicate in many ways through many media.
Movements of people, animals, and things can be acted out.

1. Choose four friends to help you.
2. Make a costume for an octopus out of an old sheet, butcher paper,

or newspapers. Tape it and crayon it. Remember that an octopus has eight tentacles.

3. Read "The Amorous Octopus" (p. 160) and decide on the motions you and your friends can make to pantomime the description given in the selection.
4. Let one be the reader and the other four the actors when you perform for your class.

Many Moods

LANGUAGE CONCEPTS

People communicate in many ways through many media.
Feelings of people and animals are described with words.

1. Make a stack of mood cards. Write on each one a word that expresses a mood.

Examples	afraid	sad	proud
	angry	anxious	lonesome
	troubled	wicked	pleased
	upset	happy	tearful

2. Choose friends to play with you.
3. Shuffle the mood cards and stack them face down.
4. Each player in turn draws a card and makes facial expressions to represent the mood. Other players decide whether or not the mood is acted out well enough.
5. The player keeps the card if he or she acted out the mood satisfactorily. If not, the card goes to the bottom of the stack.
6. The winner is the one with the most cards at the end of the game.

Rhyming Friends

LANGUAGE CONCEPTS

There are words for the many movements of people, animals, and things.
Many words rhyme with other words.

1. Act out something you do when you are playing.
2. Ask some friends to guess what you are doing.
3. Have someone act out something that rhymes with the first action.

Example swing/sing

4. Begin again with a third and fourth friend acting out two rhyming words.

Examples slide/ride ski/flee dive/drive

5. Keep score to see who can guess the most words.

Animal Party

LANGUAGE CONCEPTS

We can use language for fun and nonsense.
Movements of people, animals, and things can be acted out.

1. Choose three friends to play with you.
2. Elect one player the leader.
3. Act out an animal party. Here is a suggested procedure.

FIRST PLAYER:	I'm going to an animal party.
LEADER:	How are you going to get there?
FIRST PLAYER:	I'm going to hop like a rabbit. (*The player hops.*)
SECOND PLAYER:	I'm going to an animal party.
LEADER:	How are you going to get there?
SECOND PLAYER:	I'm going to hop like a rabbit and swing like a monkey. (*The player hops and swings.*)
THIRD PLAYER:	I'm going to an animal party.
LEADER:	How are you going to get there?
THIRD PLAYER:	I'm going to hop like a rabbit, swing like a monkey, and gallop like a horse. (*The player hops, swings, and gallops.*)

4. Each player in turn repeats what all the players before have said and done.
5. When a player misses, he or she is out of the act. The last one in is the star actor.
6. You may use any animal and its way of moving in your replies.

Chapter 10

The Viewing/Listening Center

What Is a Viewing/Listening Center?

A Viewing/Listening Center is a place

for listening to the voices of many people
for taping and listening to one's own voice
for listening to multiple languages
for expanding vocabularies and enriching meanings
for sharpening perception of the many ways people say things
for encountering new ideas without having to read and write
for providing common experiences for discussions

The Viewing/Listening Center does not require that participants be able to read and write. It promotes a high degree of success and interest. Children learn many things as they listen to stories and music recorded by many voices and view filmstrips, films, study prints, fine art prints, and other available materials.

Books with accompanying records should be available at all times. Children whose oral reading is halting and slow can learn to follow the print as they listen to models of good reading. Books and records can be provided in more than one language.

Tape recordings can be made of books that do not have commercially prepared records. The teacher, a parent, older children, or effective readers in the class can make tapes of stories and poems.

Children who write books can tape the stories and poems and place a copy in the Viewing/Listening Center so other children can hear the author's voice while following along with the reading.

Information that children cannot read independently but that is essential to understanding social studies and science can be put on tapes for the Viewing/Listening Center. The information might accompany sets of study prints, collections of magazine pictures, or sections from social studies or science textbooks.

Tapes made by the teacher can be used to give simple directions for activities children enjoy—activities involving body movement, visual scanning of the classroom, visual scanning of the outside, drawing with crayon, and fun and nonsense activities. Such activities assure success for all participants.

The Viewing/Listening Center should be considered a recreational center as well as a study center. A collection of filmstrips and study prints should be available for viewing with no assignments attached. Children who lack competence in the English language can enjoy this activity and profit from the exposure to new ideas.

Filmstrips without words printed on them should be available along with a tape recorder. Children can compose their own commentary to go with the filmstrips and then share it with the class.

A filmstrip collection of stories can serve for reading instruction. If no child in the class can read the filmstrip text effectively, older children can be asked to help. In their own classes the older children can practice correct pronunciation, enunciation, emphasis, pause, modulation of voice, and other oral reading techniques.

Visual materials, such as collections and artifacts that represent the ethnic background of some of the children, should be in the Viewing/Listening Center from time to time. Children can introduce the items during a discussion period and then make a tape to leave with the collection.

Fine art prints should be included as a continuing part of the Viewing/Listening Center. Local artists and teachers can provide tapes to accompany the paintings. Viewing and discussing fine art prints provides a basis for children to perceive their world in new ways and say new things about it. The perceptual skills inherent in the viewing and discussing are closely related to those inherent in reading and writing.

Visual materials accompanied by language lend themselves to the extension of vocabularies of names, color, size, shape, texture, and motion. They provide real experiences in the use of the language of contrast and comparison. They provide a basis for production of the same classes of words that are found often in reading materials.

The Viewing/Listening Center is usually in a specific place in the room. It must be near electric outlets. Audiovisual equipment and materials are a part of the resources required for effective operation. Some that are desirable, if not necessary, are

a record player and records
a tape recorder and tapes
a filmstrip projector
a movie projector
photographs and other study prints
fine art prints
a camera
an overhead projector
a continuing collection of pictures brought by pupils

Language Skills Developed and Practiced

The child improves speech patterns through imitation.
The child increases speed in oral reading by following models of good reading.
The child develops comprehension abilities through listening.
The child increases ability to follow directions for a variety of activities.
The child increases ability to listen to literature and music for specific purposes.
The child adjusts to the many ways people express their ideas using the same language.
The child listens to the same ideas expressed in two or more languages.
The child analyzes and evaluates his or her own speech production.
The child compares and contrasts experiences with those of others while listening and viewing.
The child extends creative writing interests and abilities by adding his or her own voice to published materials.
The child increases vocabulary by hearing names of people and things, words of motion, and words of description.

The child expands vocabulary by listening to and saying words never heard before.
The child develops unison reading skills when viewing projected filmstrips.
The child expresses his or her own interpretation of visual materials.

Group Activities

First Flight

The stewardess greets me as I board the jet.
Then I go to my seat by the window. You bet!

I fasten my seat belt and check knobs that I see
To find out how they work and how they can help me.

The light turns on bright and the air comes out cold.
A table to play on is somewhere, I'm told.

My seat can go back or go up very straight.
(Wish the pilot would hurry. It's a little bit late.)

At last our plane moves. Now we're going UP!
(Wish I could have brought along my new pup.)

The mountains grow smaller and look like to me
They are made of rows and rows of colored tepees—

Some yellow, some purple, some blue, some black—
So many colors I just can't keep track.

The roads on the mountains look like great long earthworms.
There's a lake! Next a river that turns, even squirms.

We're going up higher, and all that I see
Is a parade of clouds—all looking at me.

Two big shaggy poodles and a great giant snail
Fly by with a monster flapping his tail.

Oh, look out, Mr. Pilot! There comes a big cloud!
But he's not afraid. Into it he just plowed!

We're coming out now, so guess I won't fuss.
There's a tub full of bubble-bath clouds below us.

Look up! The sky's darker and bluer up high.
(Could you ever reach the top of the sky?)

There go three baby clouds on a blanket of blue.
There's a small dirty cloud. What did it find to do?

I can peek through that cloud and see mountains below.
Look how they're shirred with patches of snow.

Those canyons look like a giant elephant's toes.
There's a city down there with houses—rows, rows, and rows!

We're coming down now. Oh! I see Mom and Dad!
I can't wait to tell them about the ride I just had!

LANGUAGE CONCEPT

People use similes and metaphors to compare and contrast things and ideas.

1. Talk about figurative language.

similes—comparisons using *like* and *as* to show a commonality of quite dissimilar things
metaphor—a comparison very much like a simile, but without words such as *like* and *as*.
personification—the assignment of human attributes to inanimate objects.

Invite examples from students.

Read "First Flight" and ask students to listen for figurative language.

2. Tape "First Flight" for the Viewing/Listening Center so it will be ready for students to listen to and record some figurative language.

On a record sheet with the tape, enter three column headings.

Similes **Metaphors** **Personification**

As students play the tape, they jot down their interpretation of the figurative language.

3. Assign students to listen for figurative language

on TV
when talking to others
when listening to stories in the Viewing/Listening Center

What X-actly Did You Zee?

A careful investigation of all that **smashing** and **crashing** might reveal that it was almost everything from A to Z!

Or could I just think that I saw what I really didn't see?

Would you think me confused if I say I saw—

alligators acting like acrobats in the attic
or—
brontosauruses browning biscuits for breakfast
or—
caribou clicking castanets in Chinatown?

Maybe it was
deer driving ducks to disaster
and—
elephants eating eggs in elevators
and—
flamingos fabricating fiddles for frogs.

Could it be that I saw—
goats giggling at giraffes in the garage
and—
hens hissing harshly at horses?

I think what I really saw was—
ibexes imitating insects with incandescent ideas
and—
jackrabbits jumping joyfully toward Jupiter
and—
kudus kicking keyboards in kilts.

Maybe it wasn't all that, but—
leopards languishing lazily in laundromats
or—
mandrills manifesting magic with masks
or—quite possibly it was
Nobody noting nothing in notebooks!

If it wasn't that, I'm sure it could have been—
opossums operating organs for operas
or—
peacocks pleating petticoats for princesses
or—
rattlesnakes ripping roses off rostrums!

Could it have been—
squid swishing smartly in sweaters in the summertime
or—

turtles twisting tight tourniquets for turkeys on Thursday
or—
unicorns unlacing unsightly uniforms in unison?
If not all that, I'm certain that I saw—
vampires vaulting viciously over viaducts
and—
weasels waving weird welcomes with weapons.
That's **x-actly what I saw!**
X-cept perhaps . . .
yaks yanking yellow yams from yuccas
and I'm sure I saw
zebra zestfully zeroing in on the zodiac!!
Zound Zilly? Ziz!

LANGUAGE CONCEPTS

Alliteration is the use of two or more words together that begin with the same sound.

Descriptive words and phrases help make meanings clear.

There are words for the many movements of people, animals, and things.

1. Say a tongue twister students know. Ask them to respond with ones they know.
2. Read "What X-actly Did You Zee?" with expression. Make it both convincing and humorous.
3. Make a chart of animals from A to Z with space for students to add a descriptor and an action word beginning with the same letter as the beginning sound of the animal name. They will need to use dictionaries.

   ____
   anteater
   ____

   ____
   buffalo
   ____

4. Play games looking in indexes, dictionaries, and other reference material for key words that require knowledge of the alphabet letters in sequence. Notice which students have not mastered the use of the alphabet as a reference tool and play follow-up activities with them.

5. As a group, compose and record alliterative statements on any topic the students choose.
6. Choose a consonant and try to write a nonsense story using only words beginning with that letter. Allow a few function words to keep the story going.
7. Let students read "What X-actly Did You Zee?" into a tape recorder for listening experiences. It will be hilarious.
8. Talk about alliterative language and how it feels rolling off the tongue. Notice the use of alliteration in stories. It is a literary strategy many authors use.

When Can I Eat?

At 7:00 I saw a dove at the bird feeder.
At 8:00 I saw a dove and a quail at the bird feeder.
At 9:00 I saw a dove, a quail, and a wren at the bird feeder.
At 10:00 I saw a dove, a quail, a wren, and a finch at the bird feeder.
At 11:00 I saw a dove, a quail, a wren, a finch, and a woodpecker at the bird feeder.
At 12:00 I saw a cat at the bird feeder! All the birds flew away!
At 1:00 the dove came back to the bird feeder.
At 2:00 the quail came back to the bird feeder.
At 3:00 the wren came back to the bird feeder.
At 4:00 the finch came back to the bird feeder.
At 5:00 the woodpecker came back to the bird feeder.
At 6:00 I saw the dove, the quail, the wren, the finch, and the woodpecker at the bird feeder.
At 6:15 the cat came back! The dove, the quail, the wren, the finch, and the woodpecker FLEW AWAY IN A FLASH!

LANGUAGE CONCEPTS

The same language patterns are used over and over in writing.
Some symbols other than our alphabet communicate meaning.

1. Make or find a clock face for students to use when reading the selection "When Can I Eat?"
2. Read the first two stanzas and ask if anyone has an idea of the pattern. Do the ideas of an hour later and another bird come through to them?

3. Ask students to join in saying what they can. They can pause while you read the name of the new bird. They can repeat the stanza and include the new bird's name.
4. After the woodpecker has been introduced, let them be on their own to add other birds they know.
5. Introduce the cat, then begin the pattern of the birds returning.
6. Let children take the parts of the birds and the cat and act out the selection. Make name tags to pin on the characters. If possible, tape the language children use as they act out the selection.
7. Make a tape of "When Can I Eat?" for the Viewing/Listening Center. Encourage children to get well acquainted with the selection so they can use the pattern in other writing.
8. Play records or tapes of bird calls.
9. Let students add a second day to the tape.

   At 7:00 I saw a sparrow _________
   At 8:00 I saw a sparrow and a cardinal _________

Bill Henley and the Magic Bus

Something about the school bus reminded the children of a mischievous boy. Was it the blinking headlights that at times seemed to wink at those passing by? Was it the jumping skeletons that came out of the glaring red stop lights if a car came too close to the rear of the bus? Was it the very special seat belts that hugged one tight—but not too tight—or that occasionally pinched if someone got too frisky on the bus?

It was true that Bill Henley, the driver of School Bus Number 70, Happyville, not only was a very good driver with the best safety record in the state, but was also the most inventive mechanic in the state. Too, he was an amateur magician that performed at all the picnics, talent shows, and clubs of Happyville.

Some children and adults alike felt that Bill Henley combined all these talents when he worked on Bus 70 or when he drove it. If you watched him some days, you would almost believe the bus was driving itself. In fact, Bill often said, "I've got this bus so well trained that it could make this drive by itself." Of course, no one took the statement seriously—that is, none of the passengers. But deep down inside, the jolly school bus wished more than anything that a day would come when he could just try that. He knew that he could make the drive and deposit each small passenger just where Bill had taught him to stop. That was the day he dreamed about.

But the excellent driver never missed a day's work. Always he came right on time, dressed in his dark blue slacks and shirt freshly washed and ironed, bringing his broad grin, his magic laugh that was so catching, and his big brown mysterious eyes that seemed to see everything. Bill prided himself on his perfect safety record and he intended to keep it.

When anything went wrong with Bus 70, Bill talked to the bus as he worked with it just as if it were a child with a hurt knee. This pleased the children, for each one of them had a strong feeling for the bus. Somehow it was different from other buses and they knew it.

Inside the bus was the big surprise. Every seat was covered in a dark red material that looked and felt almost like velvet. Every piece of metal had been padded so that no child could be hurt on Number 70. The dashboard was covered with a tremendous number of small knobs and buttons. Each one seemed to be connected in some way to a large red heart-shaped knob.

Number 70 had not always been used to transport school children. Several years ago Happyville School District needed a bus. No one could figure out how they could buy one, for this was a little town and people in it had very little money. One night a bus and two cars collided not far from town. The Company officials who came to examine the wreck said that the bus was too damaged to ever run again. They gladly gave it to Bill just to get it off the highway, for it looked ready for the junk pile.

Bill brought his fine new tow truck to take the injured bus back to his garage. Week after week he worked to make it look as good as new. He carefully smoothed out the deep dents. He patched the badly worn upholstery. Night after night he worked on the strange-looking dashboard. When he worked on this, he always locked the garage doors so that no one knew exactly what the knobs and buttons were for. Some people said they were strictly for decoration. Some people said they were part of the weather conditioning on the bus. Others, who would not dare express their views openly for fear of being made fun of, felt that this was really the heart of the bus.

After months of hard work Bill announced, "Happyville will have transportation for its school children now."

All the community turned out to see the fine, new-looking bus.

"What comfortable seats!" said the women.

"My, that bus handles easily!" said the men.

"We love it," said the children.

Bill grinned with delight. His mysterious eyes took on a mischievous look as people asked him about the dashboard. "It's just a fancy part of my toy," was all Bill would say.

After the village streets were rolled up and all the children tucked into beds, Bill would take the bus out for long rides. Fanciful stories began to be heard about things the bus could do. One villager said, "I know I saw that bus flying close to the moon last night." Another said, "I'd swear that bus was driving itself when I saw it."

"Don't be silly! Next time you'll tell me it took the children home by itself!" said another.

"And I will!" came from somewhere near the garage of Bill Henley.

LANGUAGE CONCEPTS

We perceive our own meanings from our experiences.

Simple stories have a beginning, an elaboration of the beginning, and an ending.

Authors describe characters in ways that let readers form a mental image of them.

1. Read "Bill Henley and the Magic Bus" to the class. Put magic in your voice to make the characters come alive for the audience.
2. Ask students to list or tell all the descriptions of the bus they can remember from the reading.
3. Read the selection a second time. Add to the bus description list, then describe Bill Henley from what was heard in the story.
4. Work together to add a chapter to the story, or let volunteers continue with the story and then share their endings with the class.
5. If students have had experience riding a school bus, ask them to tell or write about those experiences. They can tape their stories and put them in the Viewing/Listening Center along with "Bill Henley and the Magic Bus." Their own stories might draw heavily on their imaginations.

Independent Activities

What Do You Hear?

LANGUAGE CONCEPTS

The words we say are written with the letters of the alphabet.

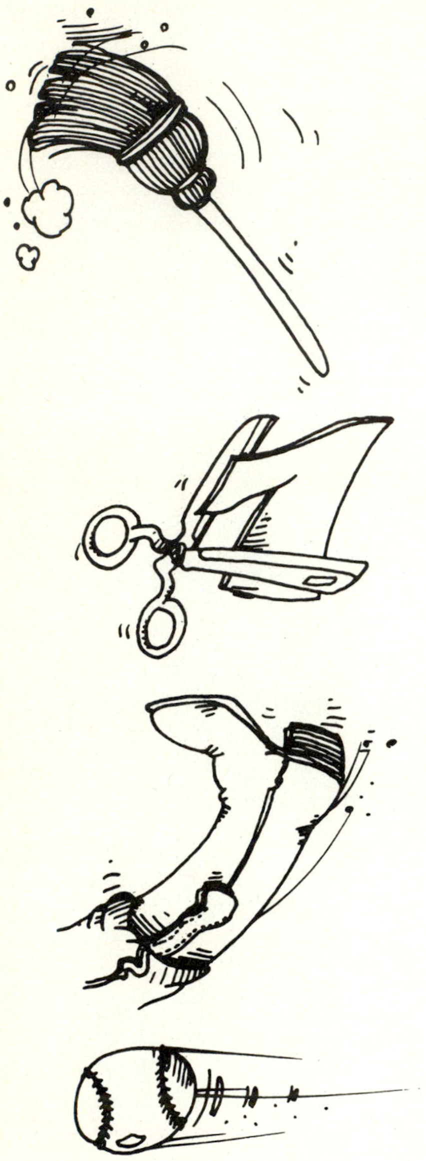

Any sound that can be spoken can be represented with letters of the alphabet.
New words can be created by anyone.

What sounds do the objects in the illustration make?

1. Make your own sound words for each object.
2. Use your own spelling. There is no correct way to spell words that represent sounds.
3. Illustrate some of the words.

Mother Goose in My Town

LANGUAGE CONCEPTS

Language can be expressed in rhythmic patterns.
Words can be used for pleasure only.
The same language patterns are used over and over in writing.
Many poets use unusual language to describe something usual.

1. Listen to a Mother Goose record or tape.
2. Recite or sing along with the recording to fix the pattern in mind.
3. Copy the first line of one of the rhymes.
4. Now continue it in your own words to express your own feelings.

Examples

Little Jack Horner sat in a corner
With thoughts about pollution.
He scratched his head once,
And said, "What a dunce!
I can't think of a good solution!"

There was a crooked man
Who worked in our fair city.
For the sick and needy there
The man had little pity.

I Like Music

LANGUAGE CONCEPTS

People communicate in many ways through many media.
Proper nouns begin with a capital letter.
Titles are used to tell the main idea of a production.

1. Listen to recordings of musical selections.
2. Choose one you like very much.
3. Write the name of your choice on the I Like Music chart.*
4. Find out how capital letters are used in titles.

I Heard Music

LANGUAGE CONCEPTS

People communicate in many ways through many media.
People communicate by speaking and writing in sentences.
Words can be used for pleasure only.

1. Listen to a recording with or without words.
2. Find the title of the recording in the I Heard Music book or make a new page for the title of your recording.*
3. Write one or more sentences about what you heard that would make others want to listen to it.

Imaginary Walk

LANGUAGE CONCEPTS

The same picture suggests different words or ideas to different people.
Descriptive words and phrases help make meanings clear.
Imagination promotes picturesque speech.
There are words for the many movements of people, animals, and things.

1. Choose a picture from a magazine or from a collection of fine art prints.†
2. Imagine that you are taking a walk into the picture.

* *To the teacher:* Provide a large piece of chart paper for children to record their favorite selections. At times, let them tell why they selected the ones they list on the chart.

† *To the teacher:* Prepare a book with the titles of music recordings available in the Viewing/Listening Center. Make a page for each title. Encourage children to make written statements after they listen. Add blank pages for new titles.

3. Talk about your walk into a tape recorder or write about it.
4. Remember that you have five senses and that there are words to describe

   what you see
   what you hear
   what your feelings are when you touch
   what you smell
   what you taste

5. Share your imaginary walk with friends.

Bird Calls

LANGUAGE CONCEPT

Sounds are imitated and described with words.

1. Listen to a record of bird calls.
2. Listen for the calls of the

dove	finch
quail	woodpecker
wren	

3. Put the calls down in words or syllables as nearly as you can. One dove seems to say, "Who cooks for you?"
4. Learn the calls and say them as you and your friends read "When Can I Eat?"

What a Contrast!

LANGUAGE CONCEPTS

People communicate in many ways through many media.
The same picture suggests different words or ideas to different people.
Antonyms are words that have opposite meanings.

---

* *To the teacher:* Collect pictures for the Viewing/Listening Center that children can relate to and talk about as if they were actually in them. Try some abstract paintings to heighten imagination.

1. Look at an art print.*
2. Study the contrasts used by the artist, as in the use of large and small areas, cool and warm colors, and lights and darks.
3. After studying the art print, talk about it to the class or to a small group. Point out the importance of contrast in art.
4. Look for contrast in designs all around you—in fabrics, woven patterns, book covers, and other decorated things.

Folk Songs

LANGUAGE CONCEPTS

Language can be expressed in rhythmic patterns.
The same language patterns are used over and over in writing.

1. Choose a favorite folk song.
2. Listen to the words and the rhythm.
3. Tap out the rhythm with your fingers or your feet.
4. Try to write another stanza for the folk song that has the same rhythm as the other stanzas. The new stanzas can be another beginning, another ending, or it can be used in the middle of the folk song.

Trifold Listening

LANGUAGE CONCEPT

Simple stories have a beginning, an elaboration of the beginning, and an ending.

1. Listen to a story.
2. Review it and make notes on the beginning, the climax, and the ending.
3. Write your answers to the questions that are on the trifold in the Viewing/Listening Center and put them in the pockets.†

---

* *To the teacher:* Fine art prints are available in many public libraries, school collections, art books, and sections of children's encyclopedias. Some should be placed in the Viewing/Listening Center for children to enjoy and study.

† *To the teacher:* Prepare a trifold with pockets at the bottom of each section to hold pupil responses.

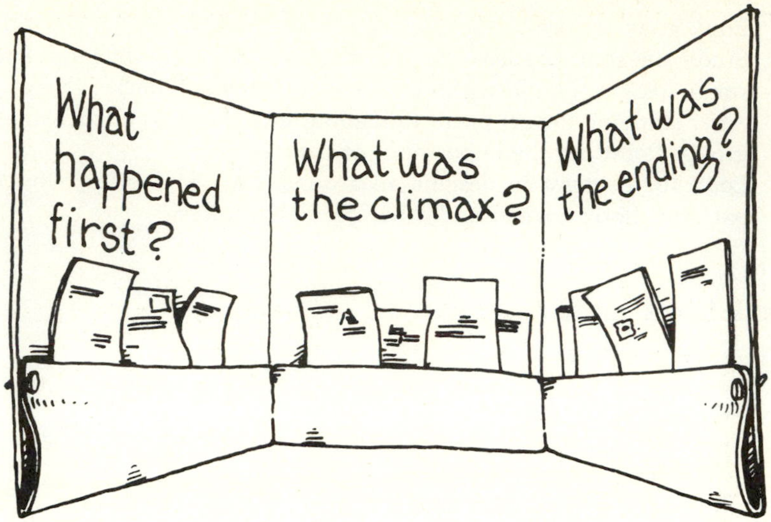

My Own Slides

LANGUAGE CONCEPTS

Abstract forms may suggest ideas that can be expressed in words.
People express feelings and emotions through creative activities.
Imagination promotes picturesque speech.

1. Cut oak tag into squares the size of slides for your projector. Use an art knife or a razor blade to cut the center openings. Two squares are needed for one slide.
2. Cut clear plastic squares just a bit larger than the inside square. Two squares are needed for one slide.
3. Put bits of colored cellophane between the plastic squares for an abstract design, or draw designs with permanent markers on the plastic squares, or do a combination of both.
4. Put the plastic squares between the frames and put tape around the edge.
5. Project your slide for others to see.
6. Talk with your classmates about the slide. Discuss your feelings, your impressions, and your artistry in combining color, shape, and line.

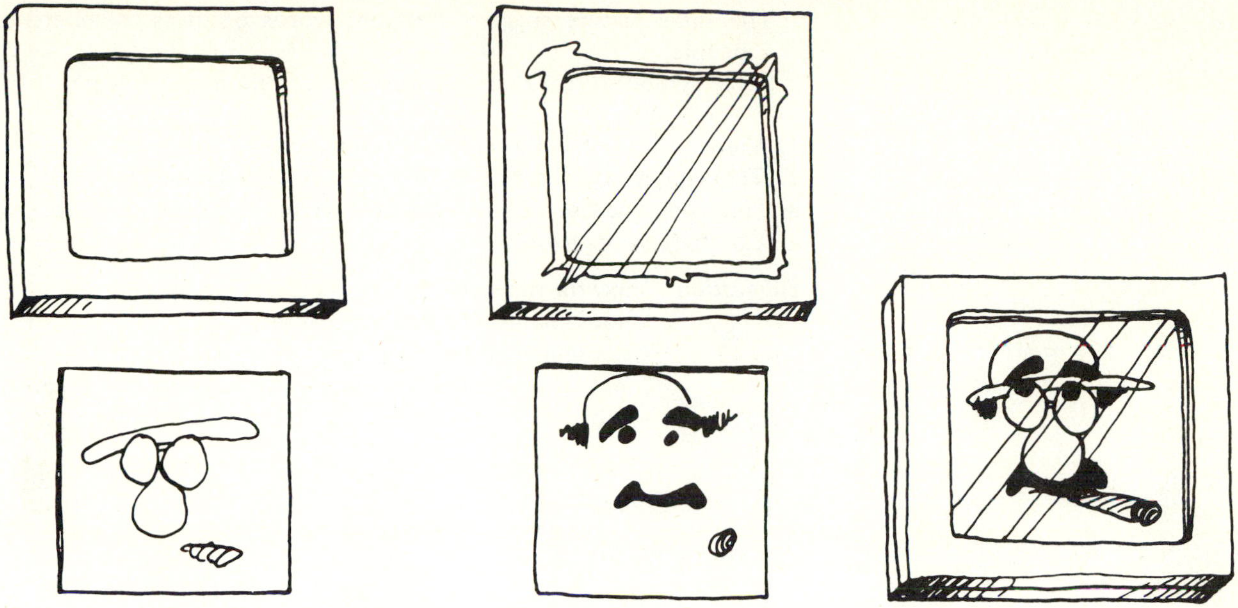

Listening for Rhyming Words

LANGUAGE CONCEPTS

Many words end with the same sound and symbol.
Many words rhyme with other words.

1. Listen to records of songs.
2. Write down the ending sound when you hear two or more words that rhyme.
3. Listen to the song enough times to remember the words that go with the endings. Write them down.
4. Put your list in the Writing Center for use in writing rhyming poetry.

Filmstrip Stories

LANGUAGE CONCEPTS

People communicate some information in sequence.
A sequence of pictures can tell a story without words.

The same picture suggests different words or ideas to different people.
Some symbols other than our alphabet communicate meaning.

1. View a filmstrip without words printed on it.
2. Tell a story into the tape recorder to go with the filmstrip.
3. Find someone else who has told a story for the same filmstrip.
4. Compare your stories.

Suggestion View the filmstrip rapidly once.
Choose names for the characters.
Choose names for the places.
Make a list of words you might want to use in your story.

My Own Clicks

LANGUAGE CONCEPTS

Stories and poems can grow out of real experiences.
Stories and poems can grow out of imagination.

1. Look through your family's collection of color slides and choose a series of slides with people or animals in them.
2. Write a real story or an imaginary story to go with the slide series.
3. Tape your story, using a special sound, such as a knock, to indicate that the next slide is to be projected.

What's the Title?

LANGUAGE CONCEPTS

We perceive our own meanings from our experiences.
We can describe things without telling their names.
Titles are used to tell the main idea of a production.

1. Find a picture that you like in a magazine.
2. Cut it out and mount it attractively.
3. Write titles for the picture:

Examples

one-word title	"Victory"
two-word title	"Marcus Wins"

three-word title	"A Proud Winner"
Can you go to four?	"_______ _______ _______ _______"

A Mood Picture

LANGUAGE CONCEPTS

Abstract forms may suggest ideas that can be expressed in words.
People express their feelings and emotions through creative activities.
New words can be created by anyone.

1. Collect ten or more pieces of paper of different shapes and colors.
2. Put them on a piece of construction paper that is at least 8½ in. by 11 in.
3. Listen to a musical recording.
4. As you listen, move the pieces of paper to show how the music makes you feel: rearrange them, overlap them, discard them, and contrast them.
5. When the music stops, paste down the design if it pleases you. If not, leave the pieces of paper for someone else.
6. Make up a word to describe your design and display it in the classroom.

Chapter 11

The Test-taking Center

What Is a Test-taking Center?

A Test-taking Center is a place

where students have continuous contact with the processes required for taking tests

to establish positive attitudes on the part of the teacher and students toward test-taking procedures

to introduce and make meaningful at the operational level vocabulary used in testing

to clarify special meanings of words used in testing situations: *check, letter, circle*

to demonstrate and practice processes found frequently in standardized tests

to practice in a gamelike, nonthreatening environment those procedures used most often in testing—especially those used in reading achievement tests

to identify students who need special and careful instruction in test-taking procedures so they can reflect what they really know

to identify the major categories of content in standardized tests —especially reading achievement tests—and provide ongoing activities that familiarize students with those processes

Instruction in test-taking inspires a guilt feeling in many teachers. They avoid this one language experience that is continuous and critical throughout the school life of students. Yet there are certain oracy and literacy skills and abilities in test taking that are not inherent in any curriculum area except by implication. Test taking is a valid language experience for instructional programs, and it is becoming increasingly significant in the lives of teachers as well as of students.

Much attention is given to the development of a sight vocabulary of words of highest frequency and to expanding reading vocabularies. Little, if any, attention is given to the development of an understanding of words that occur frequently in test directions. Examples of words that appear frequently are

start	mark	equal	left-hand corner
stop	letter	same	underline
circle	copy	right	choose
line	check	bottom	alike
sound	seconds	sort	different
picture	minute	draw	word
next	syllable	drew	
first	middle	put	
beginning	ready	finish	
end	score		

These words, in a test-taking context, should and must become natural in the teaching/learning vocabulary if students are to understand clearly standardized test directions. They should be used regularly in class group demonstrations. Students should repeat the words and show that they understand what they mean. Activities like the ones that follow can be prepared on transparencies and projected on the chalkboard. Students can come to the chalkboard and

mark
check
underline
circle

They can find words that are

alike
same

different
on the right
on the left
at the end
in the middle
at the beginning

They can point to the

upper left-hand corner
first
bottom

They can indicate that they understand the concept of

letter
syllable
word
ready
finish
seconds
minutes

All the above words are found frequently in directions for standardized tests. The administrator of tests must use them.

Mary may think that *mark* is a boy's name.
Jon may think that *check* means money.
Juanita may think that *left* is not to go.
Tanya may think that *letter* means mail.

These students have a built-in difficulty in taking tests that has nothing to do with knowing the content of the test items. Students who are going to take standardized tests regularly deserve to bring test-taking meaning to words that appear frequently and that hold in them success or failure in the testing situation.

Just as certain words relating to testing appear over and over, some categories of items appear over and over in standardized tests for reading. Some of the categories are

Visual memory
Word detail—matching

Word matching in context
Classification
Letter copying
Sound matching—alliteration
Blending
Sight vocabulary
Rhyming
Contractions
Compounds
Vocabulary
Decoding
Affixation
Syllabication
Comprehension

Successful response to the items in the tests does not require verbatim oral reading, yet oral reading is the experience that consumes most of the time and is given the major emphasis in most elementary classrooms. The above categories, which are not verbatim oral reading activities, relate directly to basic language concepts required of every person who reads and writes with a degree of independence. They cannot and must not be ignored if students' progress toward literacy is to be reflected by standardized tests.

Activities dealing with basic understanding of the above categories are included in the Test-taking Center. They are combined into group and independent activities. The concepts are demonstrated, illustrated, and repeated in group situations. Many of the activities have independent and small-group segments that can be placed in a Test-taking Center for review, practice, and mastery.

Group and Independent Activities

Visual Memory

LANGUAGE CONCEPT

Replicating information requires attention to details.

Play visual memory games with large cards or transparencies.

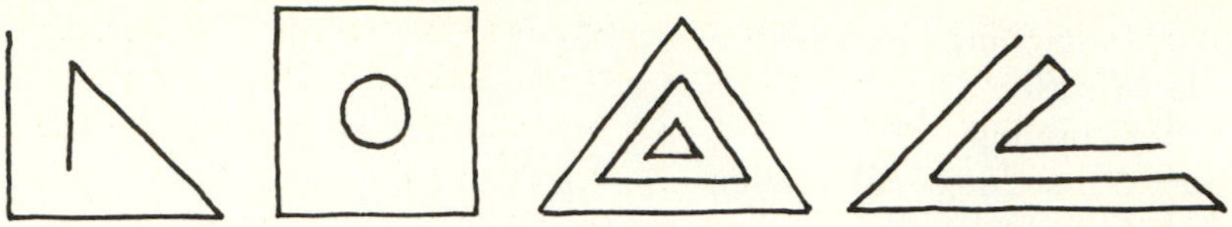

1. Make designs of increasing complexity.
2. Flash the designs with a timer—60 seconds, 30 seconds, 15 seconds, then get down to 1 second.
3. Children reproduce the designs on paper or on chalkboards. Individual chalkboards are good for this type of activity.
4. Check for accuracy, but do not create a threatening situation.
5. Make sets of cards for small-group work in the Test-taking Center.

Word Detail—Matching

LANGUAGE CONCEPTS

Some words occur frequently in our language.
The same words are spelled the same way wherever they appear.

1. Find the same words several times in newspapers, magazines, and dittoed stories that can be marked.
2. Make games like Word Hunt Game. Put three to five words of highest frequency on a card. Use the lists in Appendixes A and B. Find the words in the material furnished. Tally the number of times found.

the	than
them	house
then	horse
this	said

Matching in Context

LANGUAGE CONCEPTS

A few words in a story can carry most of the meaning.
Some words occur frequently in our language.

1. Duplicate stories and poems that have words that are repeated—especially words that are used as nouns, verbs, adjectives,

and adverbs. Use selections from group activities in Learning Centers. Duplicate selections such as "More and More Clowns" in the Reading/Research Center. Ask students to *underline, mark,* and *circle.* Use the vocabulary of testing.

2. Use duplicated stories for oral reading practice. Go through and mark the words in noun and verb positions. Read only the marked words. Read the words in noun slots that have a determiner to mark them. Read the words in noun slots that have a preposition to mark them. Notice that the nouns in prepositional phrases are not the subject of the sentence. "So Nosey Was His Name" in the Writing Center and "Click! Click! Click!" in the Reading/Research Center are good examples.

Matching Games

LANGUAGE CONCEPTS

Many words have more than one meaning.
Many words rhyme with other words.
Many words begin with the same sound and symbol.

1. Provide matching games. Many are available commercially, and they are easy to make.
2. Demonstrate with the large group before placing the games in the Test-taking Center. Games should deal with

color
shape
design
words alike but in different print
phrases
rhymes
alike beginnings
capital and lower-case letters
common endings
same number of syllables in words

Examples

Color

Make sets of color cards. Have four cards with hues of the same color.

Players choose one color and get a master card of red, green, blue, yellow, or any color for which there is a set of cards. On the reverse side is the list of the four words that make a set.
The leader calls the color words. The players ask for the card. When the player has four cards, the answers are checked on the reverse side. If they are correct, the player keeps them. If not, the cards are returned to the leader and the player gets a new master card.

Red	**Green**	**Blue**
rose	olive	sky
pink	avocado	sapphire
cherry	lime	ocean
cardinal	pea	navy
maroon	chartreuse	turquoise

Rhyming Pairs

Make sets of cards with rhyming pairs. Children arrange them in sets that rhyme. A reader can call the words for groups that do not have independent readers.

ant	mother	dish
pair	can't	curl
house	fly	brother
red	bare	joy
one	read	mouse
fish	two	sky
boy	free	bed
hair	pear	seed
three	sun	
girl	few	

Alike Beginnings

Each student has a small chalkboard or a blank sheet of paper. The teacher calls out a word and the students write another word with the same beginning sound. The teacher then says, "Everybody show." Students hold up their responses for the teacher to scan visually and respond. When appropriate, students can be the leader.

Classification Games

LANGUAGE CONCEPTS

Some words occur frequently in our language.
Some things have several names.

Provide plenty of classification games. The ability to classify is one that is on the majority of tests of reading/language.

1. Make a transparency or chart of 100 nouns of highest frequency. See Appendix B.
2. Project the list on the chalkboard or display it in front of a discussion group.
3. Choose a classification such as

   people pets food

4. Mark all the words in that class.
5. Put those words on cards.
6. Make boxes with the classification labels.
7. Children sort the cards and put them in appropriate boxes. Some cards might go in more than one box. Make the game self-checking by listing on the bottom of the box the words that fit that classification.
8. Add other noun words from time to time until the activity contains 200 nouns of highest frequency.
9. Work for 100 percent mastery *at sight* of the nouns of highest frequency. This is an essential ability for success in literacy and in taking tests at the beginning level.

Letter Copying

LANGUAGE CONCEPT

Reproduction of simple letter forms and letter sequences in words is basic to reading and writing.

1. Make transparencies with letters on them that can be flashed on a screen or chalkboard.
2. Children reproduce the letter or letters they see in the flash. Teacher says, "Everybody show," and students show their results for visual screening.

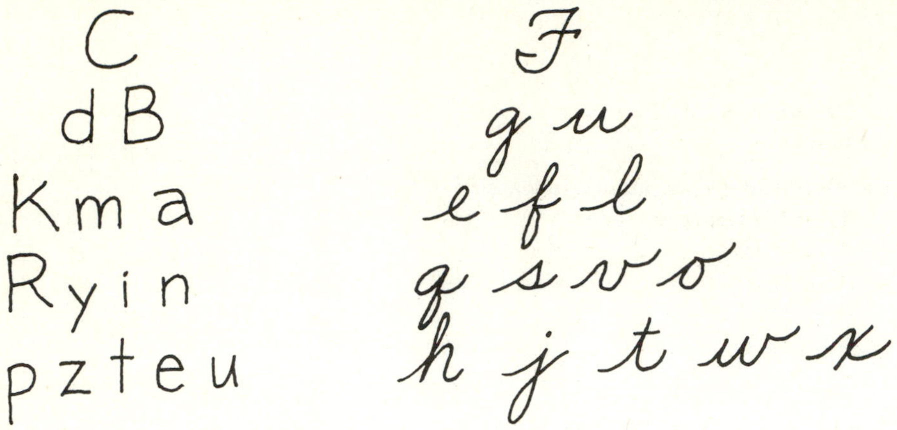

3. Increase the number of letters flashed from one to five in a sequence. Use letters that do not make a known word. Increase beyond five for older students. Use manuscript and cursive writing.

Alliteration

LANGUAGE CONCEPTS

Many words begin with the same sound and symbol.

Alliteration is the use of two or more words together that begin with the same sound.

1. Say and sing alliterative selections: "What X-actly Did You Zee?" in the Listening/Viewing Center; "The Twelve Jugglers" in the Writing Center; "Alphabet Pyramids" in the Language Study Center; "Feed the Animals" in the Language Study Center; tongue twisters known by students and teachers.
2. Locate and say the words that begin with the same sound and/or symbols. Notice the difference in consistency of vowels and consonants in initial positions of words.
3. Say and write alliterative statements to internalize initial sound/sight relationships. Mastery of these relationships is essential for literacy.
4. Play alliterative games. Make a set of five or more cards with names of animals, insects, vehicles, people, food, or other

classifications. Turn the cards down and draw in turns. Give points for the following:

one point for reading the name correctly
two points for adding a word that describes the name with an alliterative word
three points for adding two alliterative words to the name
four points for adding three alliterative words to the name
rat
red rat
red rat running
red rat running rapidly

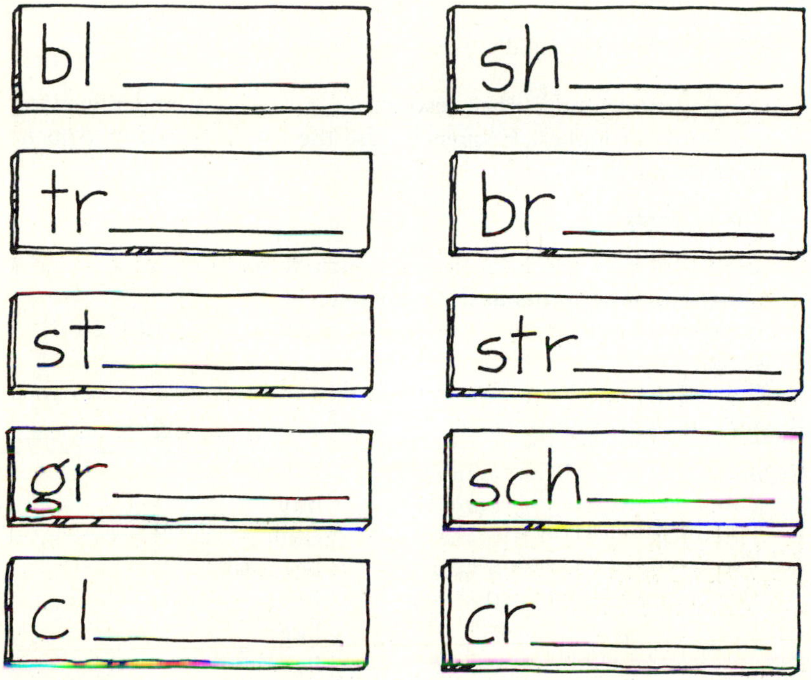

Blending

LANGUAGE CONCEPT

Consonants are sometimes blended together to represent a sound different from that of any of the single letters.

1. Demonstrate the difference in the sound of any of the single letters as contrasted with the sounds represented by the blends.
2. Provide word cards with basic consonant blends for making games. Students can collect words with different blends and make lists for practice in the Test-taking Center. They can collect words from stories and poems they write and read. In this way they conceptualize that "blending" is a characteristic of everybody's language.

High-frequency Vocabulary

LANGUAGE CONCEPT

Some words occur frequently in our language.

1. Develop games and other resources for repeating and reviewing the words of highest frequency. Use the lists featured in Appendixes B and C.

Fifteen Words

Select fifteen words from the lists. Include some nouns and verbs along with descriptors and determiners.
Students write as many sentences as possible with just the fifteen words.
The activity can be increased to twenty and twenty five words as students gain confidence.

Example

animal (s)	I
baby	buy
horse	could
a (an)	beautiful
the	my
is	like
called	have
died	

I have a horse.
I have a beautiful horse.
I have a beautiful baby horse.
I could buy an animal.
My animals died.

My horse died.
My baby horse died.
My beautiful baby horse died.
My baby is beautiful.
The baby is beautiful.
My horse is beautiful.
I called my beautiful baby horse.

2. Work for 100 percent mastery of the words of highest frequency. Keep them on display for ready reference in the Writing Center, where students will be spelling.
3. The 500 words on the lists of the 200 nouns of highest frequency and the 300 words of highest frequency will include 65 to 70 percent of all the words students will read in elementary school texts, exclusive of proper names. They need to inventory their progress toward mastery from time to time. If they do not master these words by the end of the third grade, they may be remedial readers for the remainder of their lives. *They must be able to read, write, and spell these words.*

Rhyming

LANGUAGE CONCEPTS

Many words end with the same sound and symbol.
Rhyming is the use of two or more words that end with the same sound.

1. Read rhyming poetry with students. Let them predict the rhyming word and then check out the prediction. Use selections from other Learning Centers: "I Like" from the Arts and Crafts Center; "Tongue Tinglers" from the Cooking Center; "I Move" from the Dramatization Center; "Quick Couplets" from the Writing Center; "Limericks" from the Writing Center.
2. Sing songs with rhyming patterns. Look at the spelling of the rhyming words.
3. Say a word and let students respond with any word that rhymes.
4. Substitute new rhyming words in poetry patterns.
5. Put word cards in the Test-taking Center for small groups of children to use to say rhyming words.

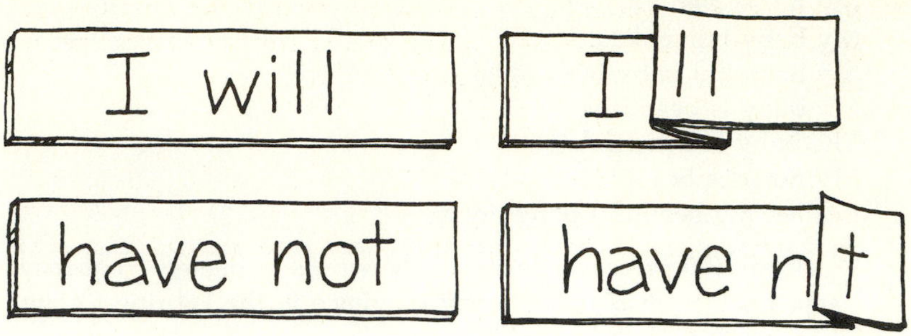

Contractions

LANGUAGE CONCEPT

Contractions are two or more words shortened and joined with an apostrophe to show that the sounds and letters are missing.

1. Demonstrate how we shorten language when we talk.
2. Show how the contracted language is printed.

I'll for I will	didn't for did not
he'll for he will	wouldn't for would not
she'll for she will	shouldn't for should not
haven't for have not	

3. Hunt for contractions in stories. Note that most contractions are found within quotation marks because they represent a person's speech.
4. Do the "I'm a Contractor" activity in the Language Study Center.
5. Make contraction cards that fold to hide the missing letter or letters. Place them in the Test-taking Center for practice.

Compounds

LANGUAGE CONCEPT

Compound words are two or more words combined into one.

1. Demonstrate how to compound words. *Butter* and *candle* are good ones to find in a dictionary. They are compounded with many other words.
2. Hunt for compound words in stories. Talk about how meanings of single words change as they are joined with other words.

3. Make cards of words that are found in several compound words and let children in the Test-taking Center say compound words that include the word on each card.

Examples fly under
pea over
milk

4. Look around the classroom to find compound words that can be observed.

Examples chalkboard bookcase
doorknob buttonhole

Vocabulary

LANGUAGE CONCEPTS

Descriptive words and phrases help make meanings clear.
There are words for the many movements of people, animals, and things.
Everything has a name.

1. Practice vocabulary expansion by saying synonyms, antonyms, and homonyms. Activities are in the Language Study Center.

   Synonyms—"Kangaroo Words"
   Antonyms—"The Opposite Pocket" and "Antonym Train"
   Homonyms—"Two-faced Words" and "Homonym Hunt"

2. Show a picture. Name it with one word, with two, and with three.
3. Take word walks around the classroom and outside. Look for hues of one color, for repeating shapes, for things that move, for things that begin with the same letter of the alphabet, for different textures, and so on.

Examples	**Color—Brown**	**Shape—Rectangle**	**Movement**
	buff	books	shake
	beige	tables	wave
	chocolate	window panes	fly
	coffee	doors	bounce
	rust	chalkboard	roll
		tablet	swish
		bulletin board	run
			walk
			skip

Summer
Summer Scene
A Picnic Spot

Decoding

LANGUAGE CONCEPTS

Any sound that can be spoken can be represented with letters of the alphabet.

Some syllables appear over and over in the language.

1. Create games for decoding nonsense words that illustrate abilities emphasized in instruction. Demonstrate the pronunciation of nonsense words as a means of testing decoding skills.

Examples

Initial Consonants

boken	soven
hupe	wibel

Blends

bleck	stame
trish	gratch

Prefixes

rewost	enpoce
unflod	preluzz

2. Place nonsense word games in the Test-taking Center.
3. Make lists of known words. When a child misses one as a sight word, sound it out using strategies that have been taught. *Talk the procedure* to clarify the thinking process involved in analysis. Keep the learning environment nonthreatening. Encourage students to take risks.
4. Plan decoding demonstrations for total group participation. Illustrate the thinking processes of analysis over and over. Use the vocabulary that is common in decoding instructions on tests students will take. Choose words and strings of words from the student's own writing to illustrate decoding strategies.
5. Choose high-frequency phonograms. Contrast the initial sound with beginning consonants and blends. Add appropriate endings to make as many words as possible.

Example

-at	cat	fat
	cats	gnat
	catty	sat
	bat	

Some High-frequency Phonograms

at	en	in	ook	un
an	ell	ill	ot	ug
am	et	ing	ow	ut
all	ed	ight	old	uff
ay	ent	it	oy	

Syllabication

LANGUAGE CONCEPTS

Some syllables appear over and over in the language.
Words have a different number of syllables or beats.
Language can be expressed in rhythmic patterns.

1. Say words and let children repeat them as they clap the number of syllables.

school	potato	umbrella
thought	Miranda	today

   Write the words on the chalkboard and point out that the number of letters in a word has little to do with the number of syllables.
2. Choose one vowel at a time. Let children find that vowel in their writing and/or dictation. Ask them to select the letters that go with that vowel to make a syllable.
3. Choose a one-syllable word. Let children suggest related words that add one syllable at a time.

1	man	1	horse
2	father	2	stallion
3	gentleman	3	thoroughbred

   Put each set of words on cards for the Writing Center. Suggest the value of these lists when writing poetry with syllabic-control patterns.
4. Have children take their own writing selections and list

   all the one-syllable words
   all the two-syllable words
   all the three-syllable words

5. Choose a high-frequency syllable such as *-an*. Read a selection and mark that syllable every time it occurs.

Rules of syllabication that might be derived from activities

Divide compound words between the component words.
Divide between the consonants when two consonants are preceded by a short vowel.
When a word has a suffix, divide between the word and the suffix.
When there is a single consonant sound spelled with double letters, between two vowels, divide between the double letters.
When there is a single consonant between two vowels, the first of which is short and stressed, divide after the consonant.
When there is a single consonant between two vowels, the first of which is long, divide before the consonant.

The greatest spelling difficulty that pupils encounter is caused by the *schwa* sound that appears in unaccented syllables. The original vowel sounds of such syllables have been obscured over a period of time, but their spelling remains.

Affixation

LANGUAGE CONCEPTS

Many words begin with the same sound and symbol.
Some are prefixes.
Many words end with the same sound and symbol.
Some are suffixes.

1. Make lists of words with prefixes and suffixes. Let children mark the root words.

rewrite	darkness
darken	tallest
unknown	decode
brighter	worthless

   Ask students to look for prefixes and suffixes in stories that they write.
2. Choose a root word and change its function (form class) by changing its suffix.

tight	(adjective)
tightness	(noun)
tighten	(verb)
tightly	(adverb)

3. Derive many words from the same root word by adding affixes.

load	reloading	unloading
reload	reloaded	unloaded
unload	reloads	unloads

script	description
prescription	transcript
scripture	describe

4. Look for suffixes that change form-class words.

-ize forms verbs
-ity forms nouns
-less forms adjectives
-ly forms adverbs

5. Develop generalizations about spelling and suffixes.

When a suffix begins with a vowel, a final *-e* is deleted from the root (nerve/nervous), and a final *-y* is changed to *-i* (mystery/mysterious).
When a root word ends in a final consonant spelled with a single letter, the letter is doubled before a suffix beginning with a vowel is added (drug/druggist).

Comprehension I

LANGUAGE CONCEPTS

Understanding and following directions helps one solve problems.
Understanding directions requires reading for details.

1. Demonstrate comprehension-question answering.

read short statements
ask a question
flash on the chalkboard from a transparency four responses: one that is ridiculous, one this is not possible but related, and two that are possible, but only one of which is correct
go through the logical reasoning process with students
let children *circle*, *underline*, or *mark* the correct response

Example It was spring in Plymouth. The winter had been a hard one. Many people had died. Those who were left were getting ready to plant gardens.

Jonathan and Mark were working near the church. All at once Jonathan whispered to Mark in a low, frightened voice, "Indians!"

Read these statements and mark an X in the box with the number of the correct answer.

1. Jonathan and Mark were glad to see the Indians.
2. Winter was a happy time in Plymouth.
3. Indians taught Jonathan and Mark how to plant their garden.
4. Jonathan and Mark were afraid.

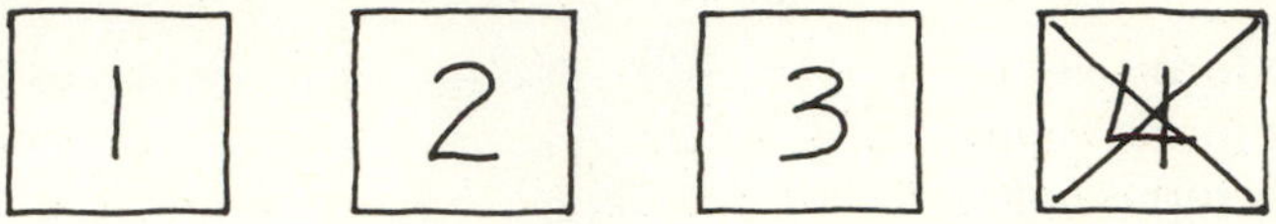

2. Build in the logical thinking process. Talk it, demonstrate it, practice it. It is a language skill required for test taking that is not automatic in general language development.

   Put short selections like those found in tests on cassettes for the Test-taking Center. Ditto answer sheets for small groups to use as they listen and respond. Provide a self-checking system.

   Practice is the goal—not rightness!

   Study the procedures required for the standardized tests the children take. Do the directions use words or phrases like *circle*, *underline*, or *mark an X?* Use that language.

Example The first settlers in Plymouth were called "pilgrims" because they left their homes in England to find a place where they could be free to worship in their own way.

When the pilgrims sailed for America they didn't know what would happen to them. They were willing to start new lives in a strange land where they could worship in their own way.

Choose the correct answer and circle the number in the box.

1. The Pilgrims didn't want to have to pay to worship.
2. America was a friendly land for the Pilgrims.
3. The Pilgrims wanted to worship in their own way.
4. The Pilgrims returned to their homes in England.

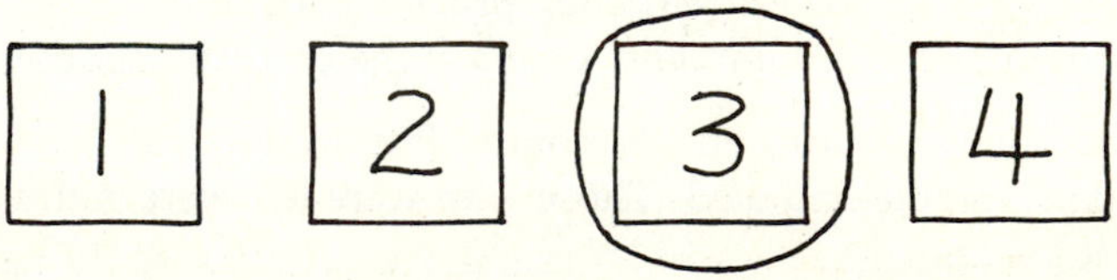

3. Children who write stories can write comprehension questions to accompany them. The questions can be duplicated and placed with the story in the Test-taking Center. Answers can be placed in a box for the author to read and correct.

Example

The Mysterious Turtle

Once there was a mysterious turtle. Well, one day the turtle was walking very slowly down the bumpy road. There was a camouflaged goat sitting on a log near the lagoon. All of a sudden the mammoth goat came right up to the turtle and stopped.

The turtle said, "Please move out of the way so I can go on my journey."

The goat refused to move. So the turtle sat and sat. The stubborn goat was still there and wasn't ready to move. Just then the turtle had an extraordinary idea. He had a scary bell in his house. He shook his house and made the bell ring. The goat got afraid of the spooky noise the bell made. He ran for the lagoon and jumped in. The turtle could then continue on his journey.

Use a pencil to fill in the space beneath the number of the correct answer.

1. The turtle met his good friend, the goat, in the camoflaged lagoon.
2. The turtle had a secret way to make a noise in his house.
3. The goat did not let the turtle continue on his journey.
4. The turtle promised the goat a gift if he would let him pass by.

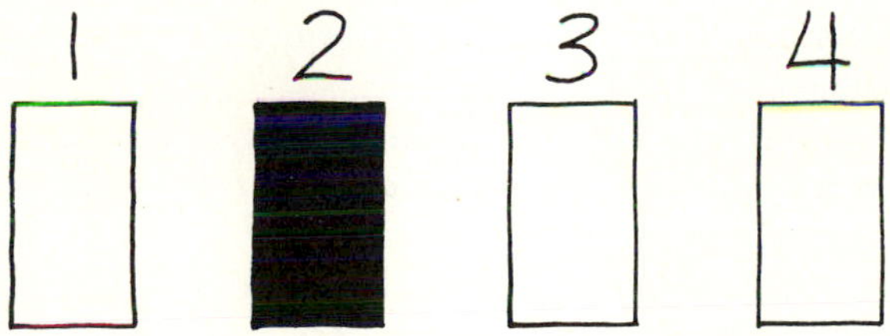

1. The goat was stubborn.
2. The noise from the turtle's house was like beautiful music.

3. The goat shook and shook the turtle.
4. The turtle sat on a log in the lagoon.

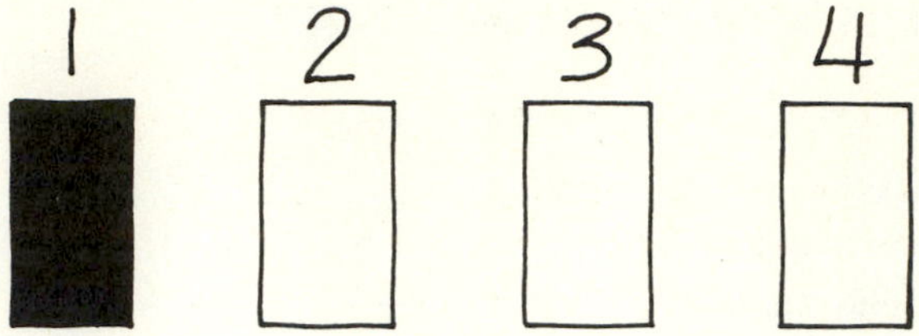

Comprehension II

LANGUAGE CONCEPTS

A few words in a story can carry most of the meaning.
Knowing about phonics is an aid to oral and silent reading.

During reading instruction, use stories to illustrate some of the strategies basic to comprehension of text.

1. Read sentences and substitute synonyms for the nouns that carry the heavy meaning loads.
2. Read orally only the nouns and verbs in sentences to demonstrate the heavy load of meaning they carry.
3. Choose a determiner such as *the* and find the noun the word marks.
4. Find prepositions in sentences and say the nouns they mark.
5. Locate pronouns and say the nouns to which they refer.
6. Change meanings by changing intonations.
7. Locate conjunctions and identify the associated words and/or ideas.
8. Summarize stories by locating main ideas and subordinate ones.
9. Retell stories with sound effects and emotional overtones that are impossible to print.
10. Repeat sequences of events as they occur in stories.
11. Discuss relationships of characters to each other.
12. Discuss the author's purpose in writing.
13. Locate and discuss figurative language used in stories and poems—simile, metaphor, personification.
14. Discuss words that have meanings other than the one used in the context of a given story.
15. Try to detect the author's point of view.

Timed Activities

LANGUAGE CONCEPTS

We can use language for fun and nonsense.

1. Help children experience 1 minute, 2 minutes, and so on.

   Talk to a friend for 1 minute.
   Hunt for the same word in a story for 2 minutes and keep a tally of the number of times it is found.

Example

for	the
and	bike
of	

   Read silently for 2 minutes and count the number of words read.
   Look at a picture for 1 minute and write or dictate into a cassette recorder the names of everything that can be remembered.

2. Use the vocabulary of timed tests, such as *start, stop, finish, complete.*
3. Engage students in estimating time after they have had several timed experiences. Read and hold up hands at the end of 2 minutes and use other ways to indicate a sense of length of time in testing situations.

An Epilogue

A Quiet Place

A Quiet Place is a place

to relax and contemplate
to renew spirit and confidence
to formulate creative ideas
to reflect on what has been seen and heard
to internalize new learnings and new pleasures

A Quiet Place can be a designated place in a classroom or an idea that makes possible individual relaxation in self-selected places in the learning environment. A designated place can be set off by a screen, bookshelves, a small rug, a large pillow, or a comfortable chair. Its purpose is to offer children a place and a time to relax, contemplate, and rest. The one essential requirement is that everyone concerned understands that there is to be no disturbing talking or noise-making.

A Quiet Place provides for rest on the basis of individual need, as contrasted with enforced periods of rest that require everyone to rest at the same time. Alternate times for activity and rest meet basic human needs in a learning center arrangement. Constant activity can destroy the notion of the organization, and children become unproductive and unruly. Children who appear to need "discipline" may have a deeper need that can be met with a few moments of peaceful relaxation.

Beautiful objects—a painting, an art print, a photograph, a flower arrangement, a very special book, an interesting rock or shell—in a Quiet Place attract children to be happy alone. Space to lie down and stretch out is desirable. A nap should be permitted and in some cases encouraged.

The ultimate in accountability for the successful operation of a learning center organization is realized when the teacher can slip away to a Quiet Place for a moment of peace and quiet and all the children honor that need.

Appendix A / Patterned Language: Models for Children's Writing

Adams, Pam. *This Old Man.* New York: Grossett and Dunlap, 1974.

Alain. *One, Two, Three, Going to Sea.* New York: Scholastic, 1964.

Aliki. *Go Tell Aunt Rhody.* New York: Macmillan, 1974.

———. *Hush Little Baby.* Englewood Cliffs, N.J.: Prentice-Hall, 1968.

———. *My Five Senses.* New York: Thomas Y. Crowell, 1962.

———. *Three Gold Pieces.* New York: Pantheon Books, 1967.

Anglund, Joan Walsh. *Spring Is a New Beginning.* New York: Harcourt, Brace and World, 1963.

———. *What Color Is Love?* New York: Harcourt, Brace and World, 1966.

Asch, Frank. *Monkey Face.* New York: Parents' Magazine Press, 1977.

Balian, Lorna. *The Animal.* Nashville, Tenn.: Abingdon Press, 1972.

Barchas, Sarah E. *I Was Walking Down the Road.* New York: Scholastic, 1975.

Baum, Arlene, and Joseph Baum. *One Bright Monday Morning.* New York: Random House, 1962.

Becker, John. *Seven Little Rabbits.* New York: Scholastic, 1973.

Beckman, Kaj. *Lisa Cannot Sleep.* New York: Franklin Watts, 1969.

Bonne, Rose, and Alan Mills. *I Know an Old Lady.* New York: Rand McNally, 1961.

Brand, Oscar. *When I First Came to This Land.* New York: G. P. Putnam's Sons, 1974.

Brandenburg, Franz. *I Once Knew a Man.* New York: Macmillan, 1970.

Brown, Marcia. *Peter Piper's Alphabet.* New York: Scribner's, 1955.

Brown, Margaret Wise. *The Bus Ride.* Chicago: Scott, Foresman, 1971.

———. *Four Fur Feet.* New York: William R. Scott, 1961.

———. *Goodnight Moon.* New York: Harper and Brothers, 1947.

———. *The Important Book.* New York: Harper and Brothers, 1949.

———. *The Inside Noisy Book.* New York: Harper and Brothers, 1942.

———. *The Runaway Bunny.* New York: Harper and Brothers, 1942.

———. *Where Have You Been?* New York: Scholastic, 1952.

———. *The Wonderful House.* New York: Harper and Brothers, 1960.

Carle, Eric. *The Grouchy Ladybug.* New York: Thomas Y. Crowell, 1977.

———. *The Mixed Up Chameleon.* New York: Thomas Y. Crowell, 1975.

———. *The Very Hungry Caterpillar.* Cleveland, Ohio: Collins World, 1969.

Charlip, Remy. *Fortunately.* New York: Parents' Magazine Press, 1964.

———. *What Good Luck! What Bad Luck!* New York: Scholastic, 1969.

Cook, Bernadine. *The Little Fish that Got Away.* Reading, Mass.: Addison-Wesley, 1976.

de Regniers, Beatrice Schenk. *Catch a Little Fox.* New York: Seabury Press, 1970.

———. *The Day Everybody Cried.* New York: Viking Press, 1967.

———. *May I Bring a Friend?* New York: Atheneum, 1972.

———. *Willy O'Dwyer Jumped in the Fire.* New York: Atheneum, 1968.

Domanska, Janina. *If All the Seas Were One Sea.* New York: Macmillan, 1971.

Duff, Maggie. *Jonny and His Drum.* New York: Henry Z. Walck, 1971.

———. *Rum Pum Pum.* New York: Macmillan, 1978.

Elgin, Benjamin. *Six Foolish Fishermen.* Chicago: The Children's Press, 1957.

Emberly, Barbara. *Simon's Song.* Englewood Cliffs, N.J.: Prentice-Hall, 1969.

Emberly, Edward. *Klippity Klop.* Boston: Little, Brown. 1974.

———. *London Bridge Is Falling Down.* Boston: Little, Brown, 1957.
———. *The Wing of a Flea.* Boston: Little, Brown, 1961.
Ets, Marie Hall. *Elephant in a Well.* New York: Viking Press, 1972.
———. *Play with Me.* New York: Viking Press, 1955.
Flack, Marjorie. *Ask Mr. Bear.* New York: Macmillan, 1932.
Francoise. *Jean Marie Counts Her Sheep.* New York: Scribner's, 1952.
Frasconi, Antonio. *The Snow and the Sun.* New York: Harcourt, Brace and World, 1955.
Galdone, Paul. *Henny Penny.* New York: Scholastic, 1968.
———. *The Little Red Hen.* New York: Scholastic, 1973.
———. *The Three Bears.* New York: Scholastic, 1972.
———. *The Three Billy Goats Gruff.* New York: Seabury Press, 1973.
Geisel, Theodore Seuss. *If I Ran the Zoo.* New York: Random House, 1950.
Grimm Brothers. *The Fisherman and His Wife.* Chicago: Follett Publishing, 1969.
———. *The Shoemaker and the Elves.* New York: Scribner's, 1960.
Hample, Stoe. *The Silly Book.* New York: Harper and Brothers, 1961.
Heller, Aaron, and Robert Deschamp. *Let's Take a Walk.* New York: Holt, Rinehart and Winston, 1963.
Hoffman, Felix. *The Wolf and the Seven Little Kids.* New York: Harcourt, Brace and World, 1957.
Hoffman, Hilde. *The Green Grass Grows All Around.* New York: Macmillan, 1968.
Hutchins, Pat. *Good-Night Owl.* New York: Macmillan, 1972.
———. *Rosie's Walk.* New York: Macmillan, 1968.
———. *Titch.* New York: Collier Books (Macmillan), 1971.
Jacobs, Leland B. *Poetry for Chuckles and Grins.* Champaign, Ill.: Garrard Publishing, 1968.
Johnson, Crocket. *Harold and the Purple Cow.* New York: Harper and Row, 1969.
Kahl, Virginia. *The Duchess Bakes a Cake.* New York: Scribner's, 1955.
Keats, Ezra Jack. *Over in the Meadow.* New York: Scholastic, 1971.
Kent, Jack. *The Fat Cat.* New York: Scholastic, 1971.
Kraus, Robert. *Whose Mouse Are You?* New York: Macmillan, 1970.
Kredensen, Gail, and Stanley Mack. *One Dancing Drum.* New York: S. G. Phillips, 1971.
Langstaff, John. *Frog Went A-Courtin'.* New York: Harcourt Brace Jovanovich, 1955.
———. *Oh, A-Hunting We Will Go.* New York: Atheneum, 1974.
———. *Over in the Meadow.* New York: Harcourt Brace Jovanovich, 1957.
Laurence, Ester. *We're Off to Catch a Dragon.* Nashville, Tenn.: Abingdon Press, 1969.
Lionni, Leo. *The Biggest House in the World.* New York: Pantheon Books, 1968.
Lobel, Anita. *King Rooster, Queen Hen.* New York: Greenwillow, 1975.
———. *A Treeful of Pigs.* New York: Greenwillow, 1979.
Mack, Stan. *10 Bears in My Bed.* New York: Pantheon, 1974.
Martin, Bill. *Brown Bear, Brown Bear.* New York: Holt, Rinehart and Winston, 1970.
———. *Fire! Fire! Said Mrs. McGuire.* New York: Holt, Rinehart and Winston, 1970.
Mayer, Mercer. *Just for You.* New York: Golden Press, 1975.
McGovern, Ann. *Too Much Noise.* New York: Scholastic, 1967.
McLeoud, Emilie W. *One Sail and Me.* Boston: Atlantic Monthly Press, 1961.
Moffett, Martha. *A Flower Pot Is Not a Hat.* New York: E. P. Dutton, 1972.
Myller, Rolf. *Rolling Around.* New York: Atheneum, 1963.
Oppenheim, Joan. *Have You Seen Trees?* New York: Young Scott Books, 1967.
Peppe, Rodney. *The House that Jack Built.* New York: Delacorte, 1970.
Polushkin, Maria. *Mother, Mother, I Want Another.* New York: Crown Publishers, 1978.
Potter, Charles F. *Tongue Tanglers.* New York: World Publishing, 1962.
Preston, Edna M. *Where Did My Mother Go?* New York: Four Winds Press, 1978.
Quackenbush, Robert. *She'll Be Comin' Round the Mountain.* Philadelphia: J. P. Lippincott, 1973.
———. *Skip to My Lou.* Philadelphia: J. P. Lippincott, 1975.

Rand, Ann. *Umbrellas, Hats, and Wheels.* New York: Harcourt, Brace and World, 1961.

Roberts, Cliff. *The Dot.* New York: Franklin Watts, 1960.

Scheer, Julian, and Marvin Bilek. *Rain Makes Applesauce.* New York: Holiday House, 1964.

———. *Upside Down Day.* New York: Holiday House, 1968.

Sendak, Maurice. *Where the Wild Things Are.* New York: Harper and Brothers, 1965.

Shaw, Charles B. *It Looked Like Spilt Milk.* New York: Harper and Row, 1947.

Shulevitz, Uri. *One Monday Morning.* New York: Scribner's, 1967.

Skarr, Grace. *What Do the Animals Say?* New York: Scholastic, 1972.

Slobodkin, Louis. *Millions and Millions and Millions.* New York: The Vanguard Press, 1955.

Sonneborn, Ruth A. *Someone Is Eating the Sun.* New York: Random House, 1974.

Spier, Peter. *The Fox Went Out on a Chilly Night.* Garden City, N.Y.: Doubleday, 1961.

Stover, JoAnn. *If Everybody Did.* New York: David McKay, 1960.

Sullivan, Joan. *Round Is a Pancake.* New York: Holt, Rinehart and Winston, 1963.

Tolstoy, Alexie. *The Great Big Enormous Turnip.* New York: Franklin Watts, 1968.

Turner, Nancy Bird, and Tibor Gergely. *When It Rained Cats and Dogs.* Philadelphia: J. P. Lippincott, 1966.

Welber, Robert. *Goodbye, Hello.* New York: Pantheon, 1974.

Wellesley, Howard. *All Kinds of Neighbors.* New York: Holt, Rinehart and Winston, 1963.

Wendriska, William. *All the Animals Were Angry.* New York: Holt, Rinehart and Winston, 1970.

Wing, Henry R. *Ten Pennies for Candy.* New York: Holt, Rinehart and Winston, 1963.

———. *What Is Big?* New York: Holt, Rinehart and Winston, 1963.

Zemach, Harve. *Mommy, Buy Me a China Doll.* Chicago: Follett Publishing, 1966.

———. *The Judge.* New York: Farrar, Strauss, & Giroux, 1968.

Zemach, Margot. *Hush, Little Baby.* New York: E. P. Dutton, 1976.

———. *The Teeny, Tiny Woman.* New York: Scholastic, 1965.

Zolotow, Charlotte. *Do You Know What I'll Do?* New York: Harper and Row, 1958.

Appendix B / Names for Games

This list includes two hundred words that are used frequently in noun positions in oral and written English

names used frequently in beginning reading materials (the list does not include proper names)
names used frequently in standardized tests for primary levels
names used in literature selections for beginning readers

The list incorporates the 100 Noun List from *Language Experiences in Early Childhood* by Roach Van Allen and Claryce Allen. Chicago: Encyclopaedia Britannica Educational Corporation, 1969.

airplane
animals
answer
apartment
apple
astronaut
author

baby
ball
balloon
basement
bear
bed
bee
bell
bird
block
body
book
box
boys
bread

breakfast
brother
bus

cake
candy
car
cat
chair
children
church
circle
city
clock
clown
coat
cookies
country
cow
cup

daddy
day

dime
dog
dollar
door
dress
drum
duck

ear
earth
elephant
end
example
eyes

fall
family
father
feet
fire truck
first
five
flag

floor
flower
food
foot
four
frame
friend
frog

game
girl
guitar

hand
head
home
horse
house

ice cream

jacket
jack-o-lantern

jelly

king
kite

lamp
land
leaf
leg
letter
life
light
line
lunch

man
men
miles
money
moon
morning
mother
mouth
moving van

name
next
nickel
night
nose
nurse

one
orange

page
paper
parts
pencil
penny
people
pet
picture
pilot
place
play
poem
point
policeman
pony
purse

quarter
queen

rain
raincoat
refrigerator
road
rock
rocket
roof
room
rope

sailboat
school
sea
second
sentence
sheet
shirt
shoe
show
side
sister
sky
snow
sock
something
song
sound
spring
square
stairs
stamp
stop sign
store
story
stove
street
summer
sun
swing

table
teacher
telephone
television
things
three
times
today
tooth
top
toy
tree
truck
turkey
two

umbrella

valentine

water
way
whistle
white
wind
window
winter
witch
word
world

x-ray

yard
years

zipper
zoo

Appendix C / Words Used Frequently

This list includes 350 words not on the "Names for Games" list

most of the function words of English—those that do not pattern in sentences as nouns, verbs, adjectives, and adverbs
words used frequently as nouns, verbs, adjectives, and adverbs
words from "Words All Authors Use" in *Language Experiences in Reading,* Level II, by Roach Van Allen and Claryce Allen. Chicago: Encyclopaedia Britannica Educational Corporation, 1966
words of the rank of 300 words of highest frequency (not on the other lists named above) from *Word Frequency Book* by John B. Carroll, Peter Davies, and Barry Richman. Boston: Houghton Mifflin Company, 1971.

a
about
after
again
all
almost
along
alphabet
also
always
am
an
and
another
any
are
around
art
as
ask
asked
at

aunt
away

back
bad
be
beautiful
became
because
been
before
began
best
better
between
big
black
blue
both
bring
but
buy

by

called
came
can
can't
center
class
close
cold
come
comes
coming
cook
cooking
could
couldn't
cut

dark
dear
decided

did
didn't
died
different
do
does
done
don't
down
drama
dramatics
during

each
early
eat
end
enough
even
evening
every
everyone

everything

far
farm
fast
fell
finally
find
finished
first
fish
for
found
friend
from
front
full
fun

gave
get
getting

give
given
glad
go
goes
going
gone
good
got
grade
grand
great
green
guess

had
hair
half
happened
happy
hard
has

have
having
he
hear
help
her
here
high
him
his
hit
hold
hope
hot
how
hundred

I
ice
if
I'll
I'm

important
in
interesting
into
is
it
its
it's

jet
just

keep
kept
killed
kind
knew
know

language
large

last
late
learned
leave
left
let
like
little
live
lived
long
look
looked
lots
love

made
make
many
may
me
meat
might
milk
mine

minutes
Miss
more
most
Mr.
Mrs.
much
music
must
my

near
never
new
nice
no
north
not
now

of
off
oh
old
on

once
only
open
or
other
our
out
over
own

paint
painting
part
party
person
playing
please
pretty
put

quite

ran
read
reading

ready
real
red
rest
ride
right
run

said
same
saw
say
see
seen
send
sent
she
should
sick
since
small
so
some
something
sometimes

soon
started
stay
still
stop
study
such
supper
sure
swim

take
tell
ten
than
that
the
their
them
then
there
these
they
think
third

this
those
thought
through
till
times
to
together
told
too
took
top
tried
trip
try
turn

under
until
up
upon
us
use
used

vacation
very
visit
vocabulary

walk
want
wanted
war
warm
was
wasn't
we
weather
week
well
went
were
what
when
where
which
while
who
why

will
window
wish
with
without
won't
wood
woods
work
world
would
wouldn't
write
writing
wrong
wrote

yes
yet
you
young
your
yours

Appendix D / Allen List of 100 High-frequency Words in Rank Order*

The words in this list are mostly words of structure. They are found very frequently in text, but by themselves they do not have any meaning. Students must acquire these words in their sight vocabularies in order to be literate. The words are useful in making many games and other language study activities for group and independent activities.

1. the	21. I	41. when	61. then	81. new
2. of	22. this	42. will	62. these	82. after
3. and	23. by	43. said	63. its	83. most
4. a	24. from	44. her	64. than	84. way
5. to	25. they	45. do	65. two	85. down
6. in	26. had	46. has	66. time	86. see
7. is	27. not	47. him	67. could	87. people
8. that	28. or	48. if	68. your	88. any
9. was	29. have	49. no	69. many	89. where
10. he	30. but	50. more	70. like	90. through
11. it	31. one	51. can	71. first	91. me
12. for	32. what	52. out	72. each	92. man
13. as	33. were	53. up	73. only	93. before
14. on	34. an	54. about	74. now	94. back
15. with	35. which	55. so	75. my	95. much
16. his	36. there	56. them	76. how	96. just
17. at	37. we	57. our	77. may	97. little
18. be	38. all	58. into	78. over	98. very
19. are	39. their	59. some	79. made	99. long
20. you	40. she	60. other	80. did	100. good

* Roach Van Allen: *Language Experiences in Communication,* p. 217.

Index to Selections